Luther's Wittenberg World

The Reformation in Switzerland

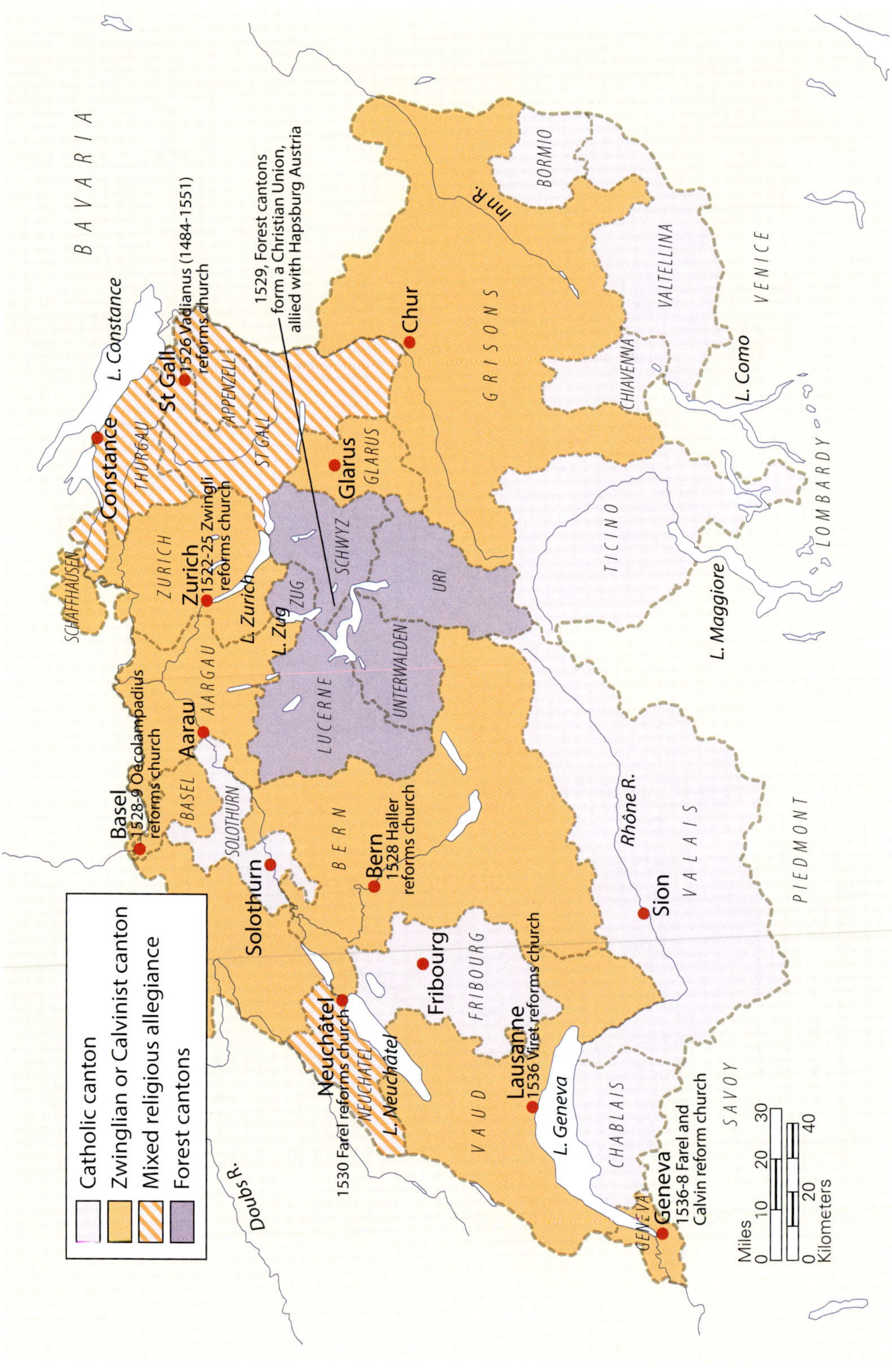

Introduction

> No man is an island, entire of itself;
> Every man is a piece of the continent, a part of the main.
>
> John Donne, 1624

As the life and thought of Martin Luther are being celebrated around the world in 2017, it is tempting to fall back into the half-a-millennium-old habit of seeing him as a lonely figure, standing without support against pope and emperor, defying and destroying the old order in the manner of Hercules, a role into which the painter Hans Holbein cast him. Nothing could be further from the truth. It was indeed through his own insights and discoveries in reading Scripture that Luther took the lead in introducing significant changes into church and society in his day. But he led in those efforts both because of the intellectual, ecclesiastical, and pastoral endeavors of predecessors and because family, friends, and followers surrounded and supported him during his own career. Even foes shaped the way he formulated his vision of the biblical message and of society.

His visions of church and society arose from his engagement with God's word in Holy Scripture. The Bible had exercised a presence and influence in his childhood and youth and in his days as student and friar in the Augustinian cloister in Erfurt. But his first fascination with stories such as Daniel in the lion's den and David slaying Goliath merged in his mind with the story of Saint George slaying the dragon, depicted in the church up the hill from his parents' smelter in Mansfeld, where he went to mass week in and week out. Furthermore, his parents and priests, teachers and professors, led him to believe that the Bible, supplemented by the traditions of the church and ecclesiastical prescriptions of religious activities, gave him instructions on how his best efforts could please God—with the help of grace, without doubt, but as the key element in building a beneficial, profitable relationship with God.

When Luther followed the commands of his superiors in the Augustinian Order of Hermits to pursue studies that would make him a "Doctor in Biblia," a teacher of Scripture and theology, against his better judgment and his deep convictions of his own unworthiness, he gradually came to see the shape of the world in a different way. It is not human creatures who must approach God with their sacred works but rather God who approaches humans with God's holy word, thereby securing the relationship of love and trust that God intended to mark the bond that unites them at creation. Luther began to see the world as a world in which the relationship of the Creator to creatures is the foundation of reality and that human life centers on conversation and community with the speaking Creator. This is the message, centered on God's climaxing word in the Word made flesh, Jesus Christ, that informed and drove Luther's entire reforming activity. It aimed at transforming the Christian culture of Europe not only in its ecclesiastical practice but in the daily lives and worldviews of its people.

Luther sought to create and cultivate a culture based upon the conversation of congregations and villages, families and individuals, with God. He sought to do that by preaching, teaching, and providing printed materials so that others could preach and teach in order to bring this way of life to the people of God. In 1531, he rejoiced that reforms launched in Wittenberg in the previous decade had made a difference in the lives of those who had heard the Wittenberg message: "It has, praise God, come so far that men and women, young and old, know the catechism and how they should believe, live, pray, suffer, and die."[1]

In his Small and Large Catechisms, Luther adapted the "catechism," the ancient Christian outline of fundamental biblical teaching that was to form the basis of Christian faith and life, to reflect his plan and desire for delivery of God's Law and Gospel to the common people. His goal was for their lives to overflow with the fruits of faith in their prayers and service to the neighbor, as the Small Catechism's "Table of Christian Callings" laid the foundation for community life in the family and economic circles, in the sphere of the

---

1. Martin Luther, *D. Martin Luthers Werke*, 127 vols. (Weimar: Böhlau, 1883–2009), 30:3:317:32–34. Martin Luther, *Luther's Works*, ed. Jaroslav Pelikan and Helmut T. Lehmann, 55 vols. (Saint Louis and Philadelphia: Concordia and Fortress Press, 1958–86), 47:52.

larger society, and in the midst of the congregation of Christ's people. Such fruitful lives could only arise in response to the Holy Spirit's promise of a new life in Christ that gives peace and certainty through its bestowal of the forgiveness of sins. This forgiveness liberates those who trust in Christ to live truly human lives. Luther understood this kind of life as one that is not, in his words, "curved in upon itself" but rather finds stability and security in Christ and thus is free to serve the neighbor's needs. Such a way of life, Luther imagined, could emerge from the proper proclamation and study of God's word in the midst of God's people.

Luther himself was not an island. Parents, priests, friends, and family, as well as his teachers, shaped him as a child and young man. Colleagues and professors at the universities at Erfurt and Wittenberg influenced his education, and monastic brothers his formation. Later, a team of Reformers assembled around him, some in Wittenberg and some spread across German lands and beyond. All shared a commitment to the reform that he had sketched, some adhering to his patterns of speech and action more closely than others. Fellow citizens in Wittenberg and correspondents from afar, onetime and frequent visitors to Wittenberg, even critics and opponents all contributed to constructing Luther's way of thinking just as he had stimulated them.

Print enabled a level of conversation in the sixteenth century that Europe had never previously experienced, and events unfolded in Wittenberg and across Europe that sometimes aided, sometimes impeded, the progress of the Wittenberg Reformation. Without the efforts of his printers, we might not know Luther's name. Nonetheless, preachers delivered the message to a largely illiterate population across wide stretches of Europe. Governmental leaders also played decisive roles in giving his call for reform room to breathe and supporting its implementation.

As happens with most such movements, contemporaries of Luther interpreted his message and acted on it in different, sometimes even contradictory ways, and another generation of students and followers had to work out the interpretation of what it meant to be in the "Wittenberg circle" in their own contexts. But there certainly was a "Wittenberg circle" that endured into the late sixteenth century. Its members shared a common commitment to Luther's new definition of what it meant to be Christian, in word and action. In that next generation, Gnesio-Lutherans propagated their more radical version of his thought against Philippist plans and ideas, which brought these more conservative—from a medieval perspective, at least initially—adherents into conflict with their more radical fellow students (see especially chapter 4). Their debates were enlivened with views from the Swabians, who developed JOHANNES BRENZ's interpretation of his Wittenberg colleague. Their conflict resulted from their common desire to reproduce Luther's and PHILLIP MELANCHTHON's worldviews for their own times and challenges. Despite their fiercely fought battles over critical issues, they all remained—or thought they were remaining—in the Wittenberg circle, in the line of succession to Luther and Melanchthon. That is why they fought with each other in the ways they did.

All this took place within the context of the sixteenth-century Germanic world into which Luther was born and in which he spent his entire life. That world was composed of individual people who lived within the framework of society that Luther described in his "Table of Christian Callings" in the Small Catechism.

Some sixty years, ago Walter G. Tillmanns, professor at Wartburg College in Iowa, composed a prosopographical survey of Luther's cultural setting entitled *The World and Men Around Luther*.[2] At the instigation of Will Bergkamp of Fortress Press, and following Tillmanns's example, this author has assembled some 340 brief biographical sketches of the people who shaped Luther's world and message. It presents those who shaped Luther as he was growing up and going to school and university, as well as his monastic acquaintances (chapter 1); the residents of Wittenberg he met on the streets, at the electoral court, and at the university (chapter 2); the team at the University of Wittenberg and environs that contributed to his Reform movement (chapter 3); early Reformers across Germany, many of whom did not study in Wittenberg but came to embrace the Wittenberg message and plan for Reformation (chapter 4); the most prominent of the German-speaking students who carried the message of Luther, Melanchthon, and their colleagues into the next generation (chapter 5); Reformers shaped by Wittenberg theology from other European lands (chapter 6); political leaders across Europe who, for reasons of personal piety and/or political aspirations, supported Luther and his colleagues or opposed him and his call for reform (chapter 7); and theological or ecclesiastical rivals and critics of Wittenberg Reformation, who also influenced the shape of Wittenberg thinking (chapter 8).

Many readers will find in this volume individuals they regard as superfluous for the Wittenberg story, and others will wonder why some specific figure was not included. It cannot be denied that a certain amount of arbitrariness does creep in in selecting for such a volume, influenced by the author's own experience in research and reading. Each of these mini-biographies is inadequate; much more of the stories of these people could be told.

2. Walter G. Tillmanns, *The World and Men around Luther* (Minneapolis: Augsburg, 1959).

What is told, it is hoped, will contribute to a sense of the story surrounding Luther and filling in the picture that sets forth the Wittenberg Reformation.

Because each person's story has been placed in a narrative framework, many figures could have been featured in a different chapter than they have been. Therefore, an index of featured individuals is offered as a guide to readers, who may also profit from the glossary of terms. Note that names that are featured with a biographical entry appear in ***bold italic type***, usually with the person's dates of birth and death. When these feature names appear elsewhere in the volume, they will be identified by SMALL CAPS as a reminder that their full biographies are provided elsewhere. Names that appear in the story but are not featured with a biography will appear in regular type.

This volume is intended to serve as a biographical reference for those who are delving into the Wittenberg culture for the first time and for those who have long studied the period but who may have encountered a new, strange name. It is hoped that these snapshots of some of the great company who played a role in the unfolding of the Wittenberg Reformation will help readers encounter another "world"—one that has influenced cultures and ecclesiastical subcultures around the globe to this day.

Robert Kolb
Saint Louis
The Festival of the Resurrection of Jesus Christ 2017

CHAPTER 1

Child, Pupil, Student, Monk: From Mansfeld to Magdeburg, Eisenach, and Erfurt

Eisleben and Mansfeld

The story of every human being begins at home. Although Martin Luther spoke at times of his humble origins, his family had enjoyed relatively favorable conditions in the years before his birth. Luther was born and baptized in Eisleben, where his father, Hans Luder, had just begun to work his way into the metal-producing industry of the county of Mansfeld.

Hans Luder **(1458–1530)** has had a reputation as a strict if not cruel father, but his son's complaints about parental discipline probably reveal nothing other than children's normal memories of negative experiences. Luther's own experiences as a father suggest that he had a positive model for parenting in his home in Mansfeld. Hans was the eldest son of one of the four most well-off families in the Thuringian village of Möhra in the domains of the elector of Saxony. His father, Heine, and his mother, Margarethe Ziegler, grew up together in Möhra, a morning's walk from the commercial center to the north, Eisenach. How Hans found his bride, Margarethe Lindemann, in that town is not known, but his family undoubtedly had connections there. The Lindemann family may have supported the adventure Hans and Margarethe set out on when they left their own area for the county of Mansfeld to the north, where Margarethe's uncle Anton had become a smelter-master. Since according to local custom, as eldest son, Hans could not inherit his parents' holdings, the newly wedded couple followed Anton to Eisleben. There their first son, Martin, was born, shortly before they ventured to the boomtown of Mansfeld, where copper smelting provided the family income. Hans rose to leadership in the mining village as one four representatives of the populace on the village council, and he also served the counts of Mansfeld as an overseer of mining in the area. His piety was demonstrated in his helping to found a Marian brotherhood, established to provide masses for deceased members, although he also expressed the usual anticlerical criticisms of priests and monks in general. The whims of the local counts, the bankers to whom he was indebted, and the economic forces in the metals industry often left the Luder family in tight circumstances, but they were able to send Luther to the university in hopes of adding a bureaucrat trained in law to the family. Hans journeyed to Erfurt to witness his son's first mass and could not repress a reminder that Luther had displeased his parents by entering the monastic life, a course Luther acknowledged as false in his dedication of his treatise *On Monastic Vows* (1522) to his father. Hans and his wife attended their son's wedding festivities in June 1525 and visited him and his family from time to time in Wittenberg. Luther received word of his father's death at the Coburg during the Diet of Augsburg in 1530; his amanuensis VEIT DIETRICH reported that

Portraits of Hans and Margarethe Luder by Lukas Cranach the Elder (1527)

when he read the letter from his boyhood friend Hans Reinicke informing him of his loss, Luther wept so profusely that he had a headache the next day. Martin Luther followed the custom of the biblical humanists and Latinized his name from Luder to Luther, a shorthand version of "Eleutherius" (a free man), reflecting his understanding of justification by faith in Christ as he set it forth in his *The Freedom of a Christian* of 1520.

Scholarly debate over the maiden name and family origin of Hans Luder's wife, ***Margarethe Lindemann Luder* (ca. 1463–1531)**, seems solved. Some sixteenth-century authors claimed she came from a Ziegler family, which indeed, like the Luders, was among the most well-off families in Möhra, but it seems most likely that this was the family of Martin's paternal grandmother. His mother came from a merchant family in Eisenach named Lindemann, hence Luther calling Johann Lindemann the Younger his cousin. The Lindemann family had supplied leadership for their town throughout the fifteenth century. Margarethe's father, also named Johann, had at least four children, three sons in addition to Margarethe, or "Hanna" as she was sometimes called. Among Luther's cousins were a tailor, a professor of law in Leipzig, a professor of medicine in Leipzig and Wittenberg, and a pastor. As with his complaints about the strict discipline of his father, his recollections of his mother's rod seem to be no more than the usual grumblings about parental discipline. The warm relationship with his aging parents points to his having experienced a healthy family life as a child. Luther's parents visited Wittenberg fairly often and were, for instance, present for Philip and Katherina Melanchthon's wedding in 1520 as well as for festivities when Luther married Katharina von Bora in 1525. According to existent records, Margarethe and Hans had eight children, four boys, two of whom died in infancy, and four girls, three of whom grew to adulthood and married. Possibly other children died in infancy as well.

Luther's brother ***Jakob* (1490–1571)** and he grew up together in harmony, to the extent that brothers can, and maintained a close relationship throughout their lives. Jakob took over the family smelting business in Mansfeld and visited Wittenberg occasionally. Mansfeld remained home for three sisters, Dorothea, Margarethe, and another, whose name is unknown, whose son Hans Ölmer lived with the Luthers in the Black Cloister for a time and earned his uncle's sharp rebuke for excessive drinking.

The father of ***Johann (Hans) Reinicke* (d. 1538)**, Luther's boyhood and lifelong friend, owned a smelting operation just as Luther's father did, and so it was perhaps natural that the two boys not only went to school together in Mansfeld but were also sent off for further education in Magdeburg in 1496, where another Mansfelder, Dr. Paul Mosshauer, served as a cathedral canon and looked after the boys. Reinicke remained in Mansfeld thereafter and entered the smelting business of his father. He and Luther remained in close contact, and Reinicke visited Luther at the Coburg in 1530 during the Diet of Augsburg as well as on other occasions in Wittenberg. It was Reinicke's letter that informed Luther of his father's death.

As a counselor of FREDERICK THE WISE, ***Johann Rühel*** **(d. 1542)**, another native of Mansfeld and, according to Luther, a relative by marriage, was serving as counselor in the electoral Saxon government when he guided and defended Luther during the Wittenberg professor's encounter with CARDINAL CAJETAN in Augsburg in 1518. Rühel also lent Luther support at the disputation with JOHANN ECK in Leipzig in 1519. In that year, Rühel had accepted a post with the government of the counts of Mansfeld, and he aided Luther in contemplating his reactions to the Leipzig Disputation. Rühel later became an advisor to ARCHBISHOP ALBRECHT OF MAINZ alongside his service to the counts of Mansfeld. Luther kept in contact with Rühel throughout his life through letters and personal visits. Luther counted on Rühel's counsel in several critical situations and followed his advice, particularly in his public reactions to the policies and actions of Albrecht. When Luther rejected a large gift of money from Albrecht, given as a wedding gift, Rühel made certain that KATHARINA received the gift despite her husband's objection.

Magdeburg and Eisenach

Martin Luther left home in 1496 to go to one of the largest cities in the German Empire, Magdeburg, for advanced schooling. He and his Mansfeld friend HANS REINICKE spent a year together there, but little is known about the persons they met there. Thereafter, Luther proceeded to the much smaller town of Eisenach, where his mother had grown up, and there he spent four years at the school of Saint George.

Luther did not board with his relatives while a pupil at the school of Saint George in Eisenach but with another prominent family, the Schalbes. ***Heinrich Schalbe*** was mayor of the town from 1495 to 1499, while Luther lived there. He later referred to his landlady, probably Heinrich Schalbe's wife, as a model of proper conduct for the mother of a household. Later tradition associated this reference with Heinrich Schalbe's daughter, ***Ursula Cotta*** **(d. 1511)**, who was married to Kunz Cotta, one of the highest-ranking members of the town's government. The Cottas lived in the same house with Ursula's parents. Ursula's younger brother, ***Caspar Schalbe***, accompanied young Luther to school and later, after becoming involved with the biblical humanists at Erfurt while a student there, conveyed messages between Luther and Erasmus. The Schalbe family was the center of a pious sodality known as the "Schalbe collegium." The group was led by local Franciscans, who spread the influence of one of their brothers, ***Johann Hilten***, who died in the local cloister in 1500. Hilten had been confined to that house after his apocalyptic spiritualism had aroused the suspicion of authorities in the order. His attacks on the corruption of church officials included the prediction that in 1516 someone would arise who would overcome the abuses of the monks, as Luther later recalled. The extent to which Luther's own view of the struggle between God and Satan stemmed from this time cannot be determined.

A priest at the foundation of Saint Mary in Eisenach, ***Johannes Braun*** **(ca. 1450–after 1516)**, who had studied at the University of Erfurt in the early 1470s, gathered pupils at the school of Saint George into another circle, in which music played a large role alongside prayer and meditation. Luther kept contact with Braun long after he left Eisenach. In Braun's circle, the rapidly spreading veneration of Saint Anne made its mark on young Martin. Luther invited Braun to his first mass in 1507 and continued to correspond with him in the early years of his teaching career in Wittenberg.

Among Luther's teachers in Eisenach was said to be ***Johann Trebonius***, described by Luther's friend and biographer Matthäus Ratzeberger as a learned man and "poet," a designation used at the time for followers of the biblical humanists. Ratzeberger related that Trebonius doffed his hat each day as he entered the classroom, noting that among his pupils were future mayors, chancellors, professors, and other officials. Scholars doubt the accuracy of this account, but it is likely that teachers with this spirit actually did cultivate in the young Luther a sense of possibility for higher service in society as well as an openness to the new learning that was infiltrating not only the universities but also the secondary schools of the time. Another teacher, ***Wigand Güldenapf***, later became pastor in Waltershausen; Luther kept in contact with him and intervened in 1526 to win him a pension.

Erfurt

Luther left Eisenach for the university in Erfurt in early 1501, where he began the study of the liberal arts with a view—apparently his father's more than his own—toward the study of law when his bachelor's and master's degrees were safe in hand. The university existed to form servants of church and society for the higher professions, in theology, law, and medicine, though many did not go further than the study of grammar, logic, and rhetoric, along

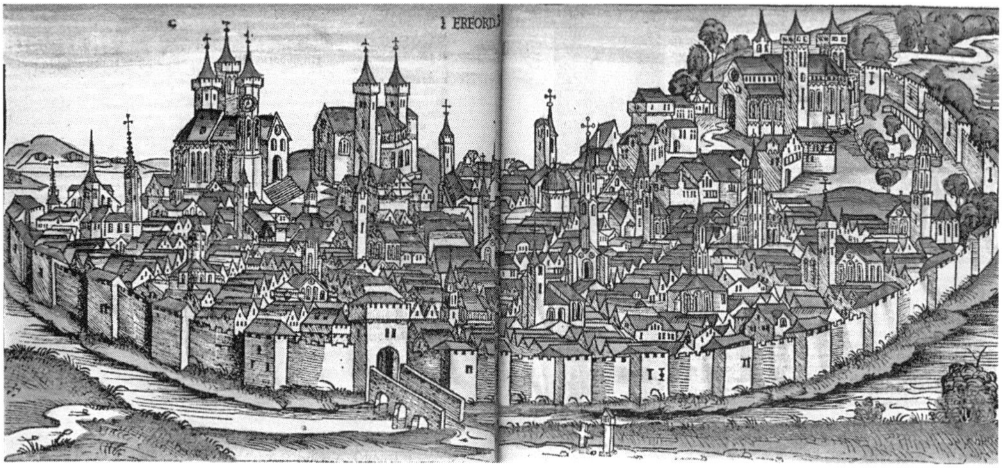

Woodcut of Erfurt from The Nuremberg Chronicle *(1493)*

with astronomy, music, arithmetic, and geometry—the trivium and the quadrivium—on their path toward becoming school teachers or serving in governmental posts. Luther's formation at the university lay in the hands of professors trained in scholastic method and, at Erfurt at that time, largely in the philosophy of the fourteenth-century thinker William of Ockham (though as in every age, Luther's instructors were somewhat eclectic in choosing the experts on whom they relied).

The University of Erfurt was not only a bastion of scholastic method and thinking, however. Around a private scholar and monk, KONRAD MUTIANUS RUFUS, a canon in nearby Gotha, there had gathered a circle of young men dedicated to the new "humanist" methods, which emphasized good rhetorical communication of ideas, not to the exclusion of logic, but placing the discipline of dialectic in the service of effective rhetoric. In addition, these "biblical humanists" endeavored to return to the sources in original languages. Thus, Greek came into the curriculum, along with more classical Latin. Hebrew followed during Luther's lifetime. These humanists strove to cleanse the academic language, Latin, from medieval accretions and return to Ciceronian style and vocabulary. They also strove to rid their disciplines of medieval diversions from the original intention of ancient authors. A number of Luther's later acquaintances, including GEORG SPALATIN, JUSTUS JONAS, JOHANN SPANGENBERG, JUSTUS MENIUS, Bartholomäus Raida, and the Reformer's first major apostate, GEORG WITZEL, were active in this circle during or immediately following Luther's time in Erfurt, but his recorded recollections do not give traces of acquaintanceship with Mutianus's "club" or the other elements of the educational reform movement now termed "biblical humanism." However, some disposition toward this movement seems to have rubbed off on the young student from Mansfeld, for in Wittenberg he practiced the humanist method from early on. As in Magdeburg, Luther experienced life in the big city—Erfurt, with some twenty thousand residents, was also among the largest German cities of the time—and Luther later made remarks, sometimes snide, about municipal politics. But his mind remained firmly planted in the small-town political thinking of Mansfeld and the electoral town of Wittenberg.

Luther's university study was temporarily interrupted by his decision to enter the Augustinian Eremites monastery, which was close to his student lodgings in the Bursa of Saint George and had a partially justified reputation for strict adherence to monastic discipline. The Augustinians were reviving the writings of their namesake at this time and also demonstrated a fresh interest in Paul's Epistles and in the educational approach of the biblical humanists. This move did not divorce Luther from the university since some instructors in both the liberal arts and theology were also residents of his monastery, members of his order. He recalled Erfurt experiences occasionally as a life that mixed a sense of satisfaction and adventure at learning with a troubled search for peace with God, who demanded the best he could produce before parceling out the grace that would enable the young student and monk to attain favor and finally heavenly salvation. Tensions between theologians and jurists and between Augustinians and other monastic orders in Erfurt, particularly the Carthusians, shaped Luther's attitudes toward monasticism in general and the legal profession, particularly the bureaucrats and courtiers among whom his father had hoped to have his son numbered, for the rest of his life.

Two professors at Erfurt impressed themselves on Luther's memory and his thinking. ***Joducus Trutvetter* (ca. 1460–1519)** came from his birthplace in Eisenach to the nearby university in Erfurt in 1476. In two years he had earned his bachelor's degree, two years later his master's degree, and in 1504 became a doctor of Bible. He served as a parish priest in Erfurt from 1493 to 1501, when he became professor at the university. In 1507, he was transferred to Wittenberg and served as university instructor and archdeacon of the castle church there for three years before returning to Erfurt. His thought was guided primarily, but not exclusively, by William of Ockham. His published works treated logic and physics rather than theological topics. By 1516, Trutvetter expressed profound discomfort over the direction of the thinking of his then Wittenberg colleague, and the formerly cordial relationship between the two generations broke.

***Bartholomäus Arnoldi of Usingen* (ca. 1465–1532)** came from his native Hesse to Erfurt to study in 1484 and, after attaining the master's degree in 1491, continued to teach there. In 1514, he earned the degree of doctor in Bible. He entered the Augustinian cloister in 1512, drawn there at least in part by his acquaintance with Luther. Luther did remember the professor once saying to the young friar, "well, Brother Martin, what is the Bible? One should be reading the ancient teachers, who extracted the sap of the truth from the Bible. The Bible just causes disturbances." The two continued to share a passionate desire for the reform of the church, but Arnoldi's model remained medieval, and he never came to terms with Luther's understanding of grace and faith. He was forced out of Erfurt in 1525 and became an advisor on the staff of Bishop Konrad von Thüringen, bishop of Würzburg, where he served until his death.

Far more important in Luther's spiritual development and the course of his career than either the scholastic or the humanist cultures of Erfurt was ***Johannes von Staupitz* (ca. 1468–1524)**, scion of a Saxon noble family with close connections to the electoral court. His studies in Cologne and Leipzig prepared him for entry into the Order of the Augustinian Eremites in 1490, in Munich. As prior of his order's house in Tübingen, he studied, lectured, and completed the course of academic theology studies by 1500, when he received his doctorate. The great Ockhamist theologian GABRIEL BIEL had died by that time, but Biel's students, Konrad Sommenhart, Heinrich Bebel, and Wendelin Steinbach, were teaching in Tübingen and provided Staupitz with the best that German higher education in theology had to offer. In Tübingen, he became a friend of Johannes Altenstaig, whose theological dictionary, published in 1517, summarized in that genre's form the scholastic theology of late fifteenth and early sixteenth centuries. By 1500, Staupitz had been

Johannes von Staupitz, engraving from Luther's Leben *by Julius Köstlin (Leipzig, 1889)*

transferred back to Munich, but his call from his family's prince, Frederick the Wise, to come to Wittenberg to assist in the establishment of the university brought him back to his native Saxony in 1502. At that time, he assumed the office of vicar-general of the observant congregation of the Augustinians in the German province of the order. His blend of scholastic theology and biblical studies offered Luther consolation in his spiritual struggles, for Staupitz emphasized God's mercy and freely given grace, based upon God's predestination of those people chosen for salvation. His plans for the reform of the church and his leadership of his Augustinian friars made Wittenberg a center for dispatching Augustinian brothers into towns in several parts of northern Germany in which the order had not yet set foot. Early on, Staupitz recognized Luther's own leadership capabilities and gave him responsibilities in administering the several houses of the order in his area. He also commanded Luther to pursue the route to the highest degree in theology, doctor in Bible, and facilitated his rapid completion of the course of studies so that his disciple could relieve him of his duties as professor of theology in Wittenberg. That took place in 1512. As Luther's own theology built on his mentor's way of thinking but took on larger dimensions that moved outside his master's framework for thinking, the relationship between Staupitz and Luther cooled, though the older man's fondness for his apprentice did not fade. Staupitz resigned his office as vicar-general of the order in 1520 and moved to Salzburg, assuming the office of court preacher for Archbishop Matthäus Lang. In 1522, Staupitz entered the Benedictine monastery there, where he died in late 1524. His understanding of the biblical message and his promotion of Luther's person as candidate for higher office within the order and then at the university made Staupitz one of the decisive factors in the formation of the Reformer.

Staupitz was not the only figure in the Augustinian cloister in Erfurt who influenced Luther in his formative years. Others, however, largely escaped mention in the contemporary sources. ***Johann Genser von Paltz* (ca. 1445–1511)** entered the Order of Augustinian Eremites in 1467 and completed his doctoral studies in 1483 at the University of Erfurt. His battle for reform within his own order and his participation in the campaign against the Hussite heresy in Bohemia marked his career. He was particularly concerned in his writings with cultivating a sense of the ease with which God's grace might be merited so that the anxieties of the pious might be set aside by the comfort of having the aid of grace insured, which would empower them to do the good works necessary for salvation. During the propagation of indulgences in behalf of a renewed crusade against the Turks in 1490, Paltz worked closely with Raimund Cardinal Peraudi, whose service to the papacy and at the court of emperors Friedrich III and MAXIMILIAN I made him a powerful figure in the church and the empire and the church's premier promoter of indulgences. Paltz preached in behalf of the indulgence sales. From 1493 to 1500, he led the organization of a new monastery in Mühlheim, but returned to Erfurt in 1500. His preaching of indulgences had been so effective that Peraudi recruited him for the task again in 1502 and 1503. He returned in 1505 to Mühlheim. His writings were dedicated particularly to popular devotional themes. Luther never mentioned Paltz but must have caught something of his spirit.

Among Luther's closest brothers in the monastery was ***Johannes Lang* (1488–1548)**, who had begun university studies in his native Erfurt in 1500. There, NIKOLAUS MARSCHALK, EOBANUS HESSUS, and others shaped his learning with their interests in the humanist pursuits of the ancient languages and good rhetorical communication. This legacy Lang passed on to Luther when they met after Lang joined the Augustinian Eremites in 1506. Ordained in 1508, he was transferred to the Wittenberg house in that year, along with Luther. Lang remained in Wittenberg until 1516. His study of theology, begun there in 1515, culminated with the award of the doctorate in Bible in 1519 in Erfurt. His service as prior of the Augustinian cloister in Erfurt (1516–18) and as district vicar for the order (1518–20) gave him opportunity to support and spread Luther's way of thinking. In 1521, his translation of Matthew's Gospel appeared in print. Lang left the cloister in January 1522 and was dismissed from his teaching position on the Erfurt faculty, so he dedicated himself to the reform of the city's church. Cooperating with the city council, he introduced extensive reform of the ecclesiastical practices in Erfurt in 1525 and headed the church there until his death. In 1537, he attended the meeting of the Smalcald League and subscribed to Luther's Smalcald Articles. His activities beyond Erfurt included advising the counts of Schwarzburg-Blankenburg on the organization of the churches in their lands in 1533 and 1539. He was in correspondence with Luther until he died.

Alongside the university and the monastery, an informal circle of biblical humanists added fresh perspectives to the intellectual life in Erfurt at Luther's time, although Luther did not record his contacts with them. Among their leaders was ***Konrad Mutianus Rufus* (1470/71–1526)**. From his native Deventer, where he went to school briefly with ERASMUS, Mutianus came to the University of Erfurt in 1486, completing his bachelor's and master's degrees by 1492. He taught in Mainz briefly and then departed for Italy to study law, winning his doctoral degree in jurisprudence at the University of Bologna in 1501. During extensive travels in Italy, he absorbed the Florentine Neoplatonism prominent in intellectual exchange at the time. Exercising the office of canon in Gotha, he influenced a large circle of students from nearby Erfurt, although there is no indication that Luther was among them, though a number of his later adherents were. Mutianus promoted moral and institutional reform in the church but did not comprehend Luther's reform of teaching and so avoided association with the Reformation embraced by many in his circle.

Among his disciples, Johannes Jäger, who took the name ***Crotus Rubeanus*** **(ca. 1480–1539/45)** in the Latinizing style of the humanists, came closest to MUTIANUS's own example. He strove ardently for reform of both learning and church life but in the end refused to follow Luther into total rebellion against the pope. He came to Erfurt to study and earned the bachelor's and master's degrees by 1508. He had by that time formed friendships with Mutianus, the Hebraist JOHANNES REUCHLIN, and ULRICH VON HUTTEN. His antipathy for monasticism infected von Hutten, but Crotus became head of the abbey school in Fulda in 1520 after serving as tutor for the family of one of the counts of Henneberg. He gathered a few friends, including von Hutten, who edited the final version of the work, and EOBANUS HESSUS, to defend Reuchlin with *The Letters of Obscure Men* (1515), a humanist declaration of war against the scholastic theologians who were pursuing the Hebraist for his use of Jewish literature. Between 1517 and 1519, Crotus served as a tutor for a German merchant family in Bologna and studied law and theology while there. His friend EOBANUS HESSUS joined him for a visit to Rome at the end of his Italian sojourn. Crotus returned to the University of Erfurt, serving as rector. In 1521, he welcomed Luther on his way to the Diet of Worms. Crotus's inclinations toward reform led him to support the secularization of the lands of the German (Teutonic) Knights in Prussia, in one published work, and through service in DUKE ALBRECHT's government in Königsberg from 1525 to 1529. Thereafter, however, he made it clear that he would not support any reform that decisively broke with the church. ARCHBISHOP ALBRECHT OF MAINZ offered him a position as a canon in Halle, where he served until his death.

Another of MUTIANUS's disciples shared much of the ambiguity of CROTUS RUBEANUS's relationship to reform, but ***Helius Eobanus Hessus*** **(1488–1540)**, probably born to a family named Koch, settled on the evangelical side of the line dividing the Reformers of his generation. He came to Erfurt in 1504 from the Latin school in Frankenberg near his birthplace in Hesse. He moved from university studies to heading a school at the church of Saint Severus in Erfurt and back again, assuming a teaching position in the liberal arts faculty in 1517. Alcoholism plagued him his entire life and plagued his large family, after his marriage in 1515, as well. In good humanist style, he renamed himself, combining the name of the day of his birth, Sunday (*Helius*), the name of the saint who claimed

OBSCVRI VIRI

Epistole Obscurorũ virorũ ad Magistrũ Ortuinũ
Gratiũ Dauentriensem Colonie latinas litteras pro
fitentẽ nõ ille q̃dẽ veteres et prius visæ: sed et nouę et illis prioribꝫ
Elegantia argutijs lepore ac venustate longe superiores.

Ad Lectorem.

Risum Heraclitæ est: vasti ridere parati
Arida mutarũt pectora Stoicidæ
Da mihi tristem animũ: ferales obijce luctus
Dispeream nisi mox omnia Risus erunt.
Exerce pulmonem.

Front page, Letters of Obscure Men (Epistolae obscurorum virorum), *1515* his birth date (*Eoban*), and the land of his birth (*Hesse*). He fulfilled his vocation as propagator of humanist learning by writing poetry, well enough to earn money for those who needed poems for special occasions or purposes. He ended his life in Marburg, where he assumed an instructorship in the liberal arts, lecturing chiefly on poetry and history. Not theologically trained, he was not active in the development of Lutheran church life and thought, but his correspondence with Wittenberg theologians reveals his standing within their circle.

Engraving of Helius Eobanus Hessus by Albrecht Dürer (1526)

Among many others, these people formed the Augustinian friar, Brother Martin, who ventured first into Wittenberg in 1508 to teach in the new university's arts faculty and, after an interlude back in Erfurt, settled into the little town on the Elbe in 1511.

CHAPTER 2

Gown and Town: Luther's Wittenberg Neighbors

When Luther first arrived at the infant University of Wittenberg in 1508, he was integrated into the life of the faculty to which he later returned and in which he found his primary orientation to questions of intellectual depth and of practical breadth. ELECTOR FREDERICK THE WISE had founded the university for his lands in 1502. When his grandfather divided the Saxon domain between his sons, Ernst and Albert, in 1485, Saxony's university in Leipzig, founded in 1409, fell to Albert while the electoral title and the larger portion of territory fell to Frederick's father, Ernst. Princedoms with any claim to prominence needed a university. For example, the dukes of Bavaria founded Ingolstadt in 1472, the elector of Brandenburg founded Frankfurt an der Oder in 1506, and the landgrave of Hesse caught up with the founding of Marburg in 1527.

The University of Wittenberg quickly gathered a requisite number of professors—minimal staffing of the arts and the higher faculties of theology, law, and medicine—but the stability of the faculty left something to be desired. It was into this adventure of organizing higher education for electoral Saxony—and for students from other territories who wished to come—that Luther was sent when JOHANNES VON STAUPITZ drew him to the "Leucorea" (Wittenberg means "white mountain" and the university claimed its name in the Greek translation thereof). Luther returned in 1511 to spend the rest of his life in the small town of Wittenberg. It had served as one of the locations of the Saxon court since 1260. Without larger commercial or industrial enterprise, however, it remained something of a backwater until Luther and Melanchthon drew both students and printers to the dusty, muddy streets of the town on the Elbe river.

Luther walked the streets of Wittenberg and shopped in its market with people of all social levels, without recording the names of most of them. Those with whom he rubbed shoulders on a daily basis included his barber Peter Beskendorf, the printers with whom he worked closely in spreading his message, and the courtiers, especially those with political, administrative, and military assignments but also the electors' court physician, music staff, and the court painters. Some of these officials were resident in Torgau or at other posts throughout the electoral domains, but they nonetheless touched Luther's existence quite directly.

The Professor's Intellectual Sources

Four individuals Luther encountered in Erfurt and Wittenberg but whom he never personally met deserve inclusion in sketching the world of the young theology instructor. He encountered them in books that shaped the way in which he understood the Christian faith and conveyed it to his hearers. The first delivered the scholastic tradition to him. ***Gabriel Biel* (ca. 1410–1495)**, a native of Speyer, was ordained during his study at the University of Heidelberg in the 1430s. He had given instruction in the liberal arts faculty there before leaving for the University of Erfurt around 1442. There, his training made him a disciple of the English-born theologian and philosopher of the early fourteenth century, William of Ockham, although Ockham's "nominalist" *via moderna* did not obliterate all influences of the "realist" positions of John Duns Scotus (ca. 1266–1308) and Thomas Aquinas (1225–1274) on Biel. Thomas's theology dominated the University of Cologne (where Biel studied and taught from 1451 to 1462) when he became cathedral preacher and vicar in the service of the archbishop of Mainz. During this time, he became a member of the Brethren of the Common Life and played a prominent role in the administration and expansion of the Brethren along the Upper Rhine. In 1484, he joined the theological faculty of the University of Tübingen, where he taught until 1491. Biel's theology was marked by strong support for the papacy and his continuation of Ockham's teaching that God is absolutely omnipotent and has made a covenant with humankind that requires individuals to "do what is in them" (or do their best) to win God's grace in order to produce the God-pleasing works that lead to salvation. Several of his works influenced Luther, both positively and negatively, as the young Augustinian struggled with his own inability to truly do his best to please his Almighty Creator. Biel's works include *Exposition of the Sacred Canon of the Mass* and his *Epitome of the Four Books of Sententiae*, a commentary on Peter Lombard's *Sententiae.*

Three other authors provided Luther with the help of the biblical humanist movement for interpreting Scripture. ***Johannes Reuchlin* (1455–1522)** supplied the young professor with a Hebrew grammar and dictionary and other aids for study of the Old Testament at the very beginning of his teaching career. Reuchlin began his schooling in his native Pforzheim, where through marriage he was connected to the family of PHILIP MELANCHTHON's paternal grandmother. After studying in Freiburg, Basel, and Paris, he dedicated himself to learning jurisprudence in Orléans and Poitier from 1479 into the early 1480s. At year's turn 1482/83, he began teaching law at the University of Tübingen. In 1485, he joined the administration of justice in the duchy of Württemberg as a judge. He was named to the imperial court in Speyer in 1502, while at the same time the Swabian League employed him as one of its three judges (until 1512). The first Christian Hebrew scholar in northern Europe, Wessel Gansfort, convinced Reuchlin of the importance of Hebrew for understanding Scripture, and in 1492 the physician of Emperor Frederick III, Jakob ben Jehiel Loans, a relative of JOSEL VON ROSHEIM, the leader of Jews in the German Empire, introduced him to the language. While in Italy in 1482, he met Giovanni Pico della Mirandola, who interested him in the cabalistic principles of interpretation that had brought Neoplatonic principles into the medieval exegesis of the Hebrew Scriptures. Reuchlin's *On the Miraculous Word* made these principles available to the scholars of northern Europe. In 1506, his grammar *On the Rudiments of Hebrew* appeared and, in 1517, his *On the Art of the Kabbalah.* In the interest of converting Jews to Christianity, he promoted study of Hebrew and defended, at the same time, the right of Jewish congregations to retain their own literature. His opposition to forced baptism of Jews and to their expulsion from Christian towns led to conflict both with the Jewish convert Johannes Pfefferkorn and with the Dominican theologians in Cologne, under the leadership of JACOB HOOGSTRATEN. CROTUS RUBEANUS and ULRICH VON HUTTEN assembled authors for a satire, *On the Letters of Obscure Men*, in defense of Reuchlin. In the midst of this controversy, Reuchlin sought refuge at the University of Ingolstadt, where he taught Hebrew; among his students was ANDREAS OSIANDER, later reformer in Nuremberg. Reuchlin recognized the talents of MELANCHTHON, whom he knew through family connections, and promoted his advancement, recommending him for the University of Wittenberg to ELECTOR FREDERICK THE WISE. However, Reuchlin opposed Luther's brand of reform and rejected Melanchthon because of his refusal to leave

Wittenberg. Reuchlin changed his will, which had left his library to Melanchthon, because of his support for his Wittenberg colleague.

The humanist scholarship of ***Jacques Lefèvre d'Étaples (Faber Stapulensis)*** **(ca. 1460–1536)** also placed at Luther's disposal important linguistic and exegetical materials that helped shape his interpretation of Scriptures. An ordained priest, Lefèvre dedicated his life to scholarship. His early exposure to Italian Renaissance scholars, including Marsilio Ficino and Giovanni Pico della Mirandola, acquainted him with both the Aristotelian and Neoplatonist schools. He edited works of mystical writers, including Pseudo-Dionysius, Richard of Saint Victor, and Hildegard of Bingen, as well as three volumes of the writings

The only (possibly) authentic portrait of Johannes Reuchlin (left) with Ulrich von Hutten (middle) and Martin Luther (right), all at far left of the title engraving of Murner's History von den fier Ketsren Prediger ordens, *printed in Strassburg, 1521*

of Nicholas of Kues. His attention turned more and more, finally exclusively, to biblical scholarship, and he published his *Five-Fold Psalter*, offering five Latin translations of the Psalms, in 1509 and three years later a commentary on the Pauline Epistles. He moved on to lecture and publish on the four Gospels and, in 1527, the Catholic Epistles. His support of reform in the circle around Bishop Guillaume Briçonnet of Meaux and the abbey of Saint-Germain-des-Prés, as well as his final sojourn at the court of the reform-minded Marguerite d'Angelouême, did not lead to his breaking with the Roman church, but his writings certainly were put to use by Luther as well as other Reformers, including Ulrich Zwingli and John Calvin.

Even more significant for Luther's life was ***Desiderius Erasmus* (ca. 1467–1536)**, the most renowned scholar of his time, at least north of the Alps. An illegitimate child, Erasmus gained from his father, a priest, a passion for Latin and Greek before the man died when Erasmus was an adolescent. Under the humanist Alexander Hegius in Deventer, Erasmus received further humanistic training and was introduced to the Brethren of the Common Life. With his older brother, he joined the Augustinian Canons and was ordained in 1492. As secretary to the bishop of Cambrai, he was sent to the University of Paris and studied theology. In 1499, as tutor of William Blount, Baron Mountjoy, he traveled to England, where he entered into humanist circles led by John Colet and Thomas More. In 1500, he returned to Paris to study Greek, and soon thereafter his *Annotations* on the New Testament took shape, an important source for new biblical scholarship that Luther used in his lectures a decade later. Erasmus's background in the Brethren of Common Life elicited his *Handbook of the Christian Soldier*; his discontent with the moral state of the church generated his *Adages* and *Praise of Folly*. After residing in Italy (1506–1509), he traveled to England, where for five years he taught Greek at Cambridge. Thereafter, he lived for the most part in Basel, teaching and editing for the printer JOHANN FROBEN, with time occasionally in England and the Low Countries. At Froben's urging, he rather hurriedly produced the first published edition of the Greek New Testament, the *Novum Instrumentum Omne*, in 1516 in order to land in the book stands before the Complutensian Polyglot of Francisco Cardinal Ximenes de Cisneros was published. Erasmus's editing work also made available the works of Jerome (1516), Cyprian (1520), Pseudo-Arnobius (1522), Hilary (1523), Irenaeus in Latin translation (1526), Ambrose (1527), Augustine (1528), Chrysostom in Latin translation (1530), Basil (1532), and Origen in Latin translation (1536). He reaped both appreciation and criticism for his scholarship, the latter because some of his interpretations challenged established readings of the Vulgate and thus teachings of the church.

Portrait of Desiderius Erasmus by Hans Holbein (1523)

Luther made much use of Erasmus's scholarship, as Erasmus later did of Luther's, in the 1520s and 1530s. The two had a somewhat tension-filled relationship from the beginning. Mutual admiration accompanied Erasmus's growing jealousy of his younger colleague. He stopped Froben from republishing a "collected works" of Luther, the first such collection of a living person's writing. The older scholar also feared the potential consequences of the younger's ever more radical critique of church practices they both found wrong. Luther perceived early on that Erasmus's concern for reform did not extend to reform of central teachings such as the doctrine of justification that were essential for Luther's vision of the church. Finally, in 1524 Erasmus broke openly with Luther on the issue of the bondage of the human will. He feared that Luther's position would undermine public morality, while Luther taught the bondage of the will's ability to choose God rather than false gods, in order to anchor assurance for troubled consciences solely in the unconditioned mercy and love of God. English acquaintances, including KING HENRY VIII and Bishop John Fisher, urged Erasmus to criticize Luther, and he did so in his *Diatribe on the Free Will* (1524). Erasmus chose the form of a university disputation, which Luther reluctantly used in his long-delayed reply in December 1525, *On Bound Choice*. Erasmus defended himself in his *Hyperaspistes* (Shield-Bearing Protector)—which was twice as long as the *Diatribe*—the first half of which was hastily prepared to be sold at the Frankfurt Book Fair in 1526. The second half appeared a year later, bringing the work to some five times longer than the *Diatribe*. Luther's *On Bound Choice* won widespread acclaim from the younger generation of biblical humanists, who continued to appreciate Erasmus's scholarship but solidly supported Luther's theology. Luther continued his criticism of the implications of Erasmus's

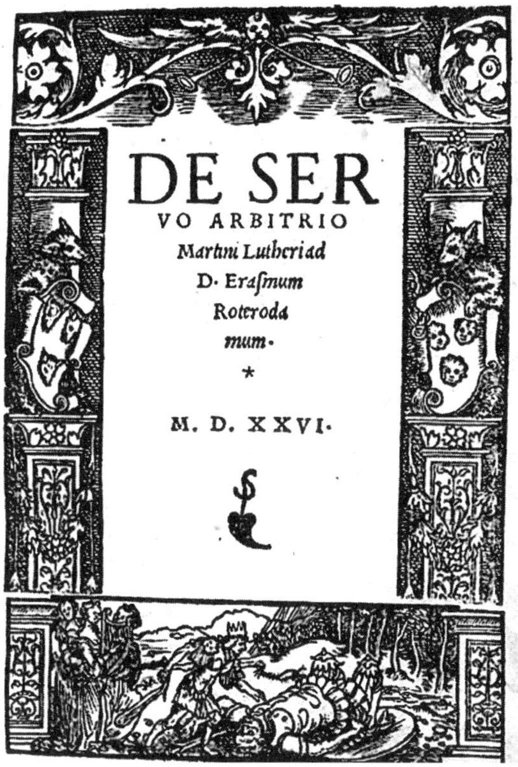

Title page of Luther's Bondage of the Will

position for moral behavior in his lectures on Ecclesiastes in 1526 (published 1532). In 1534, Luther criticized Erasmus's ecclesiology for not taking biblical teaching seriously and for seeking concord at the expense of truth.

The Professor's Initial Colleagues

Several scholars aided Luther as he began his teaching in Wittenberg, in the company of appreciative and supportive colleagues.

***Nikolaus Marschalk* (ca. 1470–1525)** had already departed Wittenberg by the time Luther first arrived in 1508, but the Erfurt humanist had made his mark on the infant university as one of its founders in 1502. After studying in Leuven/Louvain and Heidelberg, Marschalk completed his studies in Erfurt and then continued to teach there, playing a significant role in introducing the methods of biblical humanism to the university. His service to both university, as instructor in the liberal arts, and the city, as municipal secretary, had made him a prize for ELECTOR FREDERICK THE WISE when he founded his university in Wittenberg. Marschalk remained only three years as an instructor in the liberal arts and in jurisprudence on the Wittenberg faculty while serving Frederick the Wise at court, but he shaped the direction of the new university with his emphasis on humanistic methods. His private printing operation supplied textbooks for his colleagues in the university's first years. In 1505, Marschalk rejected a call from ELECTOR JOACHIM I OF BRANDENBURG to organize a faculty of law at the University of Frankfurt an der Oder in order to become a chancellor for the dukes of Mecklenburg in Schwerin. After five years, he assumed a professorship in the liberal arts at the dukes' university in Rostock. His contributions to the German scholarship of the time lay particularly in his introduction of linguistic aids for the study of Greek.

Christoph Scheurl **(1481–1542)** arrived in Wittenberg from his native Nuremberg as a professor of law in 1507. The university had lost students and instructors in its initial attempts to establish itself, but Scheurl managed to reorganize the faculty and build the Leucorea into a competitive place of higher learning in his five years of service there. His relationship with FREDERICK THE WISE insured that he would continue to play a role in Saxon policy decisions even after his departure from the university. Just before Luther's arrival in Wittenberg in 1511, Scheurl returned to Nuremberg and to the circle of biblical humanists that he served informally as secretary, the "*sodalitas Staupitziana*" that changed its name to "*sodalitas Martiniana*" as Luther replaced JOHANNES VON STAUPITZ as the center of its attention. Scheurl himself provided Luther

Portrait of Christoph Scheurl by Lukas Cranach the Elder (1509)

valuable legal advice and also provided some support for the budding Wittenberg movement, for example, in negotiating with Karl von Miltitz when von Miltitz was representing papal interests and attempting to reconcile Luther to the church in 1518–19. Nonetheless, Scheurl himself fostered suspicion among fellow members of the Nuremberg establishment because he remained in close contact with Roman Catholic theologians. His friendship with Johann Eck had arranged an initially friendly contact between Eck and Luther, and at the Leipzig Disputation in 1519 Scheurl made an introductory speech before the debate began. His diplomatic and legal service to Nuremberg as it introduced Wittenberg Reforms did not reflect fully his own religious views, which remained close to those he imbibed from Staupitz. But he was a good citizen.

Among those at the University of Wittenberg who greeted the new instructor as colleague in 1508 was ***Martin Pollich von Mellerstadt*** **(ca. 1450–1513)**. He had studied in Leipzig from 1470 to 1476 and then began to teach there, in the liberal arts—logic, astronomy, astrology—and also in the medical faculty. He became the court physician of Frederick the Wise. The elector enlisted Pollich in the organization of his new university, of which he became the first rector in 1502. Pollich's writings treated both philosophical and anatomical subjects, and he devised astronomical calendars within an astrological framework. The controversy over the origin of syphilis attracted his attention, and he criticized theories that argued for its astrological roots. His argument for returning medical studies to the texts of Hippocrates and Galen reflects his general support for the advance of humanistic studies, both in Leipzig and in Wittenberg, and his participation in the humanist sodality around Konrad Mutianus. His friends named him "*lux mundi*" (light of the world). As Luther first taught in Wittenberg, Pollich was teaching not only medical courses but also theology, representing the realist philosophy and theology of Thomas Aquinas. Of his young new colleague from Erfurt, Pollich was reported to have said, "watch this young man. He has a first-rate, clear-sighted mind, the likes of which I have not encountered in my entire life." Before his death, according to his brother Valentin, Pollich predicted of Luther, "this monk will prove all the learned doctors wrong and bring forth a new teaching and reform the entire Roman church, for he relies on the writings of the prophets and apostles and stands on the words of Jesus Christ. No one can overturn and fight against that, not with philosophy or sophistry, not with Scotism, the thought of Albert the Great, Thomas' teaching or the entire Tartaret" (Pierre Tartaret was a leading early sixteenth-century interpreter of Duns Scotus whose works were key in the study of the latter's thought).

In addition to JOHANNES VON STAUPITZ and POLLICH, several others were teaching theology when Luther arrived. Two shared Pollich's orientation grounded in the realism of Thomas Aquinas. ***Petrus Lupinus* (d. 1521)** served as a canon in the foundation of All Saints, toward the end of his life as its administrator, and also as treasurer of the university. His studies in Wittenberg brought him his theological degrees, climaxing in 1508 with the doctorate in Bible. He served as dean of the theological faculty several times and once as rector of the university. Luther recalled Lupinus's strong opposition to his cause, but their interaction won the elder colleague to his way of thinking, for which Luther thanked him in his dedication of his Galatians commentary, published in 1519. The older man contributed, however, little to the actual advance of the Reformation.

Alongside Lupinus, Thomistic theology found representation in ***Andreas Bodenstein von Karlstadt* (1486–1541)**, who had studied in Erfurt and Cologne before joining the arts faculty in Wittenberg in 1505. His training in Cologne had steeped him in the *via antiqua* and Thomistic thinking, although he also lectured on Scotist thought. In 1510, he received his doctorate in Bible and became archdeacon of the foundation of All Saints. As dean of the theological faculty, he presided at Luther's doctoral disputation in 1512. In 1515–16, he journeyed to Italy and received his doctorates in canon and civil law in Rome. Karlstadt's initial opposition to Luther's suggestions for reform of the theological curriculum and the abandonment of scholastic traditions of teaching turned to avid support under the influence of JOHANNES VON STAUPITZ and his reading of Augustine. The ancient bishop of Hippo shaped Karlstadt's new way of thinking more strongly even than he did Luther's. During his younger colleague's absence at the Wartburg in 1521 and 1522, Karlstadt led a somewhat radical revolt against medieval practice and piety within Wittenberg. On Christmas Day 1521, he celebrated the mass in a manner that clearly rejected its sacrificial character and that offered lay people both host and chalice (communion in both kinds). Tensions between Luther and Karlstadt developed after Luther's Invocavit week sermons in March 1522, which urged moderation and a slower pace in reforms. Karlstadt developed his own vision of reform, which largely repeated the patterns of dozens of medieval reform movements at the popular level, which were biblicistic, moralistic, anti-sacramental, anticlerical, and millenarian. As a canon at All Saints, he had been financially supported by the village of Orlamünde, where he assumed the pastorate in 1523, discarding all clerical vestments and presenting himself as "Brother Andreas," claiming little of the pastoral office apart from preaching and pastoral care. The electoral government found him dangerously close to the rebellious maneuvering of THOMAS MÜNTZER and removed him from his pastorate in September 1524, sending him into exile. His brother-in-law Gerhard Westerburg published Karlstadt's treatises on the Lord's Supper, which rejected Luther's understanding of the presence of Christ's body and blood in the sacramental elements. His denial of infant baptism and baptismal regeneration and of any use of images or Christian art in churches earned Luther's sharp critique in *Against the Heavenly Prophets* in 1525. In the wake of the defeat of peasant forces in the Peasants Revolt of 1524–26, Karlstadt sought to return to electoral Saxony and live as a peasant. Luther provided him refuge briefly, but the two could not reconcile. Ulrich Zwingli provided him a position in Zurich briefly and then a pastorate in Altstätten in the Rhine Valley. From 1534 until his death, he taught at the University of Basel and served as a preacher there.

***Anna von Mochau* (1505/1507–after 1545)**, the wife of Andreas Bodenstein von Karlstadt, was, according to Luther, still a young girl at the end of 1521 when Karlstadt, accompanied by Philip Melanchthon and Justus Jonas, came to her home in the village of Segrehna, near Wittenberg, to become engaged to marry her, the daughter of a poor noble family. Luther knew her previously, as a friend of the family. Karlstadt and Anna married on January 19, 1522, with a celebration worthy of a leading professor. When Karlstadt foreswore his professorship in 1523, Anna accompanied him to Orlamünde. When he was sent into exile in 1524, Anna, pregnant at the time, departed with him according to some records. According to others, she remained in Orlamünde but followed him into exile after the birth of the young Andreas, whom she refused to have baptized. The couple had at least three other sons and several daughters; Luther, his wife Katharina, Jonas, and Melanchthon served as sponsors for various of the children. Anna shared her husband's danger in 1524/25 as she traveled with him and separated from him through the Thuringian countryside with its rebellious peasants, who were suspicious of all strangers and threatened her life. She preceded her husband back to Wittenberg in mid-1525, seeking and finding refuge in Luther's Black Cloister. The reconciliation for which both men had hoped did not take place, although Luther won for the Karlstadt family the right to stay in electoral Saxony for a short time, probably in Segrehna. When Karlstadt's persistence in rejecting Luther's understanding of the sacraments earned him exile again, Luther continued to express sympathy for his wife and children, often separated from husband and father while the family moved from place to place before settling in Basel in 1534. During this period, Anna and the children were once reduced to begging for something to eat. While Karlstadt served as professor in Basel, Anna suffered from a number of ailments. At her husband's death, she turned to Luther for help in what she found to be dire economic circumstances. Whether she returned to Wittenberg for the closing years of her life is unclear.

These weren't the only instructors in theology, among them also NIKOLAUS VON AMSDORF, to welcome Luther to their midst in 1511; so did others at the university.

***Hieronymus Schurff* (1481–1554)** earned his master of arts degree in Basel and then studied law in Tübingen. His cousin Ambrosius Volland (1472–1551) and he were invited to Wittenberg at its founding, and Schurff received his doctorate in civil law there in 1503. He also became a doctor of canon law in 1507 and entered the electoral court in Wittenberg as a counselor of FREDERICK THE WISE. His legal advice at the Diet of Worms in 1521 and throughout the early years of the Reformation aided his colleagues leading reform efforts immensely. Tensions developed with Luther over the Reformer's more daring statements, and Schurff helped him set down in writing his version of what had happened in Worms.

Etching of Hieronymus Schurff by unknown artist

Schurff continued to play a prominent role in the university and government in Wittenberg into the time of both Elector Johann and Elector Johann Friedrich. Upon Johann Friedrich's defeat and Elector Moritz's assumption of control of Wittenberg, Schurff departed for the University of Frankfurt an der Oder. Schurff's influence continued through the careers of his students, including Melchior Kling (1504–1571) and Ulrich Mordeisen (1519–1572).

***Augustin Schurff* (1495–1548)**, brother of Hieronymus, began his studies in Wittenberg in 1509 and, after the completion of his master of arts degree in 1517, taught logic and physics. In 1518 he received his baccalaureate in medicine and in 1521 his doctorate in medicine. He pioneered human dissection. Among his patients were Luther, Melanchthon, Bugenhagen, and the families of electors Johann and Johann Friedrich. His publications treated, above all, the plague. One of his daughters married Lukas Cranach the Younger.

The Professor's Acquaintances at the Court

At the electoral court, which was located in the castle at the other end of Wittenberg's main street, but also in Altenburg, Weimar, and above all in Torgau, counselors administered the elector's lands and offered advice on policy matters of all kinds. Some of the counselors of the three electors who led Saxony during Luther's life had only political and administrative, including military, roles, but alongside them court physicians, musicians, and other servants of the elector also made their contributions.

***Jakob Vogt (Voigt)* (d. 1522)**, a Franciscan official and guardian of the cloister in Torgau, became the father confessor and court preacher for Frederick the Wise. He accompanied the elector on many journeys, including the pilgrimage to the Holy Land in 1493. He preached in the castle church in Wittenberg occasionally, when the elector visited the town, and aided in the assembly of the relic collection there. His initial favorable reaction to Luther's call to reform turned sour after the unrest in Wittenberg in 1521.

***Fabian von Feilitsch* (before 1457–1520)** was at Augsburg when Luther was summoned there to be brought into submission to Rome by Cardinal Cajetan in 1518. He was sent by Frederick the Wise to collect the Golden Rose, which Pope Leo X had awarded him. Von Feilitsch confronted Karl von Miltitz, the papal representative who was delivering the papal award, when he threatened Luther with ban, and von Miltitz backed down, saying that he had been joking and that no more than a hearing of the Wittenberg professor was planned. Von Feilitsch brought Luther and von Miltitz together for conversation in 1520. Von Feilitsch died in December 1520 and left Luther a legacy in his will. Luther later used him as an example of the wisdom of some courtiers.

Fabian's cousin ***Philipp von Feilitsch* (ca. 1473–after 1532)** also stood by Luther in 1518 in Augsburg, accompanying him to interviews with CARDINAL CAJETAN. Philipp von Feilitsch was among the electoral counselors at the diet of Worms in 1521, active in advising Luther on how to proceed at the diet. He protested when Luther offered to renounce safe conduct in order to publicly debate JOHANNES COCHLAEUS. Philipp von Feilitsch was one of those electoral counselors who knew of the plan to secure Luther at the Wartburg in 1521 and hinted to Luther that such a plan was in the works.

***Johann von Dolzig* (ca. 1485–1551)** joined the court of FREDERICK THE WISE in 1502 and accompanied his prince on a pilgrimage to Palestine in 1517–18. As manager of electoral funds, he paid for Luther's doctoral gown in 1512. As marshal of the Saxon court, von Dolzig commanded the troops that entered Wittenberg in 1520 to quell student-led disturbances. From the Wartburg, Luther wrote an exposition of Luke 17:11–19, in response to a request from DUKE JOHANN, the brother of FREDERICK THE WISE, and dedicated it to HAUGOLD VON EINSIEDEL; SPALATIN added the names of Hans von Dolzig and BERNHARD VON HIRSCHFELD to the dedication. Luther invited Johann von Dolzig to his wedding celebration in 1525. The advisor joined discussions with the theologians of the university in that year as Frederick's representative to negotiate on proper liturgical reform. He led the strengthening of Wittenberg's fortifications in 1526. In 1530, he took part in the discussions among the evangelical governments as part of Elector Johann's delegation. Despite accusing von Dolzig as one who was ruining Saxony, for reasons not expressed, in 1533, Luther included him in the circle that was being consulted on the translation of the Bible. Von Dolzig traveled with FRANZ BURKHARD to England in 1539, spending a month negotiating with KING HENRY VIII's government in behalf of the Smalcald League. In 1545, ELECTOR JOHANN FRIEDRICH named von Dolzig the administrator of Saalfeld district. Luther commended the courtier's eloquence.

***Haugold von Einsiedel* (ca. 1460–1522)** studied at the University of Leipzig in 1476–77 and then transferred to Ingolstadt, where he absorbed humanist influences. In 1489, he accepted ecclesiastical benefices purchased by his father, Heinrich, for him, from which he later received papal dispensation of vows, married, and entered the service of the electors of Saxony. His performance in office won the trust of both FREDERICK THE WISE and Luther. From the Wartburg, Luther dedicated an exposition of Luke 17:11–19 to von Einsiedel.

***Bernhard von Hirschfeld* (1490–1551)** entered electoral service as a page at a young age, certainly by 1503. In 1517, he accompanied Frederick the Wise on his pilgrimage to the Holy Land. He was moved into service in the administration of electoral revenue. Luther roomed with him in Worms in 1521. His support for Luther found clear expression in a letter to officials in Nuremberg, in which he said that the Edict of Worms would cause much uproar in the empire. His administrative skills and experience proved valuable in the visitation of Saxon parishes in 1528 and 1529. In 1533, Elector Johann Friedrich named him high constable at the town of Schlieben. He served as commandant of electoral Saxon forces stationed in Torgau in the 1530s and of troops charged with the defense of Wittenberg in the Smalcald War. He later joined the court of Moritz when he became elector.

Bernhard's brother ***Johann von Hirschfeld* (1504–1538)** came to Wittenberg as a page at court in 1511 and was educated by Georg Spalatin with the illegitimate son of Frederick the Wise, Sebastian von Jessen. He entered the military service of the emperor. In 1530, he was among the group of advisors Elector Johann took to Augsburg, though illness prevented him from reaching the diet. He then served Duke Johann Ernst, brother of Elector Johann Friedrich.

***Hans von der Planitz* (d. 1535)** had joined the government of Frederick the Wise before traveling with the elector to the Holy Land in 1517–18. He served at least twice as the administrator of the lands around Grimma. In 1519, von der Planitz accompanied Luther to Leipzig and encouraged Luther to remain in the confrontation with Johann Eck, insisting that withdrawal from the debate would be a loss of prestige. In 1521, Frederick had him named to the imperial administration in Nuremberg. At the Diet of Nuremberg in 1522–23, von der Planitz played a key role in the electoral Saxon plea to have Luther's case removed from the Imperial Council of Regency to the diet itself, which found that Luther's complaints about abuses should be referred to free Christian council in Germany. In 1523, Luther's attacks on Duke Georg of Saxony required diplomatic maneuverings between Wittenberg and Georg's court, and von der Planitz led the negotiations. He played a significant role in the visitation of Saxon parishes in 1528–29.

***Hans von Berlepsch* (ca. 1480–1533)** was serving as administrator of the lands around Eisenach and as castle commander at the Wartburg in 1521 when Luther was placed in protective custody under his charge. Luther reported that von Berlepsch was taking great care of him at his own expense, took him along on the hunt, and sat with him to talk of the faith. Luther later sent him copies of his writings as they appeared in print. On September

25, 1522, Luther sent von Berlepsch one of the first copies of his New Testament translation, which had taken form in von Berlepsch's castle. Similarly, Luther developed a good relationship with ***Paul Bader* (d. 1541)**, who was in charge of the Saxon castle at Coburg when Luther stayed there in April 1518 on his way to the Heidelberg meeting of his order at which the Wittenberg professor presented his theses on the theology of the cross. Bader and his wife served as good hosts, Luther thought, while he stayed there in 1530 during the imperial diet in Augsburg.

Johann Löser served as hereditary marshal of Saxony. Luther visited him in late autumn 1531 at his Castle Pretsch, at a time when the Reformer was fighting illness. Löser took him on the hunt, and although Luther had little interest in bagging animals, he had his writing materials with him, and he "bagged" a psalm, inspired to comment on Psalm 147. He dedicated the little commentary to Löser, who later served as one of the sponsors for Luther's son Paul.

***Gregor Brück Henisch (Heins)* (1485–1557)**, son of a mayor of the town of Brück, in Brandenburg, and the brother of ***Simon Heins* (ca. 1483–1523)**, an arts instructor and pastor of the Wittenberg town church, attended the universities of Wittenberg and Frankfurt an der Oder (1502–1509). In 1519, ELECTOR FREDERICK THE WISE named him a ducal counselor, and he accompanied the elector to the coronation of EMPEROR CHARLES V in Cologne and the diet in Worms in the following two years. Frederick promoted him in 1521 to the office of chancellor of his realms, and in the same year, Brück received his doctorate in both civil and canon law. He played a significant role as a bridge between the Wittenberg Reformers and the court. He was the chief author of the "*Protestatio*" of the evangelical princes in 1529 in Speyer and contributed greatly to the organization of the Smalcald League. With ELECTOR JOHANN FRIEDRICH's defeat by imperial forces in 1547, he left Wittenberg to serve Johann Friedrich's sons in Weimar. There, he helped organize the academy that became the University of Jena. In both Wittenberg and Weimar, his ideas helped shape the consistory that managed the affairs of the church.

Gregor's son ***Christian Brück* (ca. 1516–1567)** studied in Wittenberg (1532–42) and received his doctorate in jurisprudence in 1543. He married Barbara, the daughter of LUKAS CRANACH THE ELDER, in 1543. He entered the service of ELECTOR JOHANN FRIEDRICH immediately. After the Smalcald War, he followed the Ernstine government to Weimar, where he continued to serve as counselor to the elector's sons. Appointed as privy counselor in 1566, he took part in charting the young DUKE JOHANN FRIEDRICH's support of the revolt of Wilhelm von Grumbach against the imperial peace and was executed in 1567 for high treason.

Christian Beyer **(ca. 1482–1535)** studied in Erfurt (1500–1503) and then came to Wittenberg, where he became an instructor in the faculty of arts in 1507. He earned his doctorates in both canon and civil law in 1510, and in 1511 he began teaching in the university's law faculty, though he could not be an official member because he had married the previous November. In 1512 two relatives died, his wife had a stillbirth, and their house burned. But this did not prevent him from assuming the teaching responsibilities of Christoph Scheurl in the faculty and his place on the high court of the electorate. Beyer's piety revealed itself at this time through his membership in the Brotherhood of Our Dear Lady, a group that prayed for and purchased masses for the souls of deceased members. He became

Medallion depicting Christian Beyer reading the Augsburg Confession to Charles V

mayor of Wittenberg in 1513–14. He served as mayor of Wittenberg on occasion after this term in addition to duties as a counselor of Electors FREDERICK THE WISE and JOHANN. In 1528, Johann appointed him court chancellor, alongside GREGOR BRÜCK, because of the multiplication of duties. The Beyer family moved to Weimar in 1529. As Saxon chancellor, Beyer read the Augsburg Confession on behalf of the princes and city council members who had signed it at the Diet of Augsburg in 1530.

***Franz Burkhard* (1503–1560)** taught jurisprudence at the University of Wittenberg before becoming an electoral counselor. He and Luther became fast friends. Luther admired Burkhard's skill at chess. In 1534, PRINCE GEORG OF ANHALT was suffering a severe bout of melancholy, and Luther visited him often but finally had Burkhard take over the task of bringing consolation and support to the prince. When CHRISTIAN BEYER died in 1535, Burkhard assumed his duties as co-chancellor at GREGOR BRÜCK's side. Luther implored Burkhard to watch over the situation in the village of Orlamünde after Caspar Glatz retired from his office as pastor. Burkhard represented electoral Saxony on a diplomatic mission of the Smalcald League to the English royal court. Negotiations to establish a mutual commitment between the league and HENRY VIII failed.

***Johann von Metsch* (ca. 1485–1549)** served Electors FREDERICK, JOHANN, and JOHANN FRIEDRICH as a courtier. He was attracted to Luther's preaching of the gospel, and the two developed a good relationship. Von Metsch played a prominent role in the electoral governments' administration of justice, and he headed the administration of the territory in and around Wittenberg. When the elector was not residing in Wittenberg, von Metsch was in charge of all governmental activities in the area. His leadership in strengthening the defenses of Wittenberg brought the hot-tempered nobleman into conflict with many citizens of the town. Luther intervened with Elector Johann in behalf of the people. Nonetheless, von Metsch continued to cooperate with Luther in promoting evangelical teaching. Von Metsch aided the visitation of congregations in Saxony in 1527–29. However, the courtier repeatedly took advantage of women and earned Luther's severe criticism for his sexual sins. Luther refused him the Lord's Supper in 1531, calling on him to repent and abandon his exploitation of women. Von Metsch did marry in 1532 and sought absolution, which Luther gave him. Their reconciliation was, however, not long lasting. In subsequent years, Luther again criticized his heavy-handed manner of governing and his exploitation of Johann's subjects for his own gain. Particularly in 1538, during a period in which hunger threatened the town, Luther and his colleagues complained to the elector about von

Metsch's management of the distribution of food. In 1539, Elector Johann Friedrich transferred him to the administration of the territory around Colditz.

***Matthäus Ratzeberger* (1501–1558)** and Luther may have become acquainted during Ratzeberger's student days in Wittenberg (1517–25). He devoted himself to the study of medicine and became the official municipal physician in the town of Brandenburg, west of Berlin, where he enthusiastically promoted Luther's proclamation of forgiveness in Jesus Christ. In 1526, he moved to Mansfeld county to serve at the court of Count Albrecht. In 1538, Elector Johann Friedrich called him to be his personal physician. Elector and physician formed a fast friendship, and the doctor became a trusted counselor of his prince. Ratzeberger's relationship with Luther also deepened into a warm friendship. As war clouds gathered in 1546, Ratzeberger advised the elector not to go to war against Charles V, but when hostilities broke out in June of that year, the physician accompanied his prince on the military campaign that took them to south Germany and then ended in disaster in April 1547. After a brief interlude practicing medicine in Nordhausen, Ratzeberger accepted the position of city physician in Erfurt in 1550, where he remained to his death. In the 1550s, he supported the Gnesio-Lutheran criticism of the policies of Melanchthon and his colleagues in the service of Elector Moritz of Saxony. In those years the physician wrote a biography of Luther and his times. As Ratzeberger lay dying, his pastor, Andreas Poach, reported that he addressed the portrait of Luther hanging on his bedroom wall and said with a smile, "my dear Luther," and then to those at his bedside, "if God wills it, I will soon be with him. Then we will have a good conversation, and I will tell him of all the strange and curious things that have happened since he left us."

In addition, the court painter, Lukas Cranach, and court musicians discussed in chapter 3 contributed significantly to the life of the court of Frederick the Wise and his two successors, Johann and Johann Friedrich.

The Common Citizens

Few others with whom Luther had frequent contact on the streets and in the church and the stores of Wittenberg have left a record. Two who have were prominent tradesman.

The goldsmith ***Christian Döring* (d. 1533)** lived next door to Lukas Cranach the Elder, on Wittenberg's main street. The two cooperated in printing projects until they broke off their association in 1525/26. Döring provided the wagon that carried Luther to

Worms in 1521. He served as a member of the town council and as an administrator of the common chest, the town's welfare system.

***Peter Beskendorf* (d. 1538)**, Luther's barber, was one of the few citizens of Wittenberg with whom Luther had daily contact on the streets of the town whose name is known. Beskendorf handled the several aspects of his trade well enough to have served Prince Joachim of Anhalt as his "surgeon." Beskendorf was well connected with the university and conveyed greetings to CHRISTOPH SCHEURL, who had departed Wittenberg for Nuremberg, through Luther in 1517. The barber liked to engage professors in conversation about the faith and requested Luther supply him with instruction on prayer. Luther complied with his request in early 1535, shortly before tragedy befell the Beskendorf family. The treatise, *A Simple Way to Pray*, shaped an approach to meditating on the parts of the catechism that considered each part as instruction, as thanksgiving, as a guide to confession of sins, and as a petition. However, at an Easter Eve dinner at the home of Beskendorf's daughter and son-in-law, a former soldier, beer had apparently flown freely. The son-in-law boasted that he could make himself invulnerable to any wound. Peter used his knife to test the claim, and his son-in-law fell dead at his feet. Luther and his colleagues joined Beskendorf's legal representative, the electoral counselor FRANZ BURKHARD, in intervening on Peter's behalf and won the commutation of his death sentence, but Peter had to go into exile and forfeit his property. He lived out his life in poverty in Dessau.

Luther's Printers

Luther's literary activity, along with that of his colleagues, created Wittenberg's first industry, printing. For several decades, printers had occupied an increasingly important place in the life of the German university. The monastic copy centers that had produced texts on which students wrote their notes while hearing lectures slowly gave way to the more accurately printed merchandise more quickly and efficiently delivered by the press. From the founding of the university in 1502, Wittenberg had had presses, initially the private press of Professor NIKOLAUS MARSCHALK, who used a printer named Heinrich Schneider to publish texts. Two others, WOLFGANG STÖCKEL from Leipzig and Hermann Trebelius, who took over Marschalk's operation, had briefly served university needs.

The first established printer in Wittenberg, ***Johann Rhau-Grunenberg* (d. ca. 1529)** (not related to Georg Rhau), had studied in Erfurt and worked for the printer WOLFGANG STÜRMER there. He may have attained the master's degree during his studies. JOHANNES von Staupitz drew Rhau-Grunenberg to Wittenberg in 1508. For a while, his presses resided within the Augustinian monastery complex near the university building, where he largely produced texts for professors' lectures. In 1516, he published Luther's first venture into the public use of print, his edition of the late medieval "mystical" meditation, the *German Theology*, the first of several of Luther's works that he published. The aesthetically sensitive Reformer complained bitterly about the poor quality of Rhau-Grunenberg's work in 1521, alleging that his relaxed manner of dealing with his product resulted in sloppy pamphlets and books. Nonetheless, a decade later Luther recalled that he had been a pious and honest man. He continued to serve Luther, among other printers who joined him in Wittenberg, until 1527. Some four hundred titles appeared from his presses.

By 1519, it had become clear that Luther and his colleagues were making use of printed works to spread their call for reform and that whatever they printed with Luther's name and with the location listed as "Wittenberg" would sell, particularly if graced by the new form of woodcut designed by Lukas Cranach to frame the title page (what Andrew Pettegree has called "Brand Luther"). Luther himself pursued other printers to work alongside Rhau-Grunenberg and drew the son of the successful Leipzig printer, Melchior Lotter, to Wittenberg. ***Melchior Lott(h)er the Younger* (ca. 1490–ca. 1544)** had studied at the University of Leipzig and came to Wittenberg in December 1519 to establish his printing operation in the house of Lukas Cranach the Elder. He procured two presses and paper from the printer Johann Froben in Basel; later, Cranach invested in a paper mill to assure that Wittenberg printers always had raw material at hand. Among Lotter's first works were a defense of Luther by Johann Oecolampadius and the first of Luther's programmatic writings (composed between late spring 1520 and January 1522), *On Good Works*. In 1522, Lotter cooperated with Cranach and Christian Döring, who were financing the printing of Luther's translation of the New Testament, taking over the actual production from a printer whose bankruptcy ended his participation in the project. The quality of Lotter's type and his work pleased Luther. The demand for press time from the Wittenberg professors became so great that he requested the aid of his younger brother Michael in 1523. Melchior the Younger attacked one of his apprentices with a cobbler's awl and had to pay a stiff fine. This incident led to a break with Cranach and Döring. He had to move to inadequate quarters in Wittenberg, and in 1525 he returned to Leipzig and later worked in Saxon Freiberg. Luther indicated at table that Melchior Lotter the Younger's profits were "godless and intolerable gain."

His brother ***Michael Lotter* (ca. 1499–ca. 1556)** married the mayor's daughter and belonged to the upper middle class of Leipzig when he came to join his brother Melchior.

The printer's signet (mark) of Melchior Lotter (1512), father of Melchior the Younger and Michael

He remained in Wittenberg until 1528 when increasing competition within Wittenberg and the growing significance of the Reformation in Magdeburg, led by NIKOLAUS VON AMSDORF, attracted him down the Elbe to that larger city, where he continued to be an important supporting arm of the Wittenberg call for reform, publishing Luther's writings and the works of a number of his followers.

By the time Melchior Lotter the Younger left Wittenberg, ***Nickel Schirlentz*** had established his workshop in the home of ANDREAS KARLSTADT. He served Luther and his colleagues faithfully, publishing over three hundred titles between 1521 and 1547 in Wittenberg. In 1538, he was arrested for printing the *Epigrammaton* of Simon Lemnius, who had studied in Wittenberg, associated especially with MELANCHTHON, and then composed scurrilous satires attacking Luther and Melanchthon as well as the electoral government before fleeing to the court of ARCHBISHOP ALBRECHT OF MAINZ. After his release from jail, Schirlentz returned to the good graces of the Reformers, publishing a new edition of Luther's Small Catechism as his last work in 1547. Luther did comment that Schirlentz did not count his pennies but weighed them.

The father of ***Joseph Klug* (ca. 1490–1552)**, Peter, had worked in the important printing operation of Anton Koberger in Nuremberg. Joseph married Barbara Schumann, the sister of the Leipzig printer Valentin Schumann. Cranach and Döring engaged Joseph as printer in 1523, and he set up shop in Cranach's home, working together with his employers but also independently producing printed works as well. In 1524, he began to produce works with Hebrew type. By 1526, he had taken over the Cranach-Döring operation. Financial overcommitments plagued him, but he printed his way out of them.

Luther had close connections with ***Hans Lufft* (1495–1584)**, his wife, Dorothea Hermann of Leipzig, and their family. Lufft came to Wittenberg in 1523 to set up shop and won Luther's confidence quickly. The two were well-connected socially. The Luthers attended Lufft's daughter's wedding, and later her marital problems caused the Reformer concern. He thought Lufft too eager to make a hefty profit on his products and that he was thus "cursed because of unquenchable greed." Nonetheless, Luther placed the printing of the Bible, in its parts and after 1534 in whole, almost exclusively in Lufft's hands after 1526. The Wittenberg team, including Caspar Cruciger, Georg Rörer, and Christoph Walter, worked closely with Lufft. He became a member of the town council and served as a judge. Long after Luther's death, he continued to publish the Reformer's works.

Hans Lufft

***Georg Rhau* (1488–1548)** had studied at the University of Leipzig and attained the bachelor's degree in arts in 1514. From 1518 to 1520, he served as cantor at the school of Saint Thomas in Leipzig and from 1520 to 1522 as schoolmaster in Eisleben and Hildburghausen. By 1525 he had turned to the printing trade. The works that came from his presses betray his interest in music as well as theology and the cultivation of piety. The first printing of the Augsburg Confession came from his workshop. He became a member of Wittenberg's municipal council and was related by marriage to the printer Peter Seitz the Elder. He cooperated with Lukas Cranach, putting the artist's woodcuts to use frequently in his printings. Rhau worked closely with and for the electoral court in Wittenberg. When the Smalcald War broke out in 1546, Rhau took a mobile press with him as he accompanied Elector Johann Friedrich on the campaign in southern Germany. Emperor Charles V confiscated his press after the elector's defeat in April 1547. Modest in demeanor, Rhau actively supported Luther's Reform enterprise, for instance, providing

Portrait of Georg Rhau attributed to Lukas Cranach the Elder (ca. 1542)

scholarships for needy students. Among the most scholarly of the learned printers of Wittenberg, Rhau's piety was reflected in his theological knowledge and his concern for popular education in the faith. After his death in 1548, his heirs continued to publish until 1566.

***Hans Weiss* (d. ca. 1544)** had studied in Frankfurt an der Oder before coming to Wittenberg as a student in 1520. In 1525, he set up his printing operation in the town. He took over from RHAU-GRUNENBERG the printing of Luther's Postil and began to print other works by the Reformer. Among the one hundred titles he produced are many by Luther. He left Wittenberg for Berlin in 1539 as ELECTOR JOACHIM II introduced the Reformation to Brandenburg. He served as printer there until his death.

The family of ***Peter Seitz the Elder* (d. ca. 1548)**, together with his wife, Ursula nee Kersten, and their son ***Peter Seitz the Younger* (d. 1593)**, offers a good example of how deeply involved the entire family of the artisans and entrepreneurs of the sixteenth century were. Ursula, the sister of the second wife of GEORG RHAU, and later her son took over the business when her husband died in 1548. The family worked closely with Luther and MELANCHTHON and produced two hundred works over the years from 1534 to 1579.

Among the several printers who exercised their trade in Wittenberg for a briefer part of Luther's lifetime was ***Veit Kreutzer* (d. 1578)**, who began printing in Wittenberg in 1541. He cooperated with Luther and later with MELANCHTHON. His operation in Wittenberg produced the last of nearly 350 titles, mostly in the service of Wittenberg Reform. He ceased printing in 1563.

In the midst of this world, the team that supported and sustained Luther, inspired and corrected him, formed around 1520. Their stories come in the next chapter.

CHAPTER 3

The Wittenberg Team: Luther's Family, Colleagues, and Early Students

Martin Luther is often depicted as a person standing alone, and there were times when he gained insights or made decisions without anyone beside him. But his Reformation unfolded out of his insights and decisions within the context of conversations with partners who fed and nourished his ideas and associates who processed, contributed to, and carried his message further. At the heart of these efforts that are labeled "the Reformation" stand the Wittenberg colleagues and students with whom Luther lived and gained inspiration—from their critique as well as their feedback and complementary ideas. Most important in this Wittenberg was, for Luther, his own family.

Luther's Family

Katharina von Bora **(1499–1552)** sprang from a family of the lower nobility; her father, Hans von Bora, and her mother, Katharina Haubitz (or Haugwitz), had holdings near Leipzig, to which economic trends and banking practices had not been kind. At the death of her mother, she was placed in a Benedictine convent at Brehna and then transferred to the Cistercian convent at Nimbschen, where she took vows in 1515. Her superior was the sister of JOHANNES VON STAUPITZ. She escaped the convent in 1523 with eleven sisters, who were all taken by the merchant Leonhardt Koppe to Wittenberg, where Luther and his colleagues found suitable husbands and/or employment for them. Katharina was the last to be placed since her intended, HIERONYMUS BAUMGARTNER, a student from Nuremberg, was prevented by his patrician parents from marrying her. When she refused to marry another recent student and suggested instead she wed either NIKOLAUS VON AMSDORF or Luther himself, the stage was set for the Reformer himself to marry, a step he had urged others in holy orders to take but had not envisioned for himself, a condemned criminal and heretic. They married in June 1525 with little passion, Luther reported from his side, but with a rapidly growing affection and a deep sense of cooperation and dedication to the task of directing reform. Katharina's education in the cloister had prepared her to give Luther astute and keen-sighted theological advice, and her innate wisdom only increased her authority in his eyes. She complemented his lack of responsibility for money with a strong business sense and proved herself an able administrator of the Luther properties in and outside of Wittenberg. Her stewardship enabled her to repurchase a farm near Zöllsdorf that had belonged to her family. Luther summarized her activities in 1535: she drove wagon, tended the gardens, purchased cattle and tended them, and brewed beer, among other things. With the aid of a number of servants, she proved a most hospitable hostess to dozens of students and a flock of relatives who lived for a time with the Luther family in the Black Cloister. Her take-charge manner irritated a variety of those with whom she came in contact, including Melanchthon's wife, KATHARINA; one of Luther's amanuenses, VEIT DIETRICH; and GREGOR BRÜCK, the electoral Saxon chancellor. On the other hand, PHILIP MELANCHTHON and Katharina von Bora became good friends and supported each other with insights and presence in facing the rigors of daily life. Luther left a last will and testament, which, contrary to Saxon law, placed his widow in charge of all his possessions and his children. ELECTOR JOHANN FRIEDRICH intervened and appointed others as guardians for the children and provided them with financial support. As imperial armies approached Wittenberg at the end of the Smalcald War in 1547, Katharina fled first to Magdeburg and then to the domains of the dukes of Braunschweig-Lüneburg. Returning to Saxony, she resumed administration of the Black Cloister as a dormitory for students. In 1552, she fell from the wagon carrying her to Torgau, where she lingered and was taken care of by her daughter Margarethe until she died of her injuries. She provided a model of the pastor's wife for Wittenberg students and exemplified with her husband the idea of life in the pastoral ministry.

The Luthers had six children. Once he became a father, Luther's use of the designation "Father" for God increased, an indication that he also learned theology from his children.

Portrait of Katharina von Bora by workshop of Lukas Cranach the Elder (1528)

His correspondence with them and his comments on them indicate a warm relationship between parent and child. ***Hans (Johannes)* (1526–1575)**, was named for his baptismal sponsor, Johannes Bugenhagen, but the name must have pleased his grandfather as well. He was baptized two hours after his birth by Georg Rörer, who was deacon of the Wittenberg congregation, with Bugenhagen, Justus Jonas, and Lukas Cranach present. The father reported with concern the illnesses that struck his children. When young Hans was four years old, Luther wrote him a letter from the Coburg, attempting to elicit good behavior by holding forth the prospect of a garden in which he and his playmates, the sons of Justus Jonas and Philip Melanchthon, could enjoy "crossbows, whistles, and drums" if they "prayed, studied, and behaved." Nonetheless, the father exhibited a strictness with Hans that apparently was not the case with the other children. However, the eldest child knew how to press the boundaries of his father's patience. When his father told him to stop disturbing his work with loud singing, Hans simply sang very softly, and the theologian found this a wonderful example of the kind of blending of awe and joy that believers should have in God's presence. Hieronymus Weller, a Wittenberg student, served as tutor for the Luther children. In 1542, the Luthers decided to send Hans to Torgau to secondary school, along with his cousin Florian von Bora. When Luther discovered that Florian had stolen a knife from Hans's younger brother Paul, he requested suitable punishment. Luther summoned his son back to Wittenberg shortly thereafter, to be with his sister Magdalena as she lay dying. Hans, along with his brothers, stood by his father's side as he lay dying in Eisleben. In 1549, Hans was offered the opportunity to study law at the University of Königsberg. With his training as a lawyer, Hans pursued the career his grandfather had wished for Hans's father. He served the electoral Saxon government as a privy counselor throughout his career.

***Elisabeth* (1527–1528)** was reported to have had an uncomplicated birth, but illness overtook her before her first birthday. Luther related that he had never conceived of the depth of the hurt that he and Katharina experienced at the loss of their second child.

***Magdalena* (1529–1542)** illustrates the role that children played in the consciousness of their parents in the sixteenth century. Argula von Grumbach had given Luther advice on how to raise his children, suggesting ways to wean Magdalena when she visited him at the Coburg in 1530, after having earlier shared other advice on child-rearing with him. At the Coburg, Luther received a sketch of his youngest from Katharina, and he posted it on his wall. Luther's expression of grief at Magdalena's death in 1542 demonstrated the depth of sorrow at the loss of a child that accompanied his assurance of her resurrection in the completion of Christ's baptismal promise to her.

***Martin* (1531–1565)** provided the Reformer with an example of godly concentration as he played with a doll at age eight. But as he grew older, young Martin caused his father more worries than the other children, and this concern proved to be justified. In 1546, he and his brothers Hans and Paul accompanied their father to Eisleben and were with him when he died. The younger Martin studied theology but did not enter the pastoral ministry. He lived at home with his mother and then alone until his marriage in 1560. He and his wife, daughter of a prominent Wittenberg citizen, continued to live in the Black Cloister but let it go to wrack and ruin. The younger Martin avoided gainful employment and fell victim to alcohol. His alcoholism brought him to an early death at age thirty-three.

Portrait of a young girl by Lukas Cranach the Elder (1540), later identified as Magdalena Luther

***Paul* (1533–1593)** was at his father's side when he died, along with his brothers Hans and Martin. Melanchthon and Veit Winsheim gave Paul his early instruction, and at Melanchthon's advice he pursued the study of medicine, an outgrowth of his interest in nature. In 1557 the Wittenberg faculty awarded him his doctorate. He accepted a call to teach in the medical faculty at the newly founded University of Jena in 1558 and began with lectures on Galen. He served Duke Johann Friedrich the Middler of Saxony as personal court physician, and after the prince's imprisonment in 1567, Joachim II of Brandenburg appointed him court physician. At Joachim's death, August of Saxony engaged Paul as court physician. August's interest in the natural sciences was fueled in part by his love for experiments in chemistry, since August was hoping to discover the way

Paul Luther (date unknown)

in which gold might be produced through other substances. Paul was supposed to aid in the Saxon court's pursuit of such a method. When August died, Paul Luther continued his service at the court in Dresden for three years as physician for Elector Christian I, August's son. In 1589, the elector's decided drift toward Calvinistic teaching caused his physician to move to Leipzig and practice medicine there until 1592, when Duke Friedrich Wilhelm of Saxony assumed regency for the young son of Christian I, Christian II, who had ascended the throne in Saxony when his father drank himself to death. Paul Luther died in early 1593. Five of the six children that he and his wife, Anna von Warbek, had survived him.

***Margarethe* (1534–1570)** also received her father's tender care. He harshly criticized his own forgetfulness in touching the mouth of the eight-month-old child without washing his hands, and he worried about her bout with the measles and the fever it brought when she was ten. Margarethe was with her mother as Katharina suffered her fatal illness in 1552. She subsequently married a Prussian bureaucrat, Erhard von Kunheim, in 1555.

The Luther household also included a number of relatives and students who made the Black Cloister their home, and to provide for its population, Katharina and Luther had several pillars of support in addition to the servants. Among them were numbered Katharina's aunt and Luther's personal servant or *famulus*.

Magdalena von Bora **(d. 1537)**, called "Muhme Lene" by the family, was Katharina's aunt and lived with the family from 1528 on. She had earlier found her adult home in the convent at Nimbschen and fled shortly after Katharina left the cloister. She aided in the care and feeding of the many relatives, students, and other guests who boarded with the Luthers or just dropped by. Luther ministered to her as she lay dying in 1537.

Wolfgang Sieberger **(ca. 1497–1547)** came from his native Munich to Wittenberg to study in late 1515. Luther welcomed him and sought help at the electoral court for the poor young man. By 1519, he had become Luther's *famulus* or personal attendant and served in that capacity until the Reformer's death. Subsequently he continued to aid Katharina and the Luther children until his death. Luther learned how to work with wood with Sieberger at his side. The Reformer obtained an electoral pension for his servant and purchased a house in which he could live should he ever have to leave the Black Cloister. Luther wrote a satire over Sieberger's care for the finches in the 1530s.

Luther's Colleagues in Theology

Next to his own family, Luther leaned on and profited from one colleague more than others. ***Philip Melanchthon*** **(1497–1560)**, Luther's partner in leading Wittenberg Reform, was born in Bretten, the home of his mother, Barbara Reuter (1477–1529), whose father was a merchant and civic leader there. Her husband, Georg Schwarzerdt (1459–1508), had learned his trade of metalworking in Nuremberg and had become one of the best manufacturers of armor in the German lands. His products protected Emperor Maximilian, his own prince, Elector Philip the Upright of the Palatinate, and a number of others. With his father, the young Melanchthon visited Heidelberg on occasion, where he later would attend the university. In 1508 his father died, allegedly because a rival prince had poisoned him to prevent his further production of effective armor. Young Melanchthon's mother sent him and his brother Georg to Pforzheim to attend the Latin school there. There, a relative of a relative by marriage, Johannes Reuchlin, recognized his gifts and set

Portrait of Philip Melanchthon by Lukas Cranach the Elder (1537)

him on the course of learning within the framework of biblical humanism. Reuchlin took the Greek and translated his family name, Schwarzerdt (black earth) to Melanchthon. Melanchthon's university studies began in 1509, in Heidelberg, where he received his bachelor's degree before departing in 1512 for Tübingen, where he attained his master's degree and excellent instruction in the ancient languages. Reuchlin recommended him as an instructor in Greek to FREDERICK THE WISE. Apparently, the adventure that Luther's posting of the Ninety-Five Theses on indulgences was creating in the young university attracted him. His inaugural address called for extensive humanistic reform of the curriculum, in the liberal arts and the higher faculties of theology, law, and medicine. He and Luther formed a partnership that linked them in a mutual exchange of insights and information, creating a deep bond between them. Melanchthon attended the Leipzig Disputation with Luther and ANDREAS KARLSTADT in 1519. Melanchthon continued his entire career to teach courses in logic and rhetoric, history and physics, and a number of other subjects in the liberal arts faculty of the university, but he began lecturing on books of the Bible, specifically their Greek texts, upon his arrival. ELECTOR JOHANN formally appointed him to the faculty of theology in 1526, and he continued to teach in both faculties until his death. His marriage in 1520 began a thirty-seven-year relationship of affection, even if his wife was not capable of running a household in the manner of KATHARINA VON BORA. During Luther's stay in the Wartburg (1521–22), Melanchthon and his friend NIKOLAUS VON AMSDORF guided the reform in Wittenberg through a stormy period, contending with an undisciplined colleague in Karlstadt and with "heavenly prophets" from Zwickau, three young men who claimed special revelations from God. Often underway in the service of Wittenberg Reform, Melanchthon served as an ecclesiastical advisor and diplomat to electors Frederick the Wise, Johann, Johann Friedrich, Moritz, and August. With Luther and other colleagues, he supervised and conducted the visitation of Saxon parishes in 1527–28, which was designed to bring the practices of the Reformation to local congregations. Thus, Melanchthon helped form the polity of the church of the Wittenberg Reformation. His skills were put to work on drafting the explanation of these reforms on behalf of evangelical princes and town councils that was read to Emperor Charles V at Augsburg on June 25, 1530. The confession was never considered "his," but rather it belonged to the secular rulers who had staked title and life on it by opposing Emperor Charles with its presentation. The Roman Catholic party engaged the evangelicals under Melanchthon's leadership in intensive negotiations in Augsburg, and others compared Melanchthon to Daniel in the lion's den in his eloquent and determined presentation of the doctrine of justification through faith in Christ. The rejection of the Augsburg Confession by the emperor and the formal reading of the "Confutation" of the papal theologians Charles commissioned to evaluate and refute the Augsburg Confession angered Melanchthon. He set about in the fall of 1530 to compose an *Apology*, or "Defense." It was published with the text of the Confession in April 1531. After pressuring Melanchthon to publish his defense, Luther made innumerable suggestions for improvement in the published text, and Melanchthon issued a second edition in September of that year. In the 1530s, negotiations with Roman Catholic theologians commanded much of Melanchthon's time, and these efforts culminated in the colloquy in Regensburg in 1541. At the behest of Elector Johann Friedrich, Melanchthon, with assistance from his colleagues, revised the text of the Augsburg Confession, the "mission statement" of the evangelical princes and towns, to prepare for these negotiations. The defeat of Johann Friedrich in the Smalcald War and the subsequent handing over of Wittenberg to the new elector in 1547 forced Melanchthon to make a difficult decision. He chose his university over his prince because of his fear that Moritz could close the University of Wittenberg and rely alone on his own university in Leipzig. Melanchthon advised Moritz as the new elector attempted to avoid imperial wrath; he developed a policy statement, the Leipzig Proposal, which was presented to the diet of his domains in December 1548. The proposal's attempt to reintroduce some medieval customs under the guise of adherence to the imperial "Augsburg Interim" aroused fierce opposition from some of Melanchthon's closest friends and former students. The resulting controversies—over adiaphora (the neutral practices neither forbidden nor commanded by Scripture that Melanchthon and Moritz hoped would make it appear as though Saxony had adopted the Augsburg Interim) and then over the necessity of good works for salvation and the freedom or bondage of the human will in conversion—plagued Melanchthon for the last decade of his life. He rejected efforts from his opponents to reconcile because of his

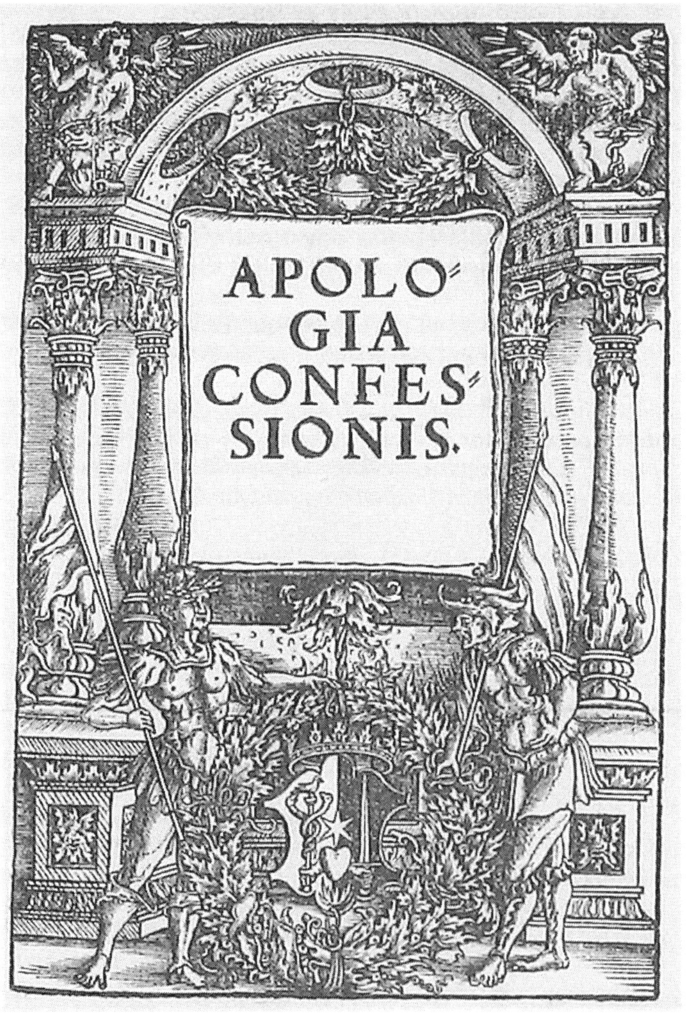

Title page of Melanchthon's Apology to the Augsburg Confession (Apologia Confessionis Augustanae), *printed in 1531*

deep suspicion and resentment against their not recognizing his good-faith efforts to save the pulpits of Saxony for Lutheran preachers by avoiding imperial invasion. Melanchthon had also long sought other ways of expressing the presence of Christ in the Lord's Supper. In 1536, he had brought together Luther with Martin Bucer and other south German theologians in the "Wittenberg Concord," which was subsequently incorporated into the *Formula of Concord*. In Melanchthon's later years, the influence of his son-in-law Caspar Peucer, whose way of thought was deeply saturated by Aristotelian physics, probably played a significant role in Melanchthon's thinking on ways of describing Christ's presence in the Lord's Supper. These later attempts to speak of the Lord's Supper aroused suspicion that Melanchthon was accepting John Calvin's understanding of a spiritual presence of Christ in the sacrament, but Melanchthon also refused to agree to Calvin's wording. These controversies embittered his last years and made him long for the death that finally delivered him from what he called "the madness of the theologians."

Melanchthon married his wife, ***Katharina Krapp*** **(1497–1557)**, daughter of Hans Krapp, a cloth merchant and member of the Wittenberg town council, in 1520. Her father had died in 1515; her brother Hieronymus followed in his father's footsteps in business and politics and was numbered later in life among the five richest citizens of Wittenberg. Katharina apparently was not gifted as a manager of the household, and that may have contributed to the tensions that kept her and Katharina von Bora at a distance despite the good relationship Melanchthon maintained with Luther's wife. The love between Melanchthon and his wife is reflected in his comments about her, particularly at her death, which occurred while Melanchthon was at the colloquy in Worms in the fall of 1557.

The Melanchthon's had four children. ***Anna*** **(1522–1547)** married a favorite student of her father, Georg Sabinus, in 1536. She bore six children. Her husband's gifts as a poet won him a position in the liberal arts faculty at Frankfurt an der Oder, and he moved his family to Königsberg to contribute to the organization of Duke Albrecht's new university in 1544. Sabinus turned out to be an abuser, but Anna stood by him. She died shortly after the birth of their sixth child, as Melanchthon was considering a trip to Königsberg to bring her back to Wittenberg. His letters to the couple and his observations to friends reveal his deep love for his daughter, his chagrin at his having falsely judged Sabinus, and his ability to find comfort in his trust in God's providence.

Philip **(1525–1605)** caused his parents grief for a different reason. While studying in Leipzig, he secretly promised to marry Margarethe Kuffner, a stepdaughter of a local pastor. His father consented, but his mother objected strenuously and sent the young Philip to Marburg to study. Philip later married a widow from Torgau, Katharina Waldener, and lived in Torgau until he became a notary for the University of Wittenberg.

***Georg* (1527–1529)** died at age two, his death eliciting deep expressions of grief from his father.

***Magdalena* (1531–1575)** married another of her father's favorite students, the professor of astronomy and later medicine, CASPAR PEUCER. The newly married couple resided in the Melanchthon home and then later in a house built for them at the back of the garden behind the Melanchthon residence. The Peucers and the first five of their ten children provided Melanchthon with much-needed psychological support in the final, troubled years of his life.

***Johannes Koch* (ca. 1492–1553)** administered Melanchthon's household from early on. He had come from Ilsfeld, near Heilbronn, to study in Wittenberg in 1516 and attained the bachelor's degree in 1518. Of his wife, who may have died young, nothing is known, but he did have two sons who seem to have lived with him in the Melanchthon household. Melanchthon praised Koch's piety; each morning he began the day with a Bible reading and prayer, and then tended to the Melanchthon children and the housekeeping duties. He accompanied the family when, during the turbulence of the late 1540s caused by the Smalcald War, they sought exile. Melanchthon demonstrated deep concern for Koch as the servant grew older and frailer in his last years.

Luther's Other Colleagues in Theology

Among the first colleagues from whom Luther gained support, even before the arrival of Melanchthon in 1518, was ***Wenceslaus Linck* (1482–1547).** He arrived in Wittenberg in 1508 at the behest of the Augustinian cloister at Waldheim, where he had been inducted into the order after studying in Leipzig from 1498 to 1502. JOHANNES VON STAUPITZ was striving to strengthen the order and make it an instrument of reform. In 1511, one year before Luther received the doctorate, four of Staupitz's friars, including Linck, were awarded the doctorate in theology at the Leucorea. As prior of the Wittenberg cloister and member of the theological faculty, Linck's friendship with Luther worked to the advantage of both in those earliest years of Luther's time in Wittenberg. A visit to Nuremberg in 1516 and his preaching there acquainted him with the city and its humanist circle, the *Sodalitas Staupitziana*, including WILLIBALD PIRCKHEIMER, LAZARUS SPENGLER, and ALBRECHT DÜRER. Linck accompanied Luther to the meeting of the order in Heidelberg in April

1518, where Luther's theses on the theology of the cross laid out his central core for teaching Scripture. In September 1518, Linck accompanied Luther to Augsburg when he was examined by Cardinal Cajetan. When Staupitz resigned his offices in the Augustinian Eremite order, Linck succeeded him as vicar-general, an office that required visitation of the sixty-six houses under his jurisdiction. In this role, he reinforced Staupitz's plans for reform with Luther's theology and put these principles into practice, including the release of brothers from their vows. In 1522, he was called to head the church in Altenburg. Luther came there to marry him to Margarethe Schweizer. Linck introduced communion in both kinds soon after his arrival in Altenburg. In 1525, his pleas for mercy for captured peasant leaders moved Elector Frederick to spare the lives of all but two of them. The city council of Nuremberg called him there in 1525, where he served until his death. Through numerous publications, he provided catechetical and exegetical helps for pastors.

Among those who preceded Luther as an instructor in Wittenberg was also ***Nikolaus von Amsdorf* (1483–1565)**. Son of a sister of Johannes von Staupitz and a minor nobleman, who served Frederick the Wise as a courtier, and the grandson of the chief secretary of Elector Frederick II's chancery, Amsdorf seemed bound for a leadership position himself. His uncle procured him a place at the new University of Wittenberg. Amsdorf's initial doubts and discomfort in reaction to Luther's shifting definition of the Christian faith turned into a fervid devotion to his colleague and his savior, Jesus. Originally a propagator of "the Scotist way" of thinking, his scholastic background in working with the image of the sovereign will of God in Duns Scotus may have prepared him for accepting Luther's announcement of the God who exhibits his power in unconditional mercy. Amsdorf may never have felt completely comfortable as university professor, and so when the city of Magdeburg asked Luther to come to introduce Reform and serve as pastor there, Amsdorf instead traveled down the Elbe. He spent over seventeen successful though conflict-filled years there as superintendent of the city's church. With two who had been studying in Wittenberg when he left, Caspar Cruciger and then Georg Major, as rectors of the municipal school, and with the aid of other pastors, he preached, catechized, and counseled, bringing the citizenry into the Lutheran worldview, in the face of continuous threats of execution for heresy from the local cathedral chapter. During his Magdeburg years, Amsdorf remained in close contact with his Wittenberg colleagues, supporting Luther and disagreeing at points with Melanchthon when he thought that Philip was placing a false emphasis on human responsibility. Close friends with his former prince, Elector Johann Friedrich, he rather unwillingly followed the elector's call to assume the bishop's office in the diocese of Naumburg and Zeitz when the elector exerted military pressure on the cathedral chapter in 1542. Ordained into that office by Luther, he struggled against the opposition of the cathedral chapter; the local Wittenberg-minded superintendent, Nikolaus Medler; and the electoral administrator of the diocese's temporal affairs, Melchior von Creutzen. Urged by Johann Friedrich to join him in Weimar when the Smalcald War broke out in 1546, Amsdorf left his residence in Zeitz, never to return. After the defeat of the evangelical Smalcald League in the war in 1547, Amsdorf was deposed by the cathedral chapter and replaced with the Erasmian Roman Catholic JULIUS PFLUG, who had the support of the new elector of Saxony, MORITZ, Johann Friedrich's cousin, who had been awarded for loyalty to EMPEROR CHARLES V with the electoral title and much of Johann Friedrich's lands. Amsdorf moved to Magdeburg and became a focal point of opposition to Moritz and the Wittenberg colleagues who supported their new prince. Moritz's proposed compromise religious policy, intended to appease Charles and his brother FERDINAND, created a crisis, and it did not help at all that Melanchthon had helped formulate the policy. This brought a number of questions that had caused tension between Amsdorf and his Wittenberg colleague into the open. Amsdorf provided at least symbolic leadership for the radical interpreters of Luther's thought in the Gnesio-Lutheran party. He repeated Luther's formulation "good works are detrimental to salvation"—when one relies on them for salvation—in a controversy over GEORG MAJOR's proposition that "good works are necessary for salvation," although Amsdorf himself prepared a pamphlet for publication (though it remained unpublished) entitled "Good Works are Necessary for the Christian Life." Amsdorf never married and lived out his last years in Eisenach with his sister, where Major, despite their fierce disagreement and public exchange of accusations of unfaithfulness to Luther and the gospel, visited him in 1564 for what the elder colleague regarded as a friendly conversation. Such was also the nature of the Wittenberg circle: passionate defense of Luther's truth, as each understood it, typified its members, who even in disagreement were linked by common experiences and concerns.

Luther also counted on the aid of a member of the staff of his prince, FREDERICK THE WISE, in his earliest days in Wittenberg and throughout his life. ***Georg Spalatin (Burckhardt)* (1484–1545)**, two months younger than Luther, came from a family in the tanning business in Spalt to the Saint Sebald school in nearby Nuremberg before beginning studies at the University of Erfurt in 1498. There, he joined the circle around NIKOLAUS MARSCHALK that was inspired by the humanistic impulses of KONRAD MUTIANUS. He followed Marschalk to Wittenberg and into the study of law. At Mutianus's instigation, he became an instructor at the Cistercian monastery of Georgenthal and supervised the library there. He came into possession of a Bible and began a lifelong study of Scripture. Ordained in 1508, he assumed duties the same year at the court of Frederick the Wise as tutor for the elector's nephews, his brother Johann's sons, Johann Friedrich and Johann Ernst, and later for their cousins Otto and Ernst of Braunschweig-Lüneburg and Frederick's own illegitimate son, Sebastian of Jessen. His prince entrusted to him the continuation of the *Saxon Chronicle* begun by Adam of Fulda. In 1512, Frederick placed Spalatin in charge of organizing a library for the electoral court and the university. His friend from his Erfurt days, Johannes Lang, brought him together with Luther, and they formed a fast friendship for the rest of their lives. Spalatin occupied key positions at Frederick's court from 1516 on when he became the elector's private secretary. He assumed the function of a confessor and, in 1522, the post of Frederick's court preacher. During the years following the posting of the Ninety-Five Theses, he served as the middleman between his prince and Luther, gently guiding Frederick into policies that protected and supported the reforms that his professor and colleagues were promoting. Spalatin's earlier contacts with Erasmus, including his translations of several of Erasmus's works into German, led Spalatin to believe that he could enlist the Dutch humanist for Luther's cause, but Erasmus disappointed him. Spalatin's counsel aided Luther in planning his course at the Diet of Worms, and during his months at the Wartburg Castle, Spalatin received and sent on correspondence to and from "Knight Jörg," Luther's code name while he was at the Wartburg. By 1523, Spalatin's sermons reveal his conversion to an evangelical interpretation of Scripture. He became anxious to leave the court but was persuaded by Luther to remain until Frederick's death in 1525. He then

Portrait of Georg Spalatin (Burkhardt) by Lukas Cranach the Elder (1509)

entered the parish ministry in Altenburg but remained active in the service of Frederick's brother and successor, Elector Johann, accompanying him to the imperial diet in Speyer in 1526 and the diet in Augsburg in 1530. His participation in negotiations leading to the Nuremberg Armistice of 1532 was critical for their success. In the administration of ELECTOR JOHANN FRIEDRICH THE MAGNANIMOUS, who succeeded his father in 1532, Spalatin played vital roles in visitations in electoral Saxony, in ducal Saxony, and other places, and frequently took part in deliberations furthering the Wittenberg Reform. From 1536, he was again in charge of the library of the university in Wittenberg. In 1544, when he fell ill with a kind of depression because of pastoral decisions he had made in regard to another pastor, Luther prayed, counseled, and cajoled him to better health. His study of Scripture never ceased, and apart from his regular preaching, he propagated the theology of Wittenberg in a variety of treatises, including a version of the "Lives of the Fathers" on figures from the early church.

AMSDORF continued to serve for a time as a professor after Luther's theology took hold of the faculty, as did ANDREAS KARLSTADT, and before they both left Wittenberg in the early 1520s, the team that actually led the Wittenberg Reformation had begun to form, with Luther and Melanchthon at its center. During the 1520s, they brought three others to the core of their reforming efforts.

***Justus Jonas* (1493–1555)** came to Wittenberg for studies in 1510–11 but then returned to Erfurt, where this native of Nordhausen had first come to study in 1506. In the humanist circle around MUTIANUS, Jonas learned the skills of the new learning, becoming especially proficient in Greek. His reputation as a learned follower of ERASMUS spread widely. He turned to the study of both canon and civil law, earning the double doctorate in the course of the 1510s. He served as a canon at Saint Severus church next to the Erfurt cathedral and assumed teaching duties in the arts faculty at the university there. Luther so impressed him at the Leipzig debate in 1519 that he became an ardent supporter of the Wittenberg professor, and in 1521 was called to teach canon law in Wittenberg. He accompanied Luther to the Diet of Worms shortly after his arrival. Caught up in the wave of excitement at the Leucorea over biblical studies, he asked to be relieved of his duties in teaching canon law and began a career as an exegetical professor. Although his commentary on Acts is his only published commentary, he lectured on Isaiah, Romans, Ephesians, Philippians, the Thessalonian Epistles, the Pastoral Epistles and Philemon, and perhaps other books. Like MELANCHTHON and BUGENHAGEN, he lectured on the text of the Vulgate but expanded the text with linguistic exposition from Greek and Hebrew. His use of the ancient fathers of the church was minimal. The proper distinction of Law and Gospel marked his preparation of his students for pastoral ministry. Jonas's chief contributions to the spread of the Wittenberg message consisted in his translations of the works of Luther and Melanchthon, some from Latin into German, some from German into Latin. He tailored his translation for specific audiences, in some cases pointing them particularly toward university-educated readers, in others altering their tone for a more popular readership. Among the works he translated were Luther's *On Bound Choice* and Melanchthon's *Apology of the Augsburg Confession*. Jonas served as dean of the theological faculty in Wittenberg from 1523 to 1533 and occasionally thereafter. His commitment to spreading Wittenberg Reform took him to the Saxon countryside in the visitations of 1527 and 1528, to the ducal Saxon visitation of 1539, to the Marburg Colloquy in 1529, to the Diet of Augsburg in 1530, and to the meeting in Smalcald in 1537 (he had served in the committee that aided Luther in the composition of the Smalcald Articles). In 1541, the city of Halle called him to be its ecclesiastical superintendent in the face of opposition from its temporal overlord, Archbishop Albrecht of Mainz. Jonas led the Reformation of the city until driven out in the Smalcald War by Spanish troops. A brief return after the defeat of the Smalcald League ended with the hostility aroused by his critique of the Leipzig Proposal of 1548, which provoked intense harassment from the government of Moritz of Saxony. One of Jonas's sons drowned in the Saale river shortly before the death of his first wife at the birth of their thirteenth child in 1542; his second wife died in 1549. His last years were spent largely without a permanent call, but he finally was given a position as pastor in Eisfeld by Duke Johann Ernst of Saxony, where he spent his last months.

Portrait of Justus Jonas

***Johannes Bugenhagen* (1485–1558)** left his native Pomerania for Wittenberg in 1521 and quickly became a member of the Wittenberg team. The attraction of Wittenberg arose out of his reading some of Luther's writings, especially on the Lord's Supper and penance, but also those on Christ and his saving work. Bugenhagen's immersion in the biblical humanism of ERASMUS had prepared him for his ever-deepening interest in interpreting Scripture, which he had begun to exercise in print as a rector of the school in Treptow and then lecturer at the Premonstratensian monastery in Belbuck in Pomerania. Hearing MELANCHTHON's lectures upon his arrival in Wittenberg influenced him profoundly, and he quickly grasped the distinction of Law and Gospel that his instructors used as the basis for biblical interpretation. Bugenhagen published a commentary on the Psalms in 1524, in which he emphasized the saving work of Christ and the nature of trust in his atoning work for salvation. He became rector of the school in Wittenberg and pastor of the town church in 1523, and a full member of the faculty of theology, in which he had been lecturing for a decade, in 1533, upon reception of his doctorate. He propagated Wittenberg teaching in a number of publications, including an exposition of the justification of sinners through Christ's work and the fruits of faith produced by the justified person in 1525. Among his other works are several treatments on the Lord's Supper, the marriage of priests, confession and absolution, and monasticism. His harmony of the accounts of Christ's passion, death, and resurrection, a work begun in Pomerania, became an important tool for pastors in conveying the significance of Christ's saving work, as were a series of commentaries on Matthew, the Pauline Epistles, and several

Portrait of Johannes Bugenhagen by Lukas Cranach the Elder (1537)

Old Testament books. Bugenhagen's primary task in spreading the Wittenberg Reform consisted of his visitation of towns and territories (and even the kingdom of Denmark) to give counsel on the reform of the teaching and practice of the church. He authored more church ordinances than any other individual within the Wittenberg movement. He stood by Melanchthon in the difficult period after the defeat of evangelical forces in the Smalcald War. His support of the Leipzig Proposal or Interim of 1548 earned him criticism from many of his former students, but he avoided becoming involved in the controversies that ensued for the most part. His son, ***Johannes Bugenhagen the Younger* (1531/32–1592)**, began lecturing in the Wittenberg theological faculty in 1560. In the discussions of the presence of Christ in the Lord's Supper within electoral Saxony in the early 1570s, the younger Bugenhagen held a moderating position and rejected the crypto-Philippist views of Peucer and others. He contributed to the restoration of Luther's teaching after 1574.

***Caspar Cruciger* (1504–1548)**, a native of Leipzig, attended the university there and studied under the humanist scholar Peter Mosellanus. He attended the Leipzig Disputation between Luther and Johann Eck in 1519. When the plague broke out in 1521, he moved to Wittenberg and began learning Hebrew. His skills quickly earned him a place in the translation team working on the Old Testament. His teachers sent him to aid their former colleague, Nikolaus von Amsdorf, in Magdeburg, where Cruciger was called to be rector of the newly founded Latin school in 1525. After three years there, he returned to Wittenberg to assist with the instruction of increasing numbers of students, in part because of the frequent absences of his former teachers and new colleagues, especially Johannes Bugenhagen. Cruciger received his doctorate in 1533 and continued to lecture, especially on

Portrait of Caspar Cruciger the Elder (in a 1654 publication)

the New Testament, to his death. His activities in promoting Wittenberg theology included participation in the visitation of ducal Saxony in 1539 and in the negotiations with papal theologians in 1540 and 1541 at Hagenau, Worms, and Regensburg. At times, Cruciger used materials prepared for classroom lectures and for public addresses by Melanchthon for his students, as was the Preceptor's custom for others in his circle. Cruciger's use of Melanchthon's phrase "contrition is necessary for salvation" elicited critique from CONRAD CORDATUS, which caused Luther to suggest the expression of this concern with "contrition or good works are necessary for the Christian life." Cruciger's wife, ELISABETH, played an important role in Wittenberg conversation, and his son ***Caspar Cruciger the Younger* (1525–1597)** served as a member of the Wittenberg theology from 1561 until his dismissal in 1574 for a spiritualizing view of the Lord's Supper.

***Elisabeth von Mersitz* (ca. 1500–1535)** left the cloister in Marienbusch near Treptow, where JOHANNES BUGENHAGEN taught. When she arrived in Wittenberg in 1522, she found a home with the Bugenhagen family until she married one of the university's most promising students, CASPAR CRUCIGER, in 1524. Luther performed the marriage, and the service was recorded as a model for evangelical marriage ceremonies. The Bugenhagens entertained the celebrating guests as if Elisabeth were their own daughter. In 1524, she composed the hymn "Lord Christ, the Only Son of God," which Luther incorporated into the hymnal he edited.

When Jonas departed Wittenberg to become the superintendent of the churches in Halle, his place was claimed by the local court preacher, who had already begun to offer lectures at the university. ***Georg Major* (1502–1574)** was among the many sons of Nuremberg who came to Wittenberg; he was nine when he became a choir boy and pupil in the local school. He completed university studies in 1529. Then, he and his wife, Margarethe von Mochau, whom he had married the previous year, moved to Magdeburg to work alongside NIKOLAUS VON AMSDORF as rector of the municipal Latin school. ELECTOR JOHANN FRIEDRICH called him back to Wittenberg as court preacher in 1537, and Major quickly was named as assessor of the electoral consistory for the church in his lands as well. In 1545, he became a professor of theology and headed the electoral Saxony theologians at the Diet of Regensburg in 1546. Alongside MELANCHTHON, he contributed to the propaganda effort in defense of the Smalcald League's defiance of EMPEROR CHARLES V in the Smalcald War, but he joined Melanchthon and other colleagues in aiding the new elector, MORITZ, in formulating a religious policy that would stave off imperial-Spanish invasion and the imposition of the full weight of the Augsburg Interim of 1548. Their "Leipzig Proposal" for the diet of Moritz's lands was quickly dubbed the "Leipzig Interim" by many former and current students and colleagues of Melanchthon. In the ensuing dispute over the propriety of the appearance of compromise when persecution threatens in order to ensure further public teaching of God's word, Major defended a line from the proposal that held that good works are necessary for salvation. This provoked a great deal of controversy for the following two decades. Major left Wittenberg to aid Prince Georg von Anhalt in Merseburg and subsequently to direct the churches in Mansfeld county in 1552–53. Opposition to his teaching on good works ended his tenure there. In 1551, Major assisted Melanchthon in preparing the statement of the Saxon government for use in the second session of the Council of Trent, translating the Latin *Repetition of the Augsburg Confession* into German. From 1560 to his death, he served as dean of the Wittenberg theological faculty. His extensive literary production served the spread and deepening of the Wittenberg Reformation on many fronts. His schoolbooks treated a variety of subjects and also provided catechetical materials for pastors. At Luther's suggestion, he began working on redeeming the stories of ancient saints and theologians, which laid down a basis, alongside Melanchthon's work, for further use of patristic literature among the Lutherans. His *On the Origin and Authority of God's Word* (1550) was the first formal treatment of the doctrine of Scripture and its inspiration from the pen of a member of the Wittenberg circle. His lectures on the Pauline Epistles and his postils provided many preachers with the biblical interpretation and homiletical models they needed to improve their own preaching and teaching.

Closely associated with the theological faculty were the liberal arts instructors who were responsible for teaching the biblical languages. The addition of Melanchthon to the faculty had solved the problem of expanding the university's offerings into the new fields of learning by filling the professorship of Greek, but the professorship for Hebrew proved more difficult in those early years, necessitating Melanchthon's instruction in both biblical languages at times. In late 1519, a Spanish-born Jewish Christian, ***Matthäus Adrian***, left Leuven/Louvain and filled the position briefly. Luther and Melanchthon arranged for housing and sought to obtain the books he needed. But by autumn, Adrian was attacking Luther's teaching on justification by faith and offering interpretations of the Old Testament that his new colleagues found perverted its teaching. Adrian departed Wittenberg after his dismissal in February 1521.

Adrian's successor as Wittenberg's Hebrew instructor, ***Matthäus Aurogallus (Goldhahn)* (ca. 1490–1543)**, was attracted to humanist learning as a teacher in his native Bohemia. In 1512, he enrolled at the University of Leipzig. After his transfer to Wittenberg in

1519, Luther and Melanchthon recognized his gifts. As Hebrew instructor, he provided good instruction for the students and invaluable aid to Luther and the other members of the translation team working on the translation of the Old Testament into German. His publications included a Hebrew and Chaldean grammar, a dictionary of Hebrew historical and geographical references, and a chronicle of the dukes and kings of Bavaria.

After MATTHIAS FLACIUS had assumed the professorship of Hebrew in the Wittenberg liberal arts faculty and then resigned it, ***Johann Förster* (ca. 1498–1556)** received the position. He had learned Hebrew under JOHANNES REUCHLIN in Ingolstadt and began teaching Hebrew at the municipal secondary school in Zwickau in 1522. He moved to Wittenberg in 1530 but was recommended as preacher in Augsburg in 1535 by Luther and MELANCHTHON. In 1539, the University of Tübingen called him to its professorship in Hebrew, but as in Augsburg his fierce opposition to local Zwinglian sympathies led to his dismissal after a year. He received a position in Nuremberg, and in 1542 he aided the introduction of the Reformation in nearby Regensburg. In 1543, he left Nuremberg for the county of Henneberg-Schleusingen, where he led in the cultivation of Luther's teaching and practice. In 1548, he became superintendent of the church in Merseburg but returned to Wittenberg the following year to teach Hebrew and replace CASPAR CRUCIGER in the theological faculty. His *New Hebrew Dictionary* offered readers Hebrew roots, syntax, and grammar, and functioned as something of a concordance. He claimed to have developed his definitions apart from rabbinic and scholastic models on the basis of biblical usage. His effort has been criticized by both contemporary and modern scholars as dependent on Luther's teaching rather than on the actual meaning of the Hebrew words.

Others occasionally offered instruction in theology in Wittenberg. One of them, ***Johann Draconites (Drach)* (1494–1566)**, became steeped in Erasmian biblical humanism while studying in Erfurt in the 1510s. There he was drawn into the circle around EOBANUS HESSUS and formed a friendship with JUSTUS JONAS. When Luther stopped in Erfurt on his way to Worms in 1521, Draconites met him and became his disciple. He came to Wittenberg and earned his doctorate in theology there in 1523. He began introducing Luther's way of thinking to his parish in Miltenberg at this time but was forced to leave the town by hostile clergy. Both he and Luther published consolations for the believers of Miltenberg at that time. His parish in Waltershausen near Gotha did not offer him an easy situation either, and in 1534 he accepted a call to be professor of theology at the University of Marburg. He began to publish his studies of the Old Testament at this time, focusing particularly on prophecies that pointed to Christ in the Prophets. LANDGRAVE PHILIP OF HESSE required his services

Portrait of Johann Draconites (1559)

in negotiations of various kinds. Draconites accompanied his prince to the Diet of Regensburg in 1541, but his treatise advocating Wittenberg Reform offended Roman Catholic opponents in the city, and they were able to have him banned from its territories. In Marburg, the accusation of antinomianism from colleagues brought his career to an end in 1548. He turned to further work on the Old Testament, including the development of a polyglot Old Testament and further studies on the prophecies of Christ, which he hoped would aid in converting Jews to faith in Christ. In 1551, the dukes of Mecklenburg called Draconites to the University of Rostock and to the superintendency of Rostock's church. His advocacy of a reverent use of Sunday led to controversy there, from which he escaped when Duke Albrecht of Prussia called him to be superintendent of the churches in the diocese of Pomesania. His burning desire to complete his work on the exposition of the Old Testament led him to gain the duke's permission to return to Wittenberg for his research and writing. He rejected the duke's demand that he return to Danzig in 1564; this led to his dismissal. His scholarly work, an example of the dedication to searching the Scriptures instilled by Luther's and Melanchthon's focus on biblical studies, did not find wide acceptance.

Luther's Colleagues in Other Disciplines

Luther also had close contact with those who succeeded Christoph Scheurl in the Wittenberg faculty of law. One member of that faculty had particularly close connections to the theologians. ***Johannes Apel* (1486–1536)**, born into a prominent merchant family in Nuremberg, came to the University of Wittenberg when it opened in 1502. He pursued the study of canon law there and at the University of Leipzig. Among his early acquaintances were Luther, MELANCHTHON, and GEORG SPALATIN in Wittenberg; his interest in humanistic educational reform also brought him into contact with JUSTUS JONAS, WILLIBALD PIRCKHEIMER from his native Nuremberg, ULRICH VON HUTTEN, and CROTUS RUBEANUS. In 1519, he began working for Bishop Konrad of Thüringen, the bishop of Würzburg. After a short stay in Wittenberg in 1520, Apel married a young Würzburg nun from a noble family. In June 1523, the bishop imprisoned Apel and another canon from his cathedral staff, Friedrich Fischer, who had also married. The families of the two canons appealed to imperial courts on the basis of an edict issued by the imperial diet in March 1523, which permitted the abrogation of vows of celibacy at the price of losing all clerical responsibilities. The bishop defied the imperial court decision ordering the release of Apel and Fischer, but intensive negotiations between the episcopal administration and the families resulted in their being set free in late September. Apel wrote a Latin "defense of my marriage" and published it after his release; Crotus Rubeanus engaged Luther's aid in bringing it to the public. To what extent his contact with Wittenberg had influenced his decision to marry and to what extent it arose out of his more general interest in reform is unclear, but Apel had clearly embraced the Wittenberg appreciation of marriage and the critique voiced by Luther and his colleagues of the abuse of God's order involved in forced adherence to vows of celibacy. LAZARUS SPENGLER, secretary of the city council in Nuremberg and a family friend, recommended Apel to ELECTOR FREDERICK THE WISE for a position in the electoral government. He was appointed to the professorship in canon law from which Justus Jonas had recently resigned. Apel taught canon law, for which very few students showed interest after Luther's recasting of the Christian world, and also assumed a position teaching civil law. In 1529, he was appointed to the bench by ELECTOR JOHANN as well. His reform of the methods for teaching law gained wide influence through his publications, some of which appeared posthumously. Nonetheless, he helped make Wittenberg a significant location for legal studies. In 1530, Apel was called to Königsberg, to serve in the administration of DUKE ALBRECHT. Albrecht had close connections to Saxony. After the secularization of the lands, he had administered as head of the Teutonic Knights, the crusading order that had controlled the eastern Baltic course for three centuries; in 1525, Albrecht looked to ELECTOR JOHANN for support and aid. After four years of service in Königsberg, Apel returned to his native Nuremberg to become city attorney and died two years later. His life demonstrates the meeting of civic responsibility in societal callings that was fostered by Luther's understanding of God calling his people to serve one another in the structures of society.

Although he did not receive a professorship of law in Wittenberg, ***Basilius Monner*** **(ca. 1497–1566)** gave the theologians support as a leading legally trained member of the Wittenberg team. Monner left the Augustinian order and attended the University of Wittenberg, perhaps beginning in 1521. He served as rector of the secondary school in Gotha from 1524 to 1535. He then assumed duties in the court of Elector Johann Friedrich. In 1538, the elector sent him on a diplomatic mission to France, and he also represented the elector in conversations with Swiss ecclesiastical leaders at this time. He served on the first Saxon ecclesiastical consistory that was formed in 1538. Soon thereafter Johann Friedrich chose him as tutor for his sons. The Saxon government sought Monner's appointment to an office at the imperial supreme court in 1539, but his commitment to Wittenberg Reform prevented his receiving the appointment. His treatises on the right of princely resistance to the emperor contributed to the Saxon propaganda campaign at the time of the Smalcald War. The results of the war brought him to the court of the sons of Johann Friedrich in Weimar, and in 1557 he became the founding member of the faculty of jurisprudence at the Academy—after 1558, University—of Jena. Matthias Flacius and his Gnesio-Lutheran colleagues in ducal Saxony found in Monner a genial colleague and avid supporter. Monner's publication of an attack on the assumption of the electorate of Saxony by the Albertine branch of the Wettin family in 1557 provoked a persistent legal assault and pursuit by the electoral Saxon government, seeking his imprisonment for what Elector August claimed slandered the Albertine family. The treatise appeared in 1557, the same year that Monner participated in the religious colloquy in Worms, where his strained relations with his former friend Melanchthon displayed themselves in the latter's cool treatment of him. In 1559, Duke Johann Wilhelm sent him on a mission to England to probe the possibilities of his marriage to Queen Elizabeth, without positive results.

Luther's contacts with the medical faculty were no less important for him. Among these colleagues was his cousin, ***Caspar Lindemann*** **(ca. 1486–1536)**, the nephew of Luther's mother. His studies, beginning in 1497 at the University of Erfurt and thereafter at the University of Leipzig, with a brief interlude at the University of Frankfurt an der Oder, ended with the completion of his master's degree in 1508 and his lecturing on logic. Medical interests attracted him to the University of Bologna, where he was awarded his doctorate in medicine in 1511. The University of Leipzig called him to its medical faculty. He witnessed his cousin's disputation with Johann Eck in 1519. In 1532, he left Leipzig for the medical faculty in Wittenberg, where he had also been serving Frederick the Wise and his brother Johann as court physician. In Wittenberg, he pursued dissection as

Portrait of Paul Eber (1869)

a means of instruction in anatomy, like his predecessor AUGUSTIN SCHURFF. The last two years of his life he served as rector of the Leucorea.

The Wittenberg theologians had daily contacts not only with their colleagues in the upper faculties of the university but also with those in the liberal arts faculty, some of whom were on their way to the theological faculty, such as Paul Eber, others of whom remained instructing in the arts their whole lives, such as VEIT WINSHEIM. ***Paul Eber* (1511–1569)** left his native Kitzingen for Wittenberg in 1532. His studies there brought him into the orbit around MELANCHTHON and launched a career that included instructing in physics, then Latin grammar, thereafter Hebrew, and finally theology. He preached regularly as deacon and then as the court preacher at the castle church. He became pastor of Wittenberg's town church and general superintendent of the electoral Saxon church at BUGENHAGEN's death in 1558. His leadership as Melanchthon's theological successor guided the theological faculty after Melanchthon's death in 1560. His support for the Philippist positions of his colleagues seldom drew him into active involvement in the controversies of the 1550s and 1560s. His attempts to introduce a more spiritualized understanding of the presence of Christ in the Lord's Supper in the early 1560s were quickly ended by an admonition from ELECTOR AUGUST OF SAXONY. His published works include a postil, a collection of sermons on the catechisms, a history of the Jewish people, a calendar of important historic dates, and neo-Latin poetry.

***Veit Winsheim (Örtel)* (1501–1570)** had gone to school in Deventer and attended the University of Vienna before arriving in Wittenberg for study in 1523. With MELANCHTHON's support he opened a private school to offer secondary education. In 1528 he began teaching rhetoric in the liberal arts faculty; in 1536 he began instructing in Greek and inherited Melanchthon's position as Greek instructor in 1541. He later taught in the medical faculty after attaining his doctorate in medicine in 1550, although he did not hold a professorship there. Not only did he serve occasionally as dean of the arts faculty and rector of the university, from 1549 to 1567 he exercised the office of town council member every third year. His son Veit became a professor of law at Wittenberg. He was among those colleagues who gave public orations praising Melanchthon at his death in 1560.

***Valerius Cordus* (1515–1544)** joined the arts faculty while studying in Wittenberg from 1539 until 1542; he had frequently visited the Leucorea since 1531. His father, ***Euricius Cordus* (1486–1534)**, had studied in Erfurt and belonged to the humanist circle around EOBANUS HESSUS. Euricius became a municipal physician in Braunschweig after attaining his doctorate in medicine in Ferrara in 1523. He later served as medical professor at the University of Marburg and as municipal physician. His interest in botany research was passed on to his son as was his dedication to Martin Luther's call for reform. Before coming to Wittenberg, Valerius had published the first pharmaceutical handbook published north of the Alps, and while in Wittenberg he wrote a work on the distillation of herbs and acids. He led his students on field-study trips, an innovation in botanical instruction at the time. Without ignoring the ancient texts that had formed the basis of botanical studies throughout the Middle Ages, Valerius developed in his students the skills involved in research on the plants themselves, plants that grew in German fields rather than those of ancient Roman and Greek gardens and forests. Valerius led one such research expedition to the southern regions of the German Empire, to Bohemia then to Regensburg, Augsburg, Tübingen, and Frankfurt am Main, from spring to

Copper engraving of Valerius Cordus (sixteenth century)

autumn 1542. With students in tow, he set out on a similar expedition for Italy in 1543. While still underway there, Valerius suffered a kick in the leg from a horse, and the complications took his life in September 1544.

***Erasmus Reinhold* (1511–1553)** began studying in Wittenberg in 1530. MELANCHTHON recognized his gifts, and by 1536 Reinhold held a professorship in mathematics. In the fields of both astronomy and mathematics, his contributions were significant. He promoted the use of Copernicus's mathematical tables and calculations and was among the first to publicly rank Copernicus with Ptolemy. His *Tabulae Prutenicae* provided the authoritative tables for astronomical calculations for a half century. He also recorded the first descriptions of several stars. From 1536 to 1538, Reinhold shared mathematical instruction with one of his students who had come to Wittenberg to study five years earlier, Georg Joachim Rheticus.

***Georg Joachim Rheticus* (1514–1574)** received his secondary education in his hometown of Feldkirch and in Zurich. He enrolled in Wittenberg in 1532 and four years later was installed in the liberal arts faculty as instructor in mathematics. In 1539, Melanchthon sent him to visit other centers of learning, and he met Nikolaus Copernicus as he journeyed toward Prussia. In 1541, while spending time in Nuremberg, he became acquainted with the printer JOHANN PETREIUS, who gave him manuscripts by Copernicus. As Petreius's representative, he traveled to visit Copernicus in Frauenburg. His attempt to move Copernicus to publish his *On the Revolution of Celestial Bodies* was successful. Through the efforts of Rheticus and Petreius, ANDREAS OSIANDER, one of the leading pastors in Nuremberg, was persuaded to edit the draft of a preface that Rheticus had prepared for the work. He did so in such a way that Copernicus's argument for the revolution of the earth around the sun was presented as a merely theoretical mathematical model, and this enabled the publication to escape censorship. Rheticus, however, defended the Copernican theory in later publications of his own. He returned to Wittenberg to teach and drew ERASMUS REINHOLD and CASPAR PEUCER, who also taught astronomy, into at least a partially supportive stance in relationship to Copernicus's work, thus making Wittenberg an important post in the spread and gradual acceptance of the Copernican system. Rheticus himself moved on to Leipzig in 1542, where a scandal with a student ended his teaching career in 1551. He settled in Cracow as municipal physician and left for a position in Hungary, where he died shortly after his arrival.

Students on Luther's Team

A number of the earlier students or members of his order who heard Luther's and, a bit later, Melanchthon's lectures contributed in various ways to the reform efforts of the Wittenberg team. Luther's first associates in Wittenberg lived with him in the Augustinian Eremite cloister, called the "Black Cloister" because the Augustinians wore black robes. ***Georg Spenlein* (1485–1563)** transferred from the Black Cloister in Wittenberg to that in Memmingen in 1515 or 1516 and joined those abandoning the monastic way of life in 1520. He spent time with Johannes Lang in Erfurt before assuming a pastorate of his own. His ministry was plagued with disputes with local officials, colleagues, and members of his congregations in at least four locales. Luther intervened from time to time on his behalf with local governments. In a letter to Spenlein written in 1516, Luther expressed his faith in the crucified Christ, who alone could bestow righteousness upon sinners.

Bartholomäus Bernhardi (ca. 1700)

***Bartholomäus Bernhardi von Feldkirchen* (1487–1551)** matriculated in Wittenberg in 1504 after studies in Erfurt the previous year. The native of the Austrian Vorarlberg pursued the course of theological education and in 1516 brought Luther's critique of scholastic teaching on the freedom of the will into public discussion by defending theses that he had written expressing Luther's ideas. This attack on GABRIEL BIEL launched an intensive debate within the faculty that gradually drew Luther's colleagues and many students to his cause. After serving as rector of the university in the winter semester 1518–19, Bernhardi accepted a call to Kemberg, just south of Wittenberg, where he married Gertrude Pannier; he was one of the first priests to marry. He was arrested for this move, paid a fine, and launched an attack on clerical celibacy. Bartholomäus's brother, ***Johannes Bernhardi (Velcurio)* (ca. 1490–1534)**, came to Wittenberg in 1512, joined his brother in promoting Luther's teaching, and attacked AUGUSTIN ALVELDT in print in 1520. Attacks of melancholy prevented him from further work on publication, but MELANCHTHON and others arranged for his commentaries on ERASMUS's *De copia* and on Aristotle's *Physica* and related works to appear in print, and their clear Latin style earned them frequent reprinting.

***Franz Günther* (d. 1528)** left his native Nordhausen to study at the University of Erfurt and earned the baccalaureate degree in the summer of 1512. In 1515, he matriculated at the University of Wittenberg, and in 1517 he defended Luther's theses against the scholastic method in the practice of theology. By 1521, he had earned the degree of licentiate of theology. In the meantime, he had been ordained by the bishop of Meissen and named a preacher in Jüterbog in 1519. There, his days were filled with controversy with local Franciscans over Luther's interpretation of Scripture. At Luther's urging, he became pastor in Lochau in 1520, where he also served as court preacher at the castle of FREDERICK THE WISE in the town. He quickly introduced communion in both kinds and married in 1522. The bishop of Meissen sent Hieronymus Dungersheim to Lochau to examine Günther. He remained in his office. When Günther baptized his first child in 1523, Frederick the Wise himself served as sponsor. Günther requested transfer to a larger parish, but the elector kept him in Lochau, where he died in 1528. At Luther's suggestion, his widow married MICHAEL STIEFEL.

***Gabriel Zwilling (Didymus)* (1487–1558)** studied at the University of Prague before his arrival in Wittenberg in 1512 as a member of the Augustinian Order. At Luther's urging, he studied in Erfurt from 1516 to 1518 and then returned to Wittenberg. During Luther's absence at the Wartburg, Zwilling committed himself to the rapid introduction of reform measures, including the abolition of private masses and the adoration of the elements of the Lord's Supper. He called for communing the laity in both kinds in 1521, supporting the radical measures advocated by Andreas Karlstadt. Zwilling led other friars out of the Augustinian cloister and preached at Christmas 1521 without clerical vestments in Eilenburg near Wittenberg. In 1522, he called for the burning of images and other material elements of medieval worship. Reacting to Luther's criticism of moving too rapidly, Zwilling quickly returned to Luther's stance, confessing that he had erred in following Karlstadt. Luther then recommended him to the town council of Altenburg as the municipal preacher, a post that the local Augustinians had the right to fill. Thereafter, Zwilling accepted a pastorate in Neustadt an der Orla, where he served for over a year before following a call to be preacher in Torgau. There, he married and introduced the reform of ecclesiastical life in Torgau. He led the reform of the school system as well. In 1549, his opposition to the Leipzig Proposal and to Elector Moritz's introduction of many of the measures it had suggested into church life in the town earned him dismissal by the elector. Moritz's mother, Duchess Katharina, then engaged the aging Zwilling as her personal pastor until his death.

One of the brightest and best of Luther's earliest students, ***Johann Agricola (Schnitter)* (1492–1566)**, disappointed Luther profoundly but nonetheless played a noteworthy role in the Wittenberg story in several respects. Agricola had studied at the University of Leipzig and taught school briefly in Braunschweig before coming to Wittenberg to study in 1516. He quickly found Luther's teaching convincing. In 1519, he served as a secretary for Luther at the Leipzig Disputation with Johann Eck. He taught at the university and was included in many of the important discussions of ecclesiastical policy and public teaching, including preparations for the visitations of Saxon parishes in 1527 and 1528. By that time his native Eisleben had called him there to serve as rector of its school; his wife, Else, provided instruction for girls as well. His power in the pulpit led Elector Johann of Saxony to take him with the electoral Saxon delegation to the diets of Speyer in 1526 and Augsburg in 1530 as his personal preacher and chaplain. Agricola had captured Luther's insistence on the killing nature of the Law's accusation of sin and its inability to contribute in any way to salvation, but he had not understood Luther's distinction of Law and Gospel as it is applied to the lives of believers, who are both righteous and sinful at the same time. Therefore, Agricola produced an oversimplified version of Luther's theology, teaching that the Law plays no part in the life of the Christian and that repentance is produced by the Gospel, not the Law; Gospel reveals the "violation of the Son of God," that is, the refusal to let Christ reign in the heart. The "violation of the Law" could not, he argued, be sufficient grounds for true repentance. This concept had appeared in his 1525 commentary on Luke's Gospel and in his catechisms, a Latin *Elements of Piety* in 1526 and a German translation for girls. He responded to criticism of its difficulty and in 1527 produced *One Hundred Thirty Questions for Christian Children*, also in German, which despite its bulkiness was reprinted some ten times in less than two years. Agricola had written his catechisms in response to Luther urging him and JUSTUS JONAS to meet the need for a primer in the faith for children. Luther's own discontent with Agricola's catechism probably helped bring him to the task himself in 1529. In 1527, as the electoral Saxon government was organizing the visitation of parishes, with Agricola involved in those discussions, he objected to MELANCHTHON's and Luther's insistence that the Law needed to be preached to believers to bring them to daily repentance. He attacked Melanchthon for this view, it was said at the time out of his disappointment at not receiving the newly created chair in theology in Wittenberg, which, in fact, Elector Johann awarded to Melanchthon. At a meeting at Torgau in November 1527, Luther worked out an agreement with Agricola, and Agricola returned to Eisleben to teach. When in late 1536 Luther invited him to come to Wittenberg to take part in the composition of an evangelical program for presenting the biblical message at the papally called council, the document that became the "Smalcald Articles," Agricola resigned his position in Eisleben and sought to become a member of the Wittenberg faculty. He was granted the right to deliver theological courses and soon was again propagating his view that the Law has no place in the Christian life, that the Gospel effects repentance and guides the life of good works. Luther patiently and then not so patiently strove to show Agricola how he was destroying the possibility of good pastoral care by not properly distinguishing Law and Gospel. In a series of disputations, Luther repudiated his former student's ideas, eliciting each time Agricola's promise to return to Luther's understanding of Law and Gospel. Agricola did not keep his promises, however. Restricted by electoral order until the matter could be resolved, Agricola secretly escaped from Wittenberg in July 1540. ELECTOR JOACHIM II OF BRANDENBURG welcomed him to Berlin and involved him immediately in the introduction of Wittenberg Reforms to his lands. Agricola became his chief court preacher and general superintendent of the churches in Brandenburg; in 1541, he publicly affirmed his adherence to Wittenberg theology. However, in 1548 Joachim had him named to the imperial commission that composed the Augsburg Interim. Agricola boasted that he had taught the papists evangelical doctrine, but his participation and support of the Interim remains inexplicable when its text is compared to what he had taught previously and continued to teach after 1548. In general, he maintained his rejection of any

IOANNES AGRICOLA ISLEBIVS THEOLOGVS.

IOannes in Saxonia natus, & in omni genere literarum optimè educatus fuit. Is cum prima artiũ fundamenta feliciter iecisset, sese ad Vuitebergensem Academiam contulit, & Theologiæ magna diligentia incubuit. Hinc factum ut sacrarum literarũ usum sibi familiarem reddiderit, & ob multifariam eruditionem postea doctissimis Theologis cõnumeratus fuerit. Id cum Ioannes elector Saxoniæ intellexisset, eum plurimùm dilexit, & aliquoties secum ad Imperij comitia perduxit, ut aduersarijs se opponeret, & doctrinam Euangelij ex uerbo Dei cõfirmaret. quod etiam Ioannes gnauiter præstitit. præsertim 1526 Spiræ, & 1530 Augustæ Vindelicorũ, ubi cum Melanchtone et Brentio idem sentiens in magna existimatione fuit. Postea uerò simultate quadam cum Luthero orta Vuiteberga discessit, & tandem ad illustriss. principem Ioachimum electorem Brandeburgicum peruenit, atq; aliquandiu latuit. Cum autem postea Carolus bello Smalkaldico uictor esset, Islebius cum suo principe 1548 Augustam uenit, & sese pontificiorum Theologis coniunxit. Ibi quoq; (ut ferebatur) unà cum Iulio Pflugio, & Michaële Sidonio nouam religionis formam composuit. quam interim dum Concilium celebraretur, omnes obseruare deberent. Vnde etiam à Cæsare & Ferdinando liberale donum tulit. Postea quoq; cum in Saxonia de Adiaphoris cõtentio esset, Islebius Ioachimi principis iussu Theologorum colloquijs interfuit, & suam sententiã copiosè proposuit. Hoc modo factum, ut non modò apud Germanos, sed etiam apud exteras nationes magnum sibi nomen compararit. Ioan. Sleid.

Image of Johann Agricola in a volume by Heinricus Pantaleon, published 1565

role for the Law in the Christian life. His contemporaries regarded him as gifted but vain, without either originality or a deeper grasp of the ideas he was trying to propagate and defend. His wife, Else, maintained a friendship with the Luther family. The theology of her sister's husband, Andreas Musculus, did not correspond to Agricola's, although through Agricola's influence Musculus obtained a firm footing in the church of Brandenburg and succeeded Agricola as its general superintendent.

***Georg Rörer* (1492–1557)** arrived in Wittenberg in 1522 after a decade of study and teaching at the University of Leipzig. His fellow students there, Stephan Roth and Caspar Cruciger, had come to the Leucorea, and Rörer joined them. He began recording in his own shorthand the sermons and lectures of Luther and in 1537 was appointed official electoral recorder of Luther's words. Luther ordained him a deacon for Wittenberg's town church in 1525, and he married the sister of Johannes Bugenhagen, his senior pastor. He remarried after her death in the plague in 1527. Rörer served as liturgist in the first legal celebration of the Lord's Supper in German later in 1525. He actively participated in the committee charged with the translation of the Bible and its revision, also recording the minutes of these discussions. Elector Johann Friedrich the Magnanimous designated him to edit Luther's collected works, the first volume of which appeared in 1539. After the Smalcald War, Rörer left Wittenberg for Copenhagen. In 1553, he followed the call of Duke Johann Friedrich the Middler to return to ducal Saxony, where he spent his final years editing the Jena edition of Luther's Works, the rival edition to the Wittenberg edition, which he had begun. Under Gnesio-Lutheran sponsorship, it arranged Luther's writings chronologically, not by topic, to aid readers in noting in the early writings where medieval theology had still played a role in Luther's teaching

***Veit Dietrich* (1506–1549)**, a native of Nuremberg, came to Wittenberg to study medicine in 1522 but soon followed Luther's insistence that he pursue the study of theology instead. Dietrich lived with the Luther family in the Black Cloister from 1528 to late 1534

Portrait of Veit Dietrich

while studying and teaching in the liberal arts faculty (serving also as its dean), until tensions with Katharina von Bora caused him to leave. His relationship with Luther continued to be warm and mutually supportive. While still in Wittenberg, Dietrich attended Luther as an amanuensis and accompanied the Reformer to the Marburg Colloquy in 1529 and to Coburg Castle in 1530 during the Diet of Augsburg. He recorded Luther's conversations at the table after supper as well and was entrusted with editing many of his sermons and other writings for publication. He continued this activity after he accepted a call to become pastor of Saint Sebald Church in Nuremberg in 1535. There, he pursued his own writing career in a number of areas, particularly pastoral care and catechesis. His last months of life were plagued by his dismissal from his pastorate by the city council in reaction to his severe criticism of the Augsburg Interim.

The last amanuensis who served Luther and later edited his works, ***Johannes Aurifaber* (ca. 1519–1575)**, came to Wittenberg for study in 1537, left in 1540 to teach in Mansfeld, but returned in 1545 to serve as Luther's amanuensis until Luther's death. Aurifaber served as a chaplain for the troops of Elector Johann Friedrich in the Smalcald War and after the defeat of the Smalcald League became court preacher for the elector's sons in Weimar. In this position, he supported the Gnesio-Lutheran teaching of university colleagues such as Matthias Flacius and Johannes Wigand and the corresponding policies of the dukes. He rejected the Augsburg Interim and the Leipzig Proposal of 1548, with its views of adiaphora and concession in times of threat. He also criticized Georg Major's defense of the proposition that good works are necessary for salvation. He was influential in the development of the final draft of the dukes' *Book of Confutation* of 1558. In 1561, Duke Johann Friedrich the Middler dismissed leading Gnesio-Lutherans on the faculty and in the ministerium because of their opposition to his plans for a lay-dominated consistory, and Aurifaber settled in Eisleben. In 1565, he accepted a pastorate in Erfurt, where he defended his colleague Johann Gallus against their colleague Andreas Poach. Gallus had accepted election as rector of the University of Erfurt even though installation services involved certain nonliturgical ceremonies in which Roman Catholic members of the university community also took part. During his service in Weimar, Aurifaber played a significant role in organizing the printing of the Jena edition of Luther's Works as a rival to the Wittenberg edition. Later, he produced two volumes of Luther's Latin letters, the first appearing in 1556, the second in 1565, from manuscript collections to which he had access. His two-volume collection of German manuscripts and single printings that had not been edited for the Wittenberg or Jena editions appeared in 1564 (with only a few publications that had actually appeared previously in the Wittenberg edition). A printed version of Luther's *Tischreden*, somewhat arbitrarily reconstructed, was issued under his editorship in 1566; it has been criticized by modern scholars for forcing the *Table Talk* notes of others into the straightjacket imposed by the loci system of organization.

The Artists and the Musicians

The graphic arts and music played a significant role in Luther's own life and in the household of the Black Cloister. The Cranachs, father and son, contributed immensely to the efforts to convey the message of the Wittenberg theologians through their woodcuts and engravings, their paintings, and their theological observations. Many other artists followed their models within the larger Wittenberg culture. In this volume, three men who contributed much to the musical elements of Wittenberg culture represent a larger group of Luther's followers who served as cantors in congregations and in other ways brought the gospel to others through their musical gifts.

***Lukas Cranach the Elder* (1472–1553)** learned the trade of artist and the skills of painting and the creation of woodcuts from his father, Hans Sunder, a painter in Kronach in Franconia. Cranach undertook an educational journey in the southern German lands, during which he spent some time among the biblical humanists at the University of Vienna around 1503. He married Barbara, daughter of Jodocus Brengbier, mayor of Gotha, and resided there briefly before being appointed court painter in Wittenberg by FREDERICK THE WISE in 1505. Cranach's growing reputation spread. His work reflected the new trends in the graphic arts north of the Alps, particularly elements shaped by ALBRECHT DÜRER, but he also developed techniques of his own that others later adopted or adapted. Early in his career, he pioneered the importation of Italian depictions of nude figures, gradually altering the way in which he portrayed the naked human body into a distinctive style of his own. Commissions for his work came from those opposed to the Wittenberg Reformation, particularly ARCHBISHOP ALBRECHT OF MAINZ, as well as other princes and towns. Cranach quickly acquired business interests in Wittenberg alongside his ever-growing studio, which employed a large group of hopeful journeymen and apprentices. He acquired the town pharmacy, and with it the right to be the sole source of sweet wine for the town. With his partner and neighbor CHRISTIAN DÖRING, a goldsmith, he formed a printing operation and later bought a paper mill to ensure his supply of material for both studio and presses. By 1519, he became a member of the town council and served several times as mayor. He

Portrait of Lukas Cranach the Elder at age seventy-seven by his son Lukas Cranach the Younger (1550)

and Luther became close friends early on in Luther's stay at the Black Cloister, and Cranach quickly absorbed Luther's new insights into the biblical message. He was able to translate them effectively into his own medium. Not only his paintings but particularly the woodcuts he prepared for published works did much to spread Luther's message. His propaganda pieces against the papacy deconstructed old ideas; his illustrations for Bible and catechisms carried depictions of the biblical stories into the homes of those who could read. Cranach accompanied Elector Johann Friedrich into prison in 1548. While the elector was being held in a prison in Augsburg, Cranach met Titian, who spent time in the company of Emperor Charles V. Cranach returned to Saxony when Johann Friedrich was released from imperial confinement in 1552 and lived in Weimar with his daughter Barbara and her husband, Christian Brück. His marriage to Barbara Brengbier had also produced two sons. The elder, Hans, died on a study journey to Italy in 1537; Luther's consolation of the grieving parents was recorded. The younger son, Lukas, took over his brother's role at his death and helped his father direct their large staff.

***Lukas Cranach the Younger* (1515–1586)**, deemed by some—but not by all—scholars a more skilled craftsman of his art than his father, had actively pursued the family trade before his brother died, but after 1537 he exercised a growing influence on the Cranach productions. When his father left Wittenberg, the younger Cranach continued to supervise the family businesses but dedicated himself largely to the production of works of art, both for religious purposes and for the decoration of public spaces and homes. Thus, both biblical narratives and the mythological figures and themes of ancient Greece and Rome are found

Copper engraving of Lukas Cranach the Younger (sixteenth century)

in his work. After Duke Moritz became elector in 1548, Cranach no longer served the electoral court but continued to prosper as a creator of artworks and illustrations for publications to his death.

***Johann Walther (Blanckenmüller)* (1496–1570)** received his family name after a couple in Kahla adopted the impoverished orphan. He attended school in Kahla and Rochlitz and became a member of the court chapel choir of Frederick the Wise, singing in Torgau, Altenburg, and Weimar. In 1525, he spent three weeks with Luther and Melanchthon in Wittenberg as Elector Johann considered discontinuation of the chapel choir at his court. Walther received warm support from both Luther and Melanchthon, from that time until their deaths. He gradually transferred the focus of his attention from the court to service to the town of Torgau as an instructor in music. In 1535, Elector Johann Friedrich granted funds for the reestablishment of the court choir. Despite his strong commitment to the theological positions of the Gnesio-Lutheran critics of Elector Moritz, Walther accepted a position at the new elector's court in Dresden in 1548 and directed its choir until he retired in 1554. Walther was instrumental in producing the first hymnal that appeared in the circle around Luther and Melanchthon in 1524. He aided Luther in his work on his *German Mass* that was printed in 1526. His hymns and other music assisted much in the spread of Luther's thought and the inculcation of his faith in the German populace.

***Konrad Rupsch* (1470–1530)** joined the court choir at Elector Frederick II's castle in Torgau in 1491 and was influenced by the importation of musical styles from the Netherlands that took place there in the 1490s. In 1505, he was ordained a priest and assumed the director's position of the court choir. His friendship with Georg Spalatin acquainted him with Luther's ideas at an early stage of the Reformation. His skills as a composer were limited, but he actively engaged in promoting the spread of hymnody. He traveled to Wittenberg in 1524 to aid Luther in developing the first hymnal that propagated Luther's ideas. Elector Johann dissolved the Torgau court choir over Luther's protests in 1527, and Rupsch assisted his friend Johann Walther, who was for a while without means.

Portrait of Ludwig Senfl attributed to Hans Schwarz (ca. 1519)

***Ludwig Senfl* (1486–1543)** came from a family with roots in Freiburg im Breisgau who had settled in Zurich. By 1496, he found a place in the court choir of Emperor Maximilian. His service to the emperor lasted until 1519, when Maximilian died. The emperor's grandsons, Emperor Charles V and his brother Ferdinand, did not employ Senfl at their courts but did grant him one-third of the annual pension their grandfather had promised his musician for life. Senfl composed and published motets and other music, often working together with his friend from his early days at the imperial court, Heinrich Isaac, on many compositions. Apparently Senfl had received ordination in minor orders at a young age, but in 1529 he abandoned his clerical status and married. After his attendance at the imperial diets in Augsburg in 1518 and in Worms in 1521, Senfl's interest in Luther's thought grew steadily even though he spent the last twenty years of his life at the court of Duke Wilhelm of Bavaria, an opponent of the Wittenberg Reformation. Senfl was also present at the diet in Augsburg in 1530. Luther admired Senfl and his development of the Bavarian choir at the Munich court of the duke. He and Senfl corresponded, and at Luther's request Senfl composed two motets for him. Senfl also began an epistolary exchange with Duke Albrecht of Prussia in 1526, and up to 1540 Senfl composed a significant number of motets and other music for the duke.

Area Pastors

Some pastors from the area surrounding Wittenberg visited the town often, sat with the Reformers at table, exchanged ideas, and therefore played a role in the shaping of Wittenberg Reform. Although ***Michael Stiefel*** **(1487–1567)** never taught at the university, his studies there demonstrate that mathematics also held a firm place in the Wittenberg curriculum. Stiefel left the Augustinian cloister in Esslingen when his sharing of a treatise by Luther with his brothers placed him in danger. Luther found him a position as preacher with Count Peter Ernst I of Mansfeld in Luther's own hometown, Mansfeld. In 1524, Stiefel accepted a call at Luther's recommendation in Austria, where he was the first to promote Wittenberg Reform, but he remained only three years; the execution nearby of LEONHARD KAISER, a follower of Luther, served as a warning that the area was not safe for preachers of Luther's Reform. Stiefel returned to parish ministry near Wittenberg, but his fascination with numbers became a preoccupation. His mathematical theorizing led him into speculation about the end times. When his prediction that the world would end at eight o'clock on the morning of October 19, 1533, did not come true, Luther remained at his side but discouraged Stiefel from such speculations, turning him instead to the composition of mathematical textbooks, the result of studies in Wittenberg. He produced the first German edition of Christoff Rudolff's classic textbook on algebra, and edited Euclid in Latin. He later became professor of mathematics at the University of Jena.

A gravure of Michael Stiefel by an unknown artist

Conrad Cordatus **(ca. 1480–1546)** came from Weissenkirchen near Wels in Lower Austria, where his peasant family shaped his early worldview with the spirit of Jan Hus's call for reform of the church. His studies at the University of Vienna, in part with the humanist scholar Conrad Celtis, led to his ordination in 1505. He earned a doctorate in theology at the University of Ferrara before assuming a parish in Ofen in the Habsburg lands. Officials jailed him for his proclamation of Luther's ideas, but he escaped to Wittenberg in 1524. He then traveled again to Hungary to spread Luther's message and was again imprisoned, escaping after nine months through the aid of a guard. He returned to Wittenberg before embarking on an extended period of seeking a place to serve. His participation in plans for founding an evangelical university in Liegnitz in Silesia ended when the attempt collapsed. In 1529, Luther arranged for his call to Zwickau; conflicts with the town council led to another return with his family to Wittenberg, and then to a call to nearby Niemegk. He attended lectures at the university and took sharp exception to Caspar Cruciger's use of Melanchthon's phrase "contrition is necessary to salvation," seeing in the phrase a defense of a human contribution and merit in the reception of forgiveness of sins. Cordatus had spent time behind bars in defending the concept of salvation by grace through faith in Christ alone. Luther worked out a reconciliation, and that such disputes did not always lead to personal breaks within the Wittenberg circle is demonstrated by Melanchthon writing a preface for the posthumously published postil that Cordatus had composed. In 1537, Luther sent Cordatus to Eisleben to assume leadership there after the departure of Johann Agricola. In 1540, Elector Joachim II of Brandenburg called him to serve as superintendent of the church in Stendal, where he led the introduction of the Wittenberg Reformation. His time in Niemegk permitted him to sit evenings at Luther's table, and his notes on the "table talk" put the best construction possible on Luther's utterances.

This circle of friends interacted with those presented in chapter 2 in daily life, but these stood closer to him and interacted in more critical fashion as the Wittenberg Reformation spread.

CHAPTER 4

German Reformers: Luther's Supporters across German-Speaking Lands

The line between those who belonged directly to the team located in Wittenberg and those who introduced and spread Luther's proclamation of the gospel and the Wittenberg team's plan for reform in other places is thin. The figures presented in this chapter include some who had studied in Wittenberg, and many who had not but who had absorbed Luther's and Melanchthon's way of thinking through occasional personal contacts and through reading their publications. Because the Wittenberg Reformation took place in specific places and took on a specific flavor in these various environments, this chapter is organized, at least roughly, by geographical location within the German-speaking lands. Two imperial knights—that is, higher nobles with responsibilities only to the emperor, not to a local duke or count—make an exception since their support of Luther did not directly transition into the establishment of an evangelical church in a locality. After recounting the lives of these two knights, whose acceptance of Luther's actual teaching was at best partial but whose enthusiasm for the spark he had ignited fit in with their own hopes and plans for reform, the chapter moves roughly from northwest of Wittenberg across northern German lands to Prussia, then to the south and to the west. Locating individuals in the Wittenberg movement is often an approximate venture since many worked in more than one location.

The Imperial Knights

Two imperial knights typify one of the groups that initially found Luther's call for reform attractive. Some of them later established their own lands as islands, sometimes in the midst of hostile territory ruled by those of the old faith, for the preaching of Luther's theology.

***Ulrich von Hutten* (1488–1523)** was sent by his family from their castle in Franconia to the nearby Benedictine abbey outside Fulda for his basic education in 1499. Six years later he began a six-year pilgrimage to the universities of Mainz, Cologne, Erfurt, Frankfurt an der Oder, Leipzig, Greifswald, Rostock, and later to Pavia and Bologna. Humanist ideas attracted him, and he formed contacts with a number of leading educational reformers of this school, including Joachim Vadian in Vienna and ERASMUS. Personal circumstances led him to publish poetry and treatises attacking his foes, and he joined in the effort

A woodcut depiction of Ulrich von Hutten (ca. 1522)

to defend Johannes Reuchlin for his pioneering work in the study of Hebrew with *The Letters of Obscure Men*, which he organized and edited, a large part of the text coming from his own pen. Emperor Maximilian crowned him poet laureate after a second trip to Italy. Von Hutten entered the service of Archbishop Albrecht of Mainz while also criticizing the vices of the papal court and the concept of celibacy. He echoed those who protested against Rome's exploitation of the German lands. His initial skepticism of Luther's call for reform turned to avid support after the Leipzig Disputation in 1519. He recognized the differences between himself and the Wittenberg professor but counted their opposition to Rome as a common cause. In 1520, Archbishop Albrecht dismissed him from his service, and von Hutten joined his friend Franz von Sickingen. He launched a campaign in print against the establishment that was supporting or complying with Roman exploitation of the Germans. His participation in efforts to arouse popular discontent met little success in the months after the Diet of Worms in 1521, and so he joined a military effort against the archbishop of Trier, Richard von Greiffenklau, which failed and sent him in flight to Basel. In 1523, von Hutten hid out in an Augustinian monastery in Mühlhausen before moving to Zurich shortly before his death. His efforts contributed little to the advance of Wittenberg Reform.

Portrait of Franz von Sickingen (sixteenth century)

***Franz von Sickingen* (1481–1523)** was sent by his prominent noble family for training at the court of the elector of the Palatinate in Heidelberg. After his service in the Landshut War of Succession in 1503–1504, which ranged two branches of the Wittelsbach family against each other for control of the area around one von Sickingen castle, Franz joined the governmental administration of the Palatinate, holding offices in Kreuznach and Böckelheim. Beginning in 1515, he indulged in minor military campaigns, particularly against the cities of Worms and Frankfurt am Main, as well as against Duke Anthony of Lorraine and the imperial city of Metz. Emperor

MAXIMILIAN declared him an outlaw in 1517, but the two reconciled the next year, and von Sickingen became an imperial field commander. As an agent of the Swabian League, he aided the Habsburg family in seizing Württemberg from the control of its duke, ULRICH. After directing security for the election of the emperor in 1519, he won appointment by CHARLES V as an imperial counselor, chamberlain, and military commander. His lack of success against the rebel forces of Robert II von der Mark, a powerful nobleman in Lorraine, led to his fall from favor, and increasingly he committed himself to offering military support for the movement for reform headed by Luther. He chose evangelical preachers for his land holdings and organized fellow nobles for his cause. On his own he attacked Archbishop Richard von Greiffenklau but was fatally wounded as forces allied with Trier defeated his troops. His enthusiasm for the idea of reform was undoubtedly stronger than his understanding of Luther's ideas.

Luther's Followers in Northern German Lands

Robert Christman has shown that JOHANNES VON STAUPITZ had launched his own movement for reform of the order of Augustinian Hermits within his province and that the young men he had raised up proved to be quite responsible to Luther's message. Several of them proclaimed that message in the Low Countries and suffered persecution for it. Three of them, HEINRICH VOES, JOHANN ESCH, and HEINRICH VON ZÜTPHEN, were martyred early and had no chance to develop ministries with impact in the Habsburg domains in the Low Countries; they are presented in chapter 5. One, JAKOB PROBST, did minister to the church of Bremen for several decades.

One of the priors in the Augustinian cloister in Antwerp, ***Jakob Probst*** **(ca. 1495–1562)**, came to Wittenberg around 1518 when he left his native Ypern in Flanders for further study. In 1519, JOHANNES VON STAUPITZ had him named prior of the Augustinian monastery in Antwerp, where he preached Wittenberg Reform. He was forced to recant in 1522 and was transferred to Ypern, where others inclined to Luther's way of thinking supported him in his desire to preach the gospel in Luther's fashion. He fled the next summons to be examined, made his way to Wittenberg, and then was called by the city government of Bremen as preacher in 1524, despite the opposition of the archbishop of the city. He furthered the reform of the city's religious life and promoted education for all children. He assumed the superintendency of the city's churches as these reforms were being introduced. A popular revolution drove him, along with the members of the municipal council, from the city in 1532, but all returned, and Probst fashioned a new ecclesiastical ordinance on the model of Wittenberg in 1533. As controversy over the Lord's Supper simmered in Bremen in the years after 1555, Probst yielded leadership of the church to Tilemann Heshusius.

Probst worked alongside a lay leader, ***Johann von der Wyck*** **(d. 1534)**, who had served Johannes Reuchlin as his attorney before the papal court in 1515 when it heard charges against Reuchlin for his defense of Jewish rights and of the need for Christian study of Hebrew literature. Von der Wyck had attained good standing among German biblical humanists by that time. Nothing is known about the further course of his career until 1528, when he was employed by the municipal government of Bremen as syndicus, or city attorney. In 1529, he argued the case of Bremen's right to introduce religious reform before the imperial supreme court, without success. At this time he also formulated an argument that justified the right of the princes of the empire to use armed resistance against the emperor should he attempt to use force to suppress reform of religious life. In the earliest years of the Smalcald League, von der Wyck played an active role as Bremen's representative. In 1532, Duke Ernst von Braunschweig-Lüneburg employed him as his representative while he remained also in the service of Bremen. In 1533, Landgrave Philip of Hesse asked him to become the syndicus for his birthplace, Münster, as the Reformation was taking hold there. By April 1534 it became clear to von der Wyck that the direction in which the leadership of Bernhard Rothmann and his associates was taking the city violated his principles, which were anchored in Luther's theology. As von der Wyck made his way back to Bremen, he was arrested at the order of Münster's bishop, Franz von Waldeck, without a hearing and subsequently died.

Leadership for reform in nearby Hamburg fell to ***Johannes Aepinus*** **(Hoeck) (1499–1553)**, who had first studied at the University of Wittenberg after secondary education in the monastery school in Belbuck headed by Johannes. Subsequently, while serving as a school rector in Brandenburg, Aepinus was briefly imprisoned by the elector of Brandenburg, Joachim I, for advocating Luther's program for reform, and upon his release he moved to Pomerania. After serving as rector of the secondary school in Stralsund, he followed a call to Hamburg in 1529, as his teacher Johannes Bugenhagen was establishing the Reformation in the city. There Aepinus served as superintendent until his death. He was active on a wider scale, aiding in negotiations with the government of King Henry VIII on behalf of Hamburg and Lübeck in 1534 and forming a relationship with Thomas Cromwell and several English clergy inclined toward the Wittenberg Reformation. He declined a call to come to England because of his rejection of the divorce of Henry VIII from Catherine of

Johannes Aepinus (Hoeck)

Aragon. His defense of the interpretation of Christ's descent into hell as the completion of his suffering for sinners led to controversy and criticism, also from Wittenberg, but not to a cooling of relationships with Luther and Melanchthon. Although he held another view of the descent into hell than Melanchthon, his preceptor urged his colleagues to accept Aepinus's opinion as no threat to the unity of the faith. Aepinus joined his fellow pastors, including Joachim Westphal, in strongly rejecting and critiquing both the Augsburg Interim and the Leipzig Proposal or Interim of 1548.

Luther's Followers in the Dukedom of Prussia

In the northeast of the German-speaking lands, beyond the borders of the empire, lay the lands of the Teutonic Knights and other crusading orders. The last grand master of the Teutonic Knights, Albrecht of Brandenburg-Ansbach, permitted preaching of Luther's views in the early 1520s, and in 1525 he secularized his lands into the duchy of Prussia. He had assembled an impressive core of theologians to execute the introduction of Wittenberg Reform. They included the following three individuals.

***Georg von Polentz* (ca. 1478–1550)**, scion of an established Saxon noble family, studied canon and civil law in Bologna and became a private secretary for the papal curia under Pope Julius II. He then became an official at the court of Emperor Maximilian I, and from there was called to Königsberg by Albrecht, at the time still head of the Teutonic Knights, to serve as palace administrator and bishop of Samland in 1518. When Albrecht was traveling in the empire from 1522 to 1525, Georg governed the territories of the Knights in his stead. He initiated Wittenberg Reform measures beginning in 1523, introducing a German liturgy and recommending reading Luther's writings. Albrecht transformed his domains into the secular duchy of Prussia under the king of Poland, and Georg sought pastors for Prussia who were inclined toward Wittenberg theology. Georg's first wife, Katharina von Wetzhausen, died the year after their marriage in 1525, and in 1527 he married Anna von Heideck.

***Paul Speratus* (1484–1551)** left his birthplace near Ellwangen in Swabia to attend the University of Freiburg. He continued studies in Paris, several Italian universities, and Vienna, earning doctorates in both law and theology. Ordained in 1506, he ministered in parishes in Salzburg and Dinkelsbühl until 1519. As cathedral preacher in Würzburg he turned to Luther's writings, and by 1522, when underway to a new position in Ofen, Hungary, he preached a sermon expressing the Reformer's theology, provoking calls for his excommunication. He found refuge in Iglau, Moravia, and there was imprisoned by the bishop of Olmütz. Three months later he escaped the death sentence by agreeing to leave the area. Wittenberg offered sanctuary at this time. There, he translated some of Luther's Latin treatises into German and composed hymns. Luther chose three of them, including "Salvation unto Us Has Come," a summary of the biblical narrative as it applies to the Christian life, for inclusion in his hymnal of 1524. The next year, Albrecht of Brandenburg-Ansbach followed Luther's recommendation to call Speratus as a preacher in Königsberg, where he participated in the first evangelical visitation of churches in Prussia in 1526 and helped edit a hymnbook for use in the duchy. In 1530, Albrecht had him made bishop of Pomesania, where he introduced the Reformation and battled against Anabaptists and followers of Kaspar Schwenkfeld. He reached out to all the ethnic groups in his diocese, Germans, Poles, Lithuanians, as well as refugees fleeing persecution in Bohemia

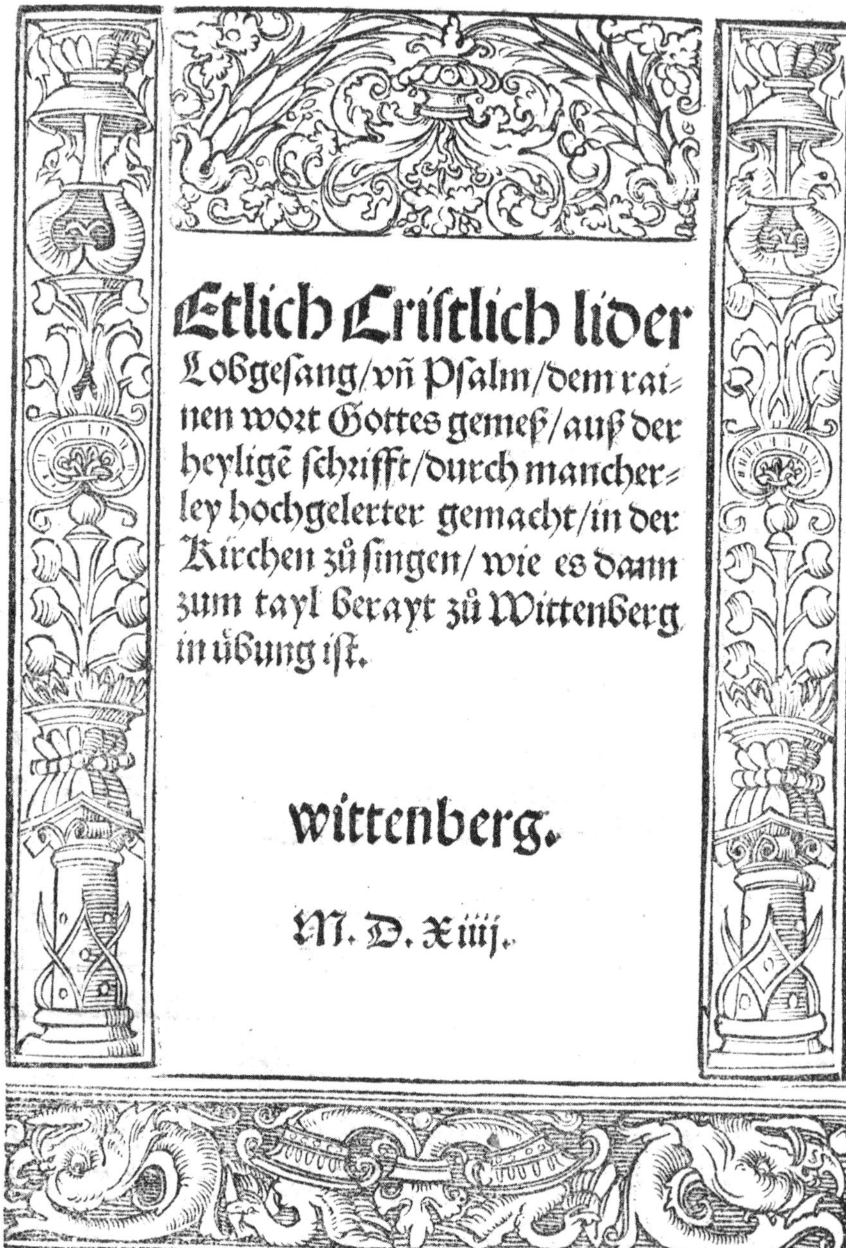

Etlich Cristlich lider
Lobgesang/vñ Psalm/dem rai=
nen wort Gottes gemeß/auß der
heyligẽ schrifft/durch mancher=
ley hochgelerter gemacht/in der
Kirchen zů singen/ wie es dann
zum tayl berayt zů Wittenberg
in übung ist.

wittenberg.

M. D. Xiiij.

The title page of Achtliederbuch *(the first Lutheran hymnal), which included hymns by Luther and Speratus* and the Netherlands. At the end of his life, he opposed the doctrine of justification of his colleague Andreas Osiander.

Johann Poliander **(Graumann) (1487–1541)** won his doctorate in theology while studying in Leipzig, where Petrus Mosellanus instilled humanist attitudes and skills in him. First a teacher and then rector at the school of Saint Thomas in Leipzig (1516–22), Poliander served Johann Eck as his amanuensis during his Leipzig Disputation with Luther and Karlstadt in 1519. He found Luther's arguments against Eck convincing. In 1522 he departed for Wittenberg, where he heard Luther preach and his colleagues lecture. In 1523 he accepted a call to a preacher's position in Würzburg, which he left during the Peasants Revolt of 1525. His response to a request for an evaluation of Luther's writings on the revolt defended the Wittenberg professor's arguments for the restoration of order in the midst of peasant violence. While preaching in Nuremberg in 1525, he attracted the attention of Albrecht of Brandenburg-Ansbach. Albrecht called him to be pastor in the heart of Königsberg, where the duke used him as a trusted counselor in the introduction and spread of the Wittenberg Reform. In the following years, Poliander countered followers of Kaspar Schwenkfeld and small groups of Anabaptists who had come to Prussia. Poliander composed a number of hymns that conveyed the heart of the Wittenberg message.

The Reformers in the Saxon Lands

A number of key supporters of the Reformation ministered in the lands of the Wettin family of Saxony or in neighboring territories. For example, ***Nikolaus Hausmann*** **(ca. 1478–1538)** left his birthplace, Freiberg in Saxony, where his father had served in the town council and as master of coinage production, for study in Leipzig. Ordained in 1503 in Altenburg, by 1519 he was serving as a preacher in Schneeberg, where he found Luther's proclamation attractive and began introducing Wittenberg Reforms. In 1521 the town council of Zwickau called him to lead the Reformation of the town. Hausmann sought Luther's counsel. He assumed the pastorate in Zwickau shortly after Thomas Müntzer had been dismissed as preacher because of his spiritualizing mysticism. Hausmann had to deal with those who had caught Müntzer's spirit, led by the weaver Nikolaus Storch. Luther came to Hausmann's aid in April 1522 to calm dissent among the citizens of Zwickau. Hausmann's faithfulness in carrying out his duties as pastor and preacher established Wittenberg Reform firmly in the town despite continuing opposition from Roman Catholic authorities in the vicinity and from their sympathizers within Zwickau. The municipal government supported Hausmann's leadership of the church but questioned his decisions frequently. At the same time he won the confidence of ELECTOR JOHANN OF SAXONY and served as a visitor of electoral Saxon churches in the visitation of 1528. In 1531, when the town council removed a pastor from his office and appointed a successor without consulting Hausmann, Luther sharply criticized the council and advised Hausmann to move to another ministry. Although Elector Johann brought about reconciliation through a meeting at his castle in Torgau, at which Luther, MELANCHTHON, and JONAS were also present, Haussmann left Zwickau, stayed at the Luther home in Wittenberg for a while, then left to stay with relatives in Freiberg. The princes of Anhalt called him in 1532 to be their court preacher in Dessau. When Duke Heinrich of Saxony wished to introduce the Reformation in Freiberg in 1538, he called Hausmann to his hometown. As he assumed office, his initial sermon was ended by a stroke, which took his life the same day. His close friendship with Luther was reflected in his faithful proclamation of Wittenberg theology throughout his ministry.

Two lay people from Zwickau illustrate other aspects of the early spread of Luther's thought. ***Stephan Roth* (1492–1546)** attended the secondary school in his native Zwickau before enrolling in the University of Leipzig in 1512. There he absorbed the new learning of the biblical humanists and became a friend of CASPAR CRUCIGER. He returned to Zwickau in 1517 to serve as rector of its secondary school; in 1520, the town council of Joachimsthal called him to lead its secondary school. He left that post in 1523 to enroll in the University of Wittenberg. During his four-year stay there, he served a time as one of the preachers in the town church. He married the sister of printer GEORG RHAU's wife. Roth took copious notes on Luther's sermons while in Wittenberg. After his return to Zwickau in 1527, during his time as municipal secretary and superintendent of schools, which began in 1528, he edited those notes into a "summer postil," sermons for the Trinity season, sometimes rather freely editing and even supplementing Luther's sermons with his own when he had no sermon from Luther for a particular Sunday. This, and his often-arbitrary criticism of the pastors in Zwickau, led to severe tensions between Roth and his mentor that were finally resolved before their deaths. Roth assembled a collection of some six thousand books, which he donated to the library of the secondary school in Zwickau.

***Ursula Weida* (Weyda) (ca. 1504–ca. 1571)** came from an old Saxon noble family; her father, Heinrich von Zschöpperitz, served the electoral Saxon government under FREDERICK THE WISE as a courtier with a variety of assignments. Ursula married Johann Weida, who also was in the employ of Duke Johann of Saxony as a tax collector at the castle at Eisenberg north of Jena and a strong supporter of Luther's Reform. After Weida's death in 1541, Ursula returned to her parental home in Zwickau to attend to her aging mother. She married her brother-in-law, Franz Behm, another official of the electoral government in Altenburg, and cared for his children, her own mother, and the brewing operation in their house. Friendship linked the Behms to Stephan Roth, the Zwickau town secretary, despite some insulting remarks Roth made about Ursula's age. In 1524, Ursula took pen in hand to issue a critique of the arguments of the abbot of the Benedictine cloister in Pegau, Simon Blick, and his brother, Wolfgang, a merchant in Erfurt, who opposed Luther and Karlstadt for their advocacy of monks and nuns leaving the monastic way of life. In a treatise entitled *Against the Unchristian Writing and Slanderous Book of Abbot Simon of Pegau and His Brother. . .* , published in 1524, Ursula marshalled her case from some eighty Scripture passages, examining and sometimes rejecting ancient patristic authorities, as she cited the Wittenberg theologians in praise of marriage and defense of the word of God as the sole foundation of the church. She assured readers who had abandoned their monastic vows of God's forgiveness and favor. An anonymous critique of her treatise employed sexual innuendo against her and other women who supported Luther. This attack was met by a likewise anonymous defense as the controversy took its course. Ursula Weida was one of the first and few women who entered into the print wars of the early Reformation. She illustrates the degree to which lay women, like lay men, developed not only a deep interest but also a perceptive understanding of Luther's message and its biblical basis.

Reform came to Gotha through the efforts of ***Friedrich Myconius (Mecum)*** **(1490–1546)**, who entered the Franciscan order in 1510 and was sent first to Leipzig and then to Weimar, where he was ordained in 1516. His sermons reflected Luther's early thinking to such a degree that his superiors frequently moved him. In 1525 he became pastor in Gotha and four years later assumed the office of superintendent of the town's churches. His frequent contacts with Luther made him one of the most important Reformers in the wider Wittenberg movement. He attended the colloquy with Zwingli and his supporters in Marburg in 1529. He took part in the negotiations that established the Wittenberg Concord in 1536 and also in the deliberations in Smalcald in 1537, the conversations with the English delegation sent by King Henry VIII to explore a possible relationship with the Smalcald League in 1538, and the preparations for the Regensburg Colloquy in Hagenau in 1540. Luther called on him to assist in the introduction of the Reformation in ducal Saxony

Illustration depicting a medallion honoring Friedrich Myconius, printed in 1699

in 1539. Myconius was strongly committed to the education of children and contributed much to the shaping of evangelical schooling in Gotha.

Nearby Saxon domains lay the imperial town of Nordhausen. There Luther's plans for reform were introduced by ***Johann Spangenberg* (1484–1550)**. He had received early schooling near his home in Hardegsen in the duchy of Braunschweig-Grubenhagen, in Einbeck and Göttingen, and he taught in Bad Gandersheim before enrolling at the University of Erfurt in 1508, where he entered into the circle of biblical humanists around Conrad Mutian. He left Erfurt in 1520 for service to the counts of Stolberg as a school rector. In 1524, the free or imperial city of Nordhausen called him to be its head pastor and to introduce Wittenberg Reform there. His leadership also built up the city's educational system. In 1527 he married Katharina Grau. Most prominent among their six children was one of the four boys, Cyriakus, a significant figure in Luther's following himself. In 1546, the counts of Mansfeld called the elder Spangenberg to supervise their churches. Shortly before his death his sharp critique of the Leipzig Proposal of 1548 alienated him from the electoral Saxon theologians, but it reinforced those who favored the Gnesio-Lutherans in the next decades, making Mansfeld one of their strongholds. Spangenberg strengthened the propagation of Luther's theology through his many publications. His textbooks for teaching grammar, music, and mathematics aided the Wittenberg educational reform. Luther urged others to expand his Large and Small Catechisms for instruction in the basics of the Christian faith, and Spangenberg did just that, publishing his catechisms in 1541 (Large Catechism) and 1542 (Small Catechism). He had already adapted Melanchthon's *Loci communes* for secondary school pupils in his *Theological Pearls* (*Margarita theologica*, 1540). In 1544 and 1545, he edited hymnals to extend the reach of new, evangelical hymnody, in German and in Latin. His pioneering work with several forms of sermons broke new homiletical ground—interpretations of hymn texts for use in preaching, collections of funeral sermons to aid pastors in the duties now associated with burial, and a postil in catechetical question and answer form as a devotional work for aiding parents in preparing their children for the Sunday morning worship service. He composed a catechism on marriage, a commentary on Acts, and evangelical explications of political ethics and economic behavior. His evangelical "art of dying" went through many editions. His edition of two meditations on the psalms by the fifteenth-century reformer in Florence, Jerome Savonarola, contributed to the Wittenberg interpretation of the history of the church.

IOANNES SPANGENBERGIVS.

IOannes Spangebergius Herdeſsianus ab adoleſcẽtia bonis literis operam dedit, & omnis generis eruditionem ſibi comparauit. In primis uerò Theologiæ incubuit, & ſacrarum literarum uſum ſibi familiariſsimũ reddidit. Itaq; Northuſij in Saxonia paſtor electus eſt. eam uocationem ipſe ſuſcepit, & magna pietate peregit. Eo etiam tempore quo ab Eccleſiaſticis negotijs uacabat, libris inhærere, atq; aliquid in uſum poſteritatis conſcribere ſolebat. Nam Pſalterium carmine Elegiacô reddidit, et Cathechiſmum maiorem cum Poſtilla Lutheri per quæſtiones explicauit. Deinde etiã Margaritham Theologicam compóſuit, & præcipuos Chriſtianæ doctrinæ locos breuiter declarauit. ſcripſit & librum de matrimonio, & multa alia huiuſmodi. Vnde Ioannes ſua eruditione & uirtute magnã ſibi inter doctos authoritatem conciliauit. Reliquit is Ciriacum filium patri quàm ſimilimum, qui & ipſe hodie in Saxonia ob multifariam eruditionem & pietatem agnoſcitur. quemadmodũ & M. Hieronymus Mentzelius, quorum tantùm nomina cum uirtutis commendatione à Vuilhelmo Eccio Radenſi Vuirtzeburgi in mea per Germaniam peregrinatione 1565 indicata fuêre. Anon.

Woodcut of Johann Spangenberg from volume printed ca. 1565

In Mansfeld, Spangenberg followed in the footsteps of one of the initial reformers of the county, ***Caspar Güttel* (1471–1542)**, who hailed from Munich and later recalled pilgrimages in his youth to the shrines to the Virgin Mary at Altötting and to Rome. In 1504, Güttel wrote a paean to the Virgin and her mother, Saint Anne. About the time of his ordination in 1494, he began studying at the University of Leipzig and attained the master's degree. He served parishes in Bohemia and in Zwickau. The Augustinian Hermits attracted him to their ranks in 1498. JOHANNES VON STAUPITZ enlisted him in his movement to bring reform measures to the order and to the areas they served, and Güttel was placed at the new cloister of the order at the edge of Eisleben in 1514 or 1515. In 1517, the theological faculty in Leipzig awarded him his doctorate of Bible. The Wittenberg critique of indulgences and the theology of the cross brought him to Luther's side very quickly. Güttel published a *Booklet on Adam's Works and God's Grace* in 1518. After preaching in Arnstadt and Zwickau, he settled in the county of Mansfeld and served as superintendent of its churches. His participation in the electoral Saxon commission for the visitation of the land's churches from 1525 to 1528 provided vital aid and insight into the process of organizing congregational life according to the Wittenberg model. In 1528 he married. The following years brought him into conflict with GEORG WITZEL as Witzel returned to the Roman obedience and with JOHANN AGRICOLA as he insisted on his "antinomian" interpretation of Luther's understanding of the Law. Güttel's devotional and polemical writings strengthened the spread of Luther's theology and its practice on the popular level significantly.

Working alongside Güttel, ***Michael Coelius (Caelius)* (1492–1559)** served as court preacher for the counts of Mansfeld from 1525 to his death. Son of a baker, Coelius enrolled in the University of Leipzig in 1509. Three years later he assumed a teaching position in the municipal school of his native Döbeln and in 1516 became rector of the school. Among his students were JOHANNES MATHESIUS, JOHANN WALTHER, and the mathematician Peter Apianus. After serving several parishes in Saxony and Bohemia, he became persona non grata because of his support for Luther in Bohemia. Luther recommended him to the counts of Mansfeld, and Count Albrecht gave him the position of court preacher. The town of Mansfeld called him as deacon and then pastor in the 1540s. During his nearly two decades of service there, he defended Luther's theology against the attacks of GEORG WITZEL, who had become priest in Eisleben after his return to the Roman obedience, on issues relating to the Lord's Supper, repentance, and good works. With his colleagues, Coelius fiercely criticized the Leipzig Proposal of 1548 and GEORG MAJOR's proposition that good works are necessary for salvation.

***Jakob Strauss* (ca. 1480–ca. 1527)** taught school in in several locations between 1506 and 1515, after receiving a basic education in his hometown Basel. In 1516 he began his studies in Freiburg, which led to a doctorate in theology, perhaps from the University of Basel. He became a member of the Dominican order. A foundation church in Berchtesgaden engaged him as its preacher, and in 1521 he began preaching a call for reform in Tirol, often against fierce opposition from the local Franciscans and others. His learning earned him great respect as he began lecturing on the Gospel of Matthew. His reform ideas caused the bishop of Brixen, Sebastian Sprenz, to forbid him to preach. Strauss's continuing efforts for reform finally made it advisable that he leave the area. He made his way to Wittenberg, where Karlstadt's radical efforts for change impressed Strauss positively. Late in 1522, he was sent to Eisenach as a preacher, and Duke Johann of Saxony promoted his career. Strauss drew Georg Witzel to his side in a parish near Eisenach and began to campaign for a restoration of Mosaic law in daily life, with support from the court preacher in Weimar, Wolfgang Stein. Luther and Justus Jonas objected to his insistence on the immediate and strict prohibition of all forms of charging interest. Melanchthon negotiated a reconciliation between Strauss and the Wittenberg colleagues. During the Peasants Revolt, Strauss pleaded from the pulpit for peace and was threatened by a peasant band, but government officials also suspected him as a rebel. He moved to Nuremberg and assumed the office of preacher for an ecclesiastical foundation in Baden-Baden, where his strong critique of the understanding of the Lord's Supper advanced by Zwingli and Oecolampadius won approval. The contempt visited upon Strauss by these two and preachers from Strasburg may have been in part responsible for Philip of Hesse's ousting several Zwinglian preachers from his land. Strauss's own final years left little or no trace. Afflicted by illness and without a call as pastor, he died without contact to Wittenberg, although rumors of his return to the Roman obedience cannot be proven.

***Ursula von Münsterberg* (ca. 1493–after 1534)**, granddaughter of King George Podiebrad of Bohemia and niece of Duke Albrecht of Saxony and his wife Zdena of Troppau, lost her parents, Duke Viktor of Troppau and Duchess Margarethe of Montferrat, at an early age and was raised at Albrecht's court in Dresden. She joined the Order of Saint Mary Magdalene of Penance in Freiberg in Saxony and fled the cloister in 1528 with two sisters of the order, the daughters of citizens of Freiberg, Dorothea Tanberg, and Leipzig, Margarete Volckmar. Ursula's defense of her leaving the monastic way of life, published in 1528, received an afterword from Luther himself. Ursula had studied the issue in detail, reading Luther's writings and those of other Reformers, and learning more from her cousin

Heinrich's wife, Duchess Katharina of Saxony. Ursula and her two sister nuns found refuge and defense in Wittenberg, where ELECTOR JOHANN dealt with her cousins, GEORG and HEINRICH. She and Dorothea Tanberg then took up residence in Marienwerder, where she continued to exchange letters with Luther. She also engaged in correspondence over her decision with her cousin, Princess Margarete of Anhalt, who defended the monastic life and criticized Urusla's renunciation of it. Ursula found support from another relative, DUKE ALBRECHT OF PRUSSIA, and a home with her cousin Duke Friedrich II in Liegnitz in 1530. Ursula died at his court some four years later.

The Wittenberg Reformation in Leipzig

Within the Wettin lands, but in the hands of Luther's hostile critic, DUKE GEORG, lay the city of Leipzig. Though in the enemy camp for most of Luther's lifetime, Leipzig had some enthusiastic supporters among the populace who remembered the Leipzig Debate between Luther and ECK, which the duke had sponsored, in 1519. Among them was ***Heinrich Stromer from Auerbach*** **(ca. 1480–1542)**, who came to the city in 1497 to study medicine. He served as rector of the university in 1508 and received his doctorate in medicine in 1511 and his professorship of medicine in 1516, the year in which his first published work, on the plague, appeared. He developed numerous contacts among the humanists of his time, including ULRICH VON HUTTEN, Petrus Mosellanus, and ERASMUS, as well as with Paracelsus. His broad interests are reflected in his textbook on algorithms (1504). He served as personal physician to Duke Georg of Saxony and to the Hohenzollern brothers, ELECTOR JOACHIM I and ALBRECHT, ARCHBISHOP OF MAINZ. His personal support for Luther in 1519 brought the two into contact, and they continued to correspond, as did Stromer and MELANCHTHON. In 1539, at the introduction of the Reformation in ducal Saxony, Stromer hosted Luther in his home.

Following the Leipzig Debate, Duke Georg's rejection of Luther's Reform efforts hardened, but initially Leipzig printers took great advantage of their connections to Wittenberg and published many of Luther's works. After 1539, when Georg's death brought his brother Heinrich to the ducal throne, Wittenberg Reform was immediately established through his lands, and the problematic printing of Wittenberg works could proceed without the hindrances that had threatened the printers under Georg's rule.

Jakob Thanner **(d. ca. 1535)** left his native Würzburg for the University of Leipzig in 1481. He married Margarethe Blumentrost, daughter of a Leipzig merchant. By 1498 he had begun to publish materials related to university instruction but turned also to popular literature. He published Luther's *Ninety-Five Theses on Indulgences* in 1517 but relatively few works from Wittenberg thereafter. His attempt to reprint Luther's New Testament translation was thwarted by episcopal mandate. Financial support for a fellow citizen who speculated in pewter brought him a time into debtors' prison, from which he returned to printing by 1529, but not in the service of the Reformation.

Many more printings of Luther's treatises came from the presses of ***Wolfgang Stöckel* (ca. 1473–1541)**, who had earned his bachelor of arts degree at the University of Erfurt before coming to Leipzig as an apprentice of the printer Arnold Neumarkt. In 1495, Stöckel began to print under his own name. His first wife had died, and he married the widow of his former employer. He spent several months in Wittenberg in 1504 at the invitation of the dean of the faculty of arts, Sigismund Epp, whom Frederick the Wise admonished to permit other works to be printed than those by scholastic scholars. Stöckel published both scholastic and humanistic works in his brief stay in Wittenberg. In Leipzig, he concentrated first on academic publishing, but with the advent of Luther's product for the market, he turned increasingly to German publications, featuring among other authors the Wittenberg professor. In 1526, the Roman Catholic theologian Hieronymus Emser drew Stöckel to the ducal court in Dresden and set him up as his private printer. Works by Emser and Johann Eck came from Stöckel's press for more than a decade, but in 1539 he turned back to Wittenberg authors, including Luther and Hieronymus Weller. His son ***Matthes Stöckel the Elder* (1526–ca. 1602)** took over the family business a year after his father's death, after his mother, Margarete, his father's third wife, had successfully managed the presses for a year. Matthes printed titles by Wittenberg Reformers until he passed the operation on to his son, Matthes the Younger, in 1586. His partnership with Gimel Bergen produced many titles in the service of Wittenberg theology, above all, the *Book of Concord* of 1580.

***Valentin Schumann* (d. 1543)**, son of a Leipzig tailor, began to print books and pamphlets in 1514, including a work by the humanist Johannes Reuchlin. Humanist and classical texts constituted his niche in the world of print until 1518, when he began to issue works by Luther. On New Year's Day 1521, some twenty young men fastened a satirical attack against Hieronymus Emser on the pulpit of the Church of Saint Thomas in the city. When it was determined that Schumann and his apprentices had printed it, they were arrested, then placed under house arrest. Only Emser's intervention in Schumann's behalf ended the drama. Schumann printed almost no works of Luther thereafter until 1539. He attempted to retain his citizenship in Leipzig but moved to Wittenberg in 1523, where the

Wittenberg council rejected the request for residency. He served Emser as a private publisher in Dresden for a while, seems to have printed briefly in other towns, but returned to Leipzig by 1526. His son Jakob could not sustain the family business after his death.

***Melchior Lotter the Elder* (ca. 1470–1549)** married Dorothea, the daughter of the Leipzig's first printer, Konrad Kachelofen, around 1490 after serving as Kachelofen's apprentice. By 1495, Lotter was publishing on his own as well as with his father-in-law and former master and was managing a steadily increasing business. He printed the indulgence for Saint Peter's Cathedral in Rome for ARCHBISHOP ALBRECHT's Magdeburg province in 1517, but also began to serve as Luther's favorite printer in Leipzig. At the Reformer's request, he sent his son MELCHIOR THE YOUNGER to Wittenberg; later, his son MICHAEL also established himself in Wittenberg. The plague drove the elder Lotter from Leipzig briefly in 1522, but in that year he also published Luther's New Testament. Arrested for printing a positive appraisal of Luther by Johannes Cellarius in 1520 without getting approval of the city council, he soon returned to printing and to publishing Luther's treatises, sixty in all by the time he ceased in 1525. In 1531, he became the first Leipzig printer with Hebrew type, and Anton Margarita's *The Entire Jewish Faith*, the convert's fierce attack on the Jewish religion from which he had converted, appeared from his press in that year. Lotter served the city as the printer of official documents and provided liturgical works, grammars, schoolbooks for children, humanistic works, medical works, classical texts, as well as theological treatises to his customers. His business interests extended well beyond his printing enterprise, the center of his commercial domain. He dealt in the paper trade and ran a tavern and a kind of general store, as well as a book dealership, which he sold in 1517. Duke Georg denied him a place on the city council, and only after the duke's death in 1539 did he assume the office, also serving briefly as a municipal judge.

Increasing pressure from Duke Georg meant that the Leipzig printers reduced or abandoned their aboveboard production, and sometimes below-board reproduction, of works by the Wittenberg Reformers. Once DUKE HEINRICH assumed the throne, that situation changed. Both above- and below-board printing of Luther and others began to expand the Leipzig book trade. ***Nikolaus Wolrab* (ca. 1500–ca. 1560)** grew up in the family of a bookbinder and bookseller in Leipzig, attended the university there, and was able to set up his own printing operation with aid from Bishop JOHANN FABRI of Vienna through the latter's friendship with JOHANNES COCHLAEUS, the defender of the old faith, who was perhaps related to Wolrab's wife. The printer published a number of Cochlaeus's works, but in 1537 and 1538, before Duke Georg's death, had begun to print works by Luther, provoking a mandate from the duke against any production of the Reformer's writings in his domains. Following his arrest by Heinrich's government for printing the work of the apostate Wittenberg student Georg Witzel, Wolrab dedicated himself solely to writings favoring reform, earning the wrath of Cochlaeus in turn. Wolrab recognized the market for Luther's Bible, which had an electoral privilege protecting it against pirating. Wolrab's pirated edition of Luther's translation won him not only Luther's harsh condemnation for his greed and contempt for authority but also another short prison sentence. He returned to printing works by Wittenberg authors and received commissions from city and court, but his financial situation drove him to flee in the face of his creditors to Frankfurt an der Oder in 1546. He returned to Leipzig in 1550 but left for Dresden in 1553 and a year later established himself in Bautzen, where he died in 1560 after expressing views aimed at attracting commissions from Roman Catholic theologians, with some success. He seems to have been more dedicated to profits from printing than to any particular confession of the faith.

When ***Valentin Bapst the Elder* (d. 1556)** began to print in 1542, he had been in the business of selling thread in Leipzig for more than a decade and a citizen for a year. He had apparently also worked as a typesetter for some printer. Among his very first published works was the *Medicine for the Soul* by Urbanus Rhegius and several popular works by Luther, including his Small Catechism, *Prayerbook* of 1522, and *Simple Way to Pray* of 1535. Because he could set musical notes, Luther turned to him for printing his *Spiritual Songs* of 1545. His son Valentin apparently could not manage the operation effectively upon his father's death because his father's apprentice, ***Ernst Vögelin* (1519–1589)**, who married Anna, daughter of Valentin the Elder, assumed direction and then ownership of the operation. Vögelin managed the business successfully until the threat of arrest drove him to flee Leipzig in 1576. He had cooperated with the theologians on the Leipzig and Wittenberg faculties who were rather secretly trying to advance a spiritualizing view of the Lord's Supper and had printed several of their works. In fear of imprisonment, he moved to Heidelberg in the lands of the Calvinistic Elector Friedrich III and openly embraced the Heidelberg Catechism, through which the elector was propagating his own blend of theology from Wittenberg, Zurich, and Geneva. Upon the elector's death, Vögelin moved to Neustadt an der Haardt, where he enjoyed the patronage of Count Johann Kasimir of the Palatinate, Friedrich's younger son, who unlike his brother, Elector Ludwig VI, also rejected Luther's way of thinking. Vögelin returned to Heidelberg to exercise various capacities in the service of Johann Kasimir when he became regent over the electorate at Ludwig's death in 1583.

Both pastors and professors led the introduction of the Wittenberg Reformation in ducal Saxony. DUKE HEINRICH entrusted the important task of leading the introduction of the Wittenberg Reformation in Leipzig to ***Johannes Pfeffinger* (1493–1573)**. Born in Wasserburg am Inn, he began his career in the church in 1515 after completing secondary school. As a preacher at a foundation in Passau, he read Luther's writings, which drove him into Paul's letters. Following two years of service in Passau, he fled to Wittenberg in 1523. After studying there, he became pastor in electoral Saxon service, in Sonnenwald, in 1527. To keep him in their own parish, its citizens arranged his marriage to a native, Elisabeth Kühlstein. One of their four children, Johannes, died at age twenty-two, and his father composed a devotional work for parents who lost children. In 1530, the bishop of Meissen drove him out of Sonnenwald. Residents of Leipzig trekked to the cloister at Eicha, where Pfeffinger then became pastor, to hear him preach. In 1532 he assumed the pastorate in Belgern, another post within electoral Saxony. His aid in introducing the Reformation in Leipzig in 1539 led to his call there the next year. He served as superintendent and attained his university degrees in a short time, culminating in the doctorate of theology in 1543. In 1544, he became a professor of theology alongside his duties as superintendent of the church. His participation in the defense of the Leipzig "Interim" earned him the suspicion of Gnesio-Lutherans, and in 1558 NIKOLAUS VON AMSDORF criticized his view of the powers of the will in conversion. Pfeffinger enforced a strict doctrinal discipline in Leipzig; he opposed a colleague who denied justification by grace through faith alone through a confession on the doctrine that the ministerium under his direction accepted as authoritative. When his friend VIKTORIN STRIGEL, for whom he had arranged a teaching post at the university in 1562, denied the true presence of Christ's body and blood in the Lord's Supper in 1567, Pfeffinger banned him from the classroom. Pfeffinger's preaching won him widespread acclaim. Heinrich Salmuth, his son-in-law, succeeded him as superintendent of the Leipzig church.

Pfeffinger's involvement with university as well as church linked him closely to colleagues in all faculties. The most prominent of them was ***Joachim Camerarius* (1500–1574).** His parents, leading citizens of Bamberg, took special pains to educate their son. At age thirteen, he continued learning with Georg Helt, who provided secondary education in Leipzig and lectured at the university. In 1516, Camerarius began his university studies and quickly mastered Greek under the guidance of several humanist lecturers, particularly Peter Mosellanus. He became friends with EOBANUS HESSUS and EURICIUS CORDUS, who drew him into the Erfurt humanist circle. During the indulgence controversy, Luther's

Hymn based on Psalm 124 by Justus Jonas, printed by Ernst Vögelin, 1563

Johannes Pfeffinger

protest and theology attracted his enthusiastic support, so in 1521 he transferred to Wittenberg, where he and MELANCHTHON formed a close, lifelong friendship. Camerarius visited ERASMUS in 1524. In 1526, Melanchthon arranged for Camerarius's call to lead the secondary school the preceptor had helped organize in Nuremberg. There, Camerarius was drawn into the humanist circle and translated *On Human Proportions* by his new friend ALBRECHT DÜRER. In 1527 he married Anna von Truchseß-Grünsberg. He was in Nuremberg's delegation to the imperial diet in Augsburg in 1530, where he aided Melanchthon as he negotiated with the Roman Catholic officials and formulated the Augsburg Confession. In 1535, the University of Tübingen called Camerarius to assist in the reform of the university as DUKE ULRICH returned to power. A similar task awaited him in 1541 in Leipzig as ducal Saxony under DUKE HEINRICH introduced the Reformation. His learning and leadership led Leipzig out of mediocrity to be a leader in German higher education during his more than thirty years there. His published works included aids for preaching, translations of classical Greek authors into Latin (including Homer, Herodotus, Demosthenes, Xenophon, Theocritus, Euclid, Sophocles, Aesop, Thucydides, and Plutarch), commentaries on the works of a number of ancient authors, textbooks on grammar and rhetoric, and commentaries on Jesus Sirach. His biography of Melanchthon helped establish his friend's reputation as a mild-mannered victim of "the madness of theologians." His son ***Joachim Camerarius the Younger* (1534–1598)** studied medicine at Padua and Bologna before returning to Nuremberg to practice medicine and compose several important contributions to the medical discussions of the time.

Among the team that aided in bringing the University of Leipzig into the Wittenberg orbit in the early 1540s were also two members of the theological faculty, ***Alexander***

Engraving of Joachim Camerarius by Johan Jacob Haid (eighteenth century)

***Alesius* (1500–1565)** and ***Bernhard Ziegler* (1496–1552)**. Alesius encountered Wittenberg theology in reading published treatises that trickled into Scotland, which he fled in the face of persecution when his interest in Luther's thinking became known. He came to the University of Wittenberg in the early 1530s. His return to England included a brief stint of instructing in Cambridge, but when KING HENRY VIII issued his Catholicizing *Six Articles* in 1539, Alesius left the king's domain. He assumed a professorship in theology at Leipzig in 1543 after teaching briefly in Frankfurt an der Oder. His published works included commentaries on the Psalms, John's Gospel, and the Pastoral Epistles. His theological orientation was set by MELANCHTHON, but he largely avoided participating in the controversies of the period after 1548. Ziegler, son of a ducal Saxon officer and local administrator, began studies at the University of Leipzig in 1516. He learned Hebrew from Anton Margarita, the rabbi's son and convert to the Christian faith, whose virulent attacks on his ancestral religion earned him the wrath of CHARLES V. In 1521, Ziegler entered the cloister at Altzella but was soon attracted to Luther's teaching. In 1525, he began working for reform in Ansbach, teaching Hebrew as well as serving as pastor. Called in 1540 to teach Hebrew at the University of Leipzig, Ziegler earned his doctorate in theology and joined the theological faculty in 1544. His intervention on behalf of his friend Matthäus Lauterwald against ANDREAS OSIANDER in the controversies that swirled around the latter in Königsberg contributed significantly to discrediting Osiander through an examination of his theology.

Engraving of Bernard Ziegler (sixteenth century)

Wittenberg Reform in Erfurt

The city of Erfurt formed an enclave under the jurisdiction of the archbishop of Mainz within Wettin territories. Luther had spent most of the years 1501–11 in Erfurt. Its pastoral leadership in the introduction of Wittenberg reforms lay in the hands of Johannes Lang and others, and its printers provided key support for Wittenberg Reformers throughout the sixteenth century. Among the pastors in the city, ***Johann Eberlin von Günzburg*** **(ca. 1470–1533)** served but a short time, but at a critical stage in the city's history. He may have studied in Ingolstadt before becoming a priest in the diocese of Augsburg. His studies in Basel began in 1489, in Freiburg in 1493. As a member of the strict element within the Franciscan Order, he served in the cloisters in Heilsbronn, Tübingen, Ulm, and Freiburg. Reading Luther's publications, he found the Wittenberg Reformer convincing, and in 1521, at the instigation of Girolamo Aleander, the papal legate, and of Charles V's father confessor, he was dismissed from the order. Soon thereafter, Eberlin wrote his *Fifteen Bundesgenossen* (Comrades), a plea for the reform of social and economic conditions in the form of a description of "Wolfaria," a utopian society. In 1522 he came to Wittenberg to study, while continuing his composition of treatises calling for reform of various kinds. Thomas Murner and Kaspar Schatzgeyer, both Franciscans, carried on a personal feud in print with Eberlin. In 1524, the city council of Erfurt called him to be a preacher there. His preaching calmed rebellious groups within the city in 1525. At the end of 1525, Count Georg II of Wertheim called him to the town of Wertheim, where his publications continued to pour forth from his pen along with a translation of Tacitus. At Georg's death, Eberlin assumed a pastorate in Leutershausen, which brought him into conflict with the establishment of the town, and there he died three years after his arrival.

The first press in Erfurt was set up in 1499, and its printers spread Luther's ideas throughout the central German lands. Among the first to follow Wolfgang Schenk in practicing the trade there was ***Wolfgang Stürmer*** **(d. after 1551)**, whose commitment to humanistic learning became clear immediately with his publication in 1506 and 1507 of seven works by Helius Eobanus Hessus. He worked together on further humanistic works with Johann Rhau-Grunenberg, who soon departed for Wittenberg. His first treatises from Luther's pen came from his shop in 1522; it quickly became clear that he was a significant distributor of Wittenberg theology. Alongside his fifty titles by Luther published through 1546, he issued works by a number of others in the Wittenberg circle, including Johann Spangenberg, Caspar Cruciger, and Justus Menius, partially in partnership with his brother ***Gervasius Stürmer* (d. after 1557)**, who later took the lead in their joint ventures. He published works by MELANCHTHON, BUGENHAGEN, JONAS, CRUCIGER, and several of their students.

***Melchior Sachse the Elder* (d. 1551)** began publishing in Erfurt in 1525 with the publication of comment on the "Twelve Articles" of the peasants by URBANUS RHEGIUS. He printed forty editions of treatises by Luther in the next two decades. In addition, works on medicine, practical handbooks of various kinds, and municipal documents came from his presses. After his death, his widow, ***Barbara* (d. 1553)**, directed the family business until her death, when her son ***Melchior Sachse the Younger* (d. 1586)** took it over, producing a new printing of Luther's Small Catechism as his first work in 1554. Both mother and son, as well as the latter's sons and heirs, continued to produce literature in the service of the Wittenberg Reformation.

Luther's Followers in Braunschweig and Hesse

In the vicinity of the Saxon lands, the territories of Hesse and the several branches of the duchy of Braunschweig profited from strong princely leadership but produced fewer theologians of wider influence in the 1520s and 1530s. Among those who ministered in these lands to the northwest and west of Saxony, however, were the following comrades of the Wittenberg Reformers.

In Hesse, in addition to ERHARD SCHNEPF and others, ***Erasmus Alber* (ca. 1500–1553)** served for a time. He came to the University of Wittenberg in 1520 after studying at the University of Mainz. Subsequent to leading a Latin school in Ursel (1525–27), he became pastor in Sprendlingen (1528–39) under PHILIP OF HESSE. ELECTOR JOACHIM II of Brandenburg called Alber to be a court preacher as the elector introduced the Reformation in 1539 but dismissed him because he criticized Joachim's taxing clergymen. Alber served briefly in several places, including Rothenburg ob der Tauber in the subsequent years and received his doctorate in theology in Wittenberg in 1543. His sharp attacks on Roman Catholics and, after 1548, on both the imperial policies set forth in the Augsburg Interim and the electoral Saxon compromise in the Leipzig Proposal or Interim set him on a pilgrimage that made for short stays in several places. Among those who found refuge in Magdeburg after the Smalcald War, he left there at the end of its siege by electoral Saxon troops. A few weeks after assuming the office of superintendent of the church in Neubrandenburg in 1553, he died. In addition to his polemical writings in defense of the Wittenberg

Reformation, his editions of Aesop's fables, a collection of animal fables under the title *Book of Virtue and Wisdom*, and his German-Latin Dictionary display his adept literary talents.

Neighboring Hesse lay the county of Nassau, where ***Erasmus Sarcerius*** **(Sorck, Schürer) (1501–1559)** helped introduce the Wittenberg Reformation. He had studied at Leipzig and Wittenberg in the 1520s and became a school teacher, finally in Lübeck, before Count Wilhelm of Nassau called him to be rector of his Latin school in Siegen in 1536. In 1537, he assumed the office of superintendent of the churches of the county and court preacher for the count's lands. In subsequent years, he constructed an organization based on consistorial governance and regular synodical meetings of pastors. At the same time, he echoed Luther's emphasis on the family and home as the focal point of catechetical instruction of the young and encouraged family devotions. In 1548, imperial pressure caused Count Wilhelm to ask Sarcerius to leave his duchy so that he could introduce partial compliance with the Augsburg Interim. Sarcerius accepted a call to be pastor in Leipzig and worked with Melanchthon on preparations for the participation of the electoral Saxon theologians on the Council of Trent, a plan that collapsed when Elector Moritz began organizing his military forces for revolt against Emperor Charles. Sarcerius's growing discomfort with the Leipzig Proposal of 1548 led to him accepting a call to be superintendent of the churches in Mansfeld county. There, he entered into controversy with Georg Major over the role of good works. The Gnesio-Lutheran government of ducal Saxony drew Sarcerius into consultations on various matters. He supported the Gnesio-Lutheran insistence on clear confession of the faith at the Colloquy of Worms in 1557 and participated in the composition of the ducal Saxon *Book of Confutation* in 1558. He was the first to issue his own dogmatics text in the form of Melanchthon's *Loci communes* (1539–40) and published a number of biblical commentaries as well as a postil to aid pastors in preaching. His works on pastoral care and on ecclesiastical law, particularly in regard to marriage, also assisted pastors in their exercise of their office.

Sarcerius's school in Siegen received a new rector from Wittenberg in 1540 when ***Georg Öhmler (Aemylius)*** **(1517–1569)** arrived after having studied in Wittenberg since 1532. He had also conducted a school there. Öhmler's father, like Luther's, operated a smelting business in Mansfeld; his mother was part of the Mansfeld smelting family Reinicke. Thus, Öhmler found a warm reception in coming to Wittenberg. His recitation of seventy-five biblical stories in Latin verse that appeared in print in 1539 was among the first of his literary efforts in behalf of the cultivation of biblical knowledge and faith. In Wittenberg, Valerius Cordus nurtured Öhmler's interest in botany, and the latter's expansion of some of his teacher's observations on specific plants were later published by his contemporary, the Swiss naturalist Conrad Gessner. Öhmler's years in Siegen produced a number of widely used publications, particularly his summary of the Gospel and Epistle lessons in Latin verse and a postil with questions on the lessons. His catechetical textbook appeared in 1557, after he had become superintendent of the church in Stolberg in the Harz mountains (1553). He received his doctorate in theology in Wittenberg (1554). His combination of skills at Latin poetry, a thorough command of Luther's theology, and a research interest in botany illustrates the breadth of Wittenberg learning.

URBANUS RHEGIUS left Augsburg to come to the court of Duke Ernst of Braunschweig-Lüneburg and to shape ecclesiastical life in the duchies of Braunschweig, as did ***Anton Corvinus*** **(1501–1553)**, who had received a humanist-shaped education at the University of Leipzig. As a Cistercian monk in Riddagshausen near the town of Braunschweig, he was attracted to Luther's understanding of the biblical message. Dismissed from the monastery, he traveled to Goslar and became active in the reform of the town's ecclesiastical life. His earlier appreciation of ERASMUS diminished after he had visited Wittenberg and conversed with Luther and MELANCHTHON. In 1529, he became pastor in Witzenhausen in Hesse and aided LANDGRAVE PHILIP from time to time, including disputing with imprisoned Anabaptist leaders after the fall of Münster in 1534 and taking part in the Regensburg Colloquy in 1541. His organizational skills were put to use in formulating church ordinances for Northeim in 1539, Braunschweig-Calenberg in 1542, Braunschweig-Wolfenbüttel in 1543, and Hildesheim in 1544, in the latter two cases in cooperation with JOHANNES BUGENHAGEN. In 1542, he left Witzenhausen to formally assume

Woodcut depicting Anton Corvinus by Master AS, 1546

duties overseeing the introduction of Wittenberg Reforms in the lands of Duchess Elisabeth of Braunschweig-Calenberg. When her son, Erich II of Braunschweig-Calenberg, introduced the Augsburg Interim to his lands in 1549, he jailed Corvinus. Corvinus wrote a widely used postil, which provided pastors with succinct notes to aid preaching on the appointed lessons of the church year.

Nuremberg's Sodality of Martin

South of Wittenberg some two hundred miles lay the imperial city of Nuremberg, a political and economic focal point of the German Empire and one of the first major centers to turn decisively toward Wittenberg Reform. Here, clergy played a secondary role to lay leadership, which included not only prominent intellectuals and artists but also printers, who quickly recognized the potential of Luther's publications.

Pastoral leadership in Nuremberg included at least two of Luther's inner circle who came to strengthen the original leadership of the Wittenberg Reformation, Wenceslaus Linck and Veit Dietrich. Among the priests who had been serving in Nuremberg when they turned to Luther's teaching was ***Andreas Osiander* (ca. 1496–1552)**. He was born in Gunzenhausen in Franconia and studied at the University of Ingolstadt from 1515 to 1520. His study of Hebrew, the Old Testament, and the cabala, the medieval, Neoplatonic hermeneutical system of medieval Jewish scholars, with Johannes Reuchlin permanently shaped his way of thinking. He was ordained and began serving as an instructor in the Augustinian cloister in Nuremberg in 1520. In 1522, the city council appointed him as the preacher at the church of Saint Lorenz. He quickly became the spokesman for the forces within the city favoring Luther's teaching. His ministry was haunted by disputes with the council, for example, over the preacher's insistence that all those receiving the Lord's Supper receive private absolution before doing so; the city council favored the use of the general absolution alongside the practice of private absolution. Tensions with those who came to his side in the Nuremberg ministerium also accompanied Osiander's pastorate. Among those who opposed him on the issue of general absolution were Linck and Dietrich. Nonetheless, Osiander played a key role inside and outside the city in the spread of the Wittenberg Reformation and its differentiation not only from medieval practices and the Roman obedience but also from Zwinglian, Anabaptist, and spiritualist tendencies. With Johannes Brenz, he authored the Brandenburg-Nuremberg church ordinances of 1533, which served as a model for other ecclesiastical constitutions in the German lands. His catechism in sermonic form and his harmony of the gospel accounts also exercised widespread influence. He participated in the Wittenberg witness to the gospel at the Colloquy of Marburg in 1529, the Diet of Augsburg in 1530, the conference of the Smalcald League in 1537 (where he subscribed to Luther's Smalcald Articles), and the negotiations in Hagenau and Worms in 1540–41, which led to the Colloquy in Regensburg in 1541. When the Nuremberg city council tried to work out a settlement that would protect the city from the harsh imposition of the Augsburg Interim, Osiander left the city and accepted the invitation of DUKE ALBRECHT OF PRUSSIA to become a pastor in Königsberg. Albrecht disregarded the statutes of his university and imposed Osiander upon the theological faculty. These measures and Osiander's own arrogance gradually alienated him from his colleagues. His own cabalistic framework for thinking became ever more evident in his teaching that it is not the justifying word of forgiveness on the basis of Christ's death and resurrection that effects the justification of sinners but rather that faith is the entryway for Christ's divine nature to dwell in believers and bestow his substantial righteousness as God upon them. Mounting criticism from every corner of the Wittenberg circle plagued Osiander's last months of life. Until shortly before his own death in 1568, Duke Albrecht made certain that only supporters of Osiander's views served as pastors in his domains, but at the end he called two early opponents of his favorite, JOACHIM MÖRLIN and MARTIN CHEMNITZ, back to Königsberg to eliminate Osiander's teaching from his duchy.

Andreas Osiander as depicted in 1854 publication Zweihundert deutsche Männer in Bildnissen und Lebensbeschreibungen

In addition to the leadership displayed by Osiander, Linck, Dietrich, and other pastors, lay people played a critical role in the reform of the city. ***Lazarus Spengler* (1479–1534)** succeeded his father as secretary of the administration of the city of Nuremberg in 1507 after serving a decade as secretary of the municipal court and manager of the city's records since 1501. His study of law at the University of Leipzig had prepared him for these positions. He took an active role in the humanist lay elite of the city that gathered in the "*Sodalitas Celtica*" and later the "*Sodalitas Staupitziana*"—named in honor of two frequent guests in Nuremberg who had won the respect of the group's some sixteen members. The theology and piety of Staupitz particularly shaped their attitudes. After two visits from Luther, as he traveled to and from Augsburg in 1518, they began calling themselves the "*Martinianer.*" Spengler quickly grasped the heart of Luther's message regarding the justification of sinners through the unconditional grace of God and the atoning work of Jesus Christ. He defended Luther in a treatise published anonymously in late 1518, the first of a series of treatises, that demonstrated his command of the intricacies of Luther's entire theology. His influence extended well beyond Nuremberg's borders, through these publications and through his activities in behalf of introducing reform, for instance, in the Brandenburg-Nuremberg church ordinances of 1533, composed by Andreas Osiander and Johannes Brenz. Spengler consistently argued against any use of force in defense of Wittenberg Reform, reflecting his sensitivity to his city's special role as an imperial city in the governing of the empire.

Another prominent member of the circle of those advancing humanist learning in Nuremberg was ***Willibald Pirckheimer* (1470–1530)**. His father had served as a legal counselor to the bishop of Eichstätt, where Willibald was born and imbibed the learning of the day. While his father later was employed by the courts of the dukes of Bavaria and the dukes of Tirol, Willibald traveled with him to Italy, the Swiss cantons, and the Low Countries. In 1488 he departed for study in Padua and Pavia, where his instructors led him ever deeper into Platonic philosophy. Elected to the Nuremberg city council in 1495, he began a career as civic leader that lasted over a quarter of a century. In 1499, he made an unsuccessful attempt at a military career as commander in the army of the emperor and the Swabian League against the Swiss. Later Charles V appointed him as an imperial advisor. Pirckheimer's wide range of interests made him a good conversation partner on the ancient classical authors and the history of the church as well as matters of the occult. When Luther visited Nuremberg in the early 1520s, Pirckheimer entertained him; he read Luther's writings avidly and supported many Wittenberg Reform measures. The bull that excommunicated Luther included Pirckheimer among those banned as well, perhaps because of his satirical criticism of Johann Eck, but in 1521 he reconciled with the papacy. His family was deeply involved in the church, with seven of his own sisters as nuns and an uncle who was a Carthusian prior. He defended Luther in correspondence and wrote against the persecution of the evangelical preachers. At the end of his life, he withdrew from public life and dedicated himself to translating ancient Greek texts into Latin, including the sermons of Gregory of Nazianzus. His history of the ancient Germans won him acclaim. He died without committing himself to Luther's way of thinking.

Willibald's older sister ***Charitas Pirckheimer* (1466–1532)**, along with their sister Clara and Willibald's daughters Katherina and Crescentia, were nuns in the convent of Saint Clara in Nuremberg, of which Charitas became abbess in 1503. She dedicated much time

Portrait (1524) of Willibald Pirckheimer at age fifty-three by Albrecht Dürer

to reading ancient Latin pagan writers as well as the church fathers. She particularly enjoyed the writings of Saint Jerome. She participated in the discussions of the circle of biblical humanists in Nuremberg and corresponded with a number of those who propagated the new learning beyond the city, including Georg Spalatin and Erasmus. She opposed Luther's teaching early on and congratulated Hieronymus Emser for his attacks on Luther. She became subject to the sharp criticism of the city council for her adherence to the old faith but resisted and maintained the cloister to the end of her life.

Portrait of woman thought to be Charitas Pirckheimer, after Albrecht Dürer by a twentieth-century artist

Hans Sachs **(1494–1576)**, a cobbler by trade, sprang from an artisan family that sent him to Latin school in Nuremberg. A local Nuremberg weaver, Lienhard Nunnenbeck, taught him the art of the Meistersänger tradition, and he became a leading author and performer of his verses and their musical settings. He spent the years 1511 to 1516 as a journeyman traveling from place to place. He returned to Nuremberg and launched a literary career that produced more than four thousand songs of the "Meistersänger" genre along with two hundred dramatic pieces, and countless poems, fables, and other literature for entertainment. His literary works criticized selfishness, envy, and greed, and praised Christian virtues; they propagated Luther's focus on Scripture and his proclamation of the justification of sinners by God's grace through faith in Christ. From 1520 on, Sachs dedicated himself to campaigning for Luther's ideas, naming the Wittenberg Reformer "the Wittenberg nightingale," and reading his works voraciously. His sharp critique of papal practices irritated Nuremberg authorities, who wished to avoid imperial threats to the city, but they added to his popularity with the masses, who continued to read his works.

Self-portrait by Albrecht Dürer (1500)

***Albrecht Dürer* (1471–1528)** followed his father into training as a goldsmith, the occupation of both his grandfathers, citizens of Nuremberg. But by the end of his apprenticeship in 1486, the young Dürer was also pursuing instruction in painting with Michael Wolgemut, the master of all Nuremberg painters of the time. Dürer also learned the craft of preparing woodcuts and engravings as illustrations for books at this time. After four years of travel to different artists, he returned in 1494 to Nuremberg to marry Agnes Frey from a leading Nuremberg family. Then he departed to Venice, where he remained into early 1495. His return to Nuremberg marked the beginning of a career that dominated the artistic scene not only in his own city but in all the German-speaking lands and beyond, both because of the fine quality of his work in the media of painting, woodcuts, and engravings, but also because of his theoretical studies of proportion and perspective. He visited Venice once again in 1505, learning and adapting the latest Italian styles to his own. Commissions from EMPEROR MAXIMILIAN and a number of other princes indicate his prominence among his contemporaries. Dürer's work always reflected his Christian faith. When he began to learn of Luther's call for reform, he greeted it enthusiastically and often expressed his concern for the Reformer's safety after EMPEROR CHARLES V outlawed him in 1521.

***Hieronymus Baumgartner* (1498–1565)** figures in Luther's story in part because he was intending to marry KATHARINA VON BORA when he encountered the opposition of his parents and did not return to Wittenberg. He married Sybilla Dichtlin, the daughter of an official of the dukes of Bavaria who had been imprisoned and stiffly fined for his support for Luther's way of thinking; Hieronymus and Sybilla raised a family of seven children. Baumgartner had come to Wittenberg in 1518 after five years of study at the University of Ingolstadt and a brief visit in Leipzig. His conversations with Luther and MELANCHTHON converted him to the Wittenberg cause. When he returned to his native Nuremberg in early 1522, he easily integrated himself into the leadership of the city as a member of a prominent family. In 1525, he became a member of the city council, and he rose to the highest levels of civil leadership in the following thirty years. His devotion to the Wittenberg Reformation made him an ideal representative of Nuremberg at the imperial diets of Speyer in 1529 and Augsburg in 1530, and at the Smalcald League's meeting in 1537. He played important roles in organizing various parts of civic life on the basis of Wittenberg theology. His talents provided key support for the founding of the secondary school of which Joachim Camerarius became rector. He also helped establish the city's municipal library. As he returned from the imperial diet in Speyer in 1544, he was taken captive by a knight, Albrecht von Rosenberg, for reasons arising out of Nuremberg's disputes with the Swabian League. After fourteen months of harsh confinement, he won release through the payment

Dürer sketch of his wife, Agnes Frey (1494)

of eight hundred gold gulden. Through correspondence and other contacts, he remained in close contact with MELANCHTHON and other Wittenberg friends throughout his life and continued to lend them support through Nuremberg's participation in the wider Wittenberg movement.

Nuremberg attracted printers early on, in part because of the *Sodalitas Staupitziana*. The son of a local baker and miller, ***Anton Koberger* (ca. 1440–1513)** commanded admiration for his publications far beyond the city and even beyond the borders of the empire. In particular, his production of Hartmann Schedel's *Chronicle of the World* (1493) earned him wide respect. His twenty-four presses exceeded the production power of almost all other printers of his time. In the next generation, several of the many printers in Nuremberg served the Wittenberg Reformers well and had extensive contacts with Luther, MELANCHTHON, and their colleagues.

The presses of ***Hieronymus Höltzel* (d. ca. 1530)** produced the works of both scholastic theologians and humanists, along with the woodcuts of ALBRECHT DÜRER and others and imperially commissioned documents. Höltzel recognized the potential of Luther's *Ninety-Five Theses on Indulgences* in 1517 and continued to print the Reformer's works. His issuance of a work by ANDREAS KARLSTADT without ascription and of another by THOMAS MÜNTZER landed Höltzel in prison, and after a long period of questioning he was released and renewed printing. A few months later, his son-in-law Hans Eichenauer was arrested for printing an anonymous tract supporting the peasants in revolt. Höltzel was exiled, but by the end of 1526 he had returned to the city and to its citizenship roles. Some scholars believe he continued to print and have his product appear under the names of other publishers. Debts plagued him, and the end of his life is clouded in uncertainty.

***Friedrich Peypus* (ca. 1485–1535)** first worked for the Nuremberg city physician, Ulrich Pinder, who also served as personal physician of ELECTOR FREDERICK THE WISE OF SAXONY, in the private press that produced works for members of the *Sodalitas Celtica*. Woodcuts of DÜRER appeared from this operation. When Peypus married Pinder's daughter Margarethe, the father-in-law set him up with a press of his own. In the stormy and uncertain days in which Luther's ideas began to ferment among the humanist and municipal leadership of Nuremberg, Peypus published several dubious works, among them Luther's *Sermon on Indulgences and Grace*. That earned him a fine that was levied but never actually imposed. He added Luther to his repertoire of publications as he continued to print the works of humanist scholars and also law books and legal studies. He at least dabbled in merchandising but dedicated most of his energies to his publishing firm.

***Jobst Gutknecht* (d. 1542)** was another among the first of the Nuremberg printers who found in Luther's writings an expression of their own convictions as well as a source of wealth. He became a citizen of the city in 1511 and was listed in records at that time as a printer. By 1514 he had his own bookstore and took over the press of Wolfgang Huber, whose father, Ambrosius, had established the family publishing business in 1497. Gutknecht printed a missal in 1514, and his interest in religious works continued as Luther's works came into the market, issuing two editions each of Luther's *Sermon on Indulgence and Grace, Short Explanation of the Ten Commandments*, and *Claim of Immunity for the Sermon on the Papal Indulgence and Grace*, all in 1518. Over the rest of his lifetime he led the production of Luther's works in Nuremberg. In 1533, he and Johann Petreius were commissioned to publish the church ordinances written for the city and the margravate of Brandenburg-Ansbach by Andreas Osiander and Johannes Brenz. Gutknecht published over five hundred titles during his twenty-eight-year career.

***Johann Petreius* (1497–1550)** attended the University of Basel and continued his studies in Wittenberg, attaining the master of arts degree in 1517. After employment by a relative, Adam Petri, in Basel, he came to Nuremberg in 1523, married Barbara Neudörffer, and thereby became a citizen. That year Melanchthon's *Hypotyposes* and his commentaries on John and Matthew were among Petreius's first publications, followed by Luther's German Psalter in 1524. The Nuremberg catechism of Andreas Osiander and the Nuremberg-Brandenburg *Church Ordinances* followed from his presses over the following years. His overall production, over six hundred titles, made him the single most important printer in the city at his time. His association with Osiander aided him in executing the commission to publish Nikolaus Copernicus's *On the Revolution of the Heavenly Spheres*, with its preface by Osiander, in 1543. Petreius's son Lorenz, offspring of his second marriage, to Anna Bauer, widow of a local merchant, became a pastor in the city.

***Hans Hergot* (d. 1527)** had only a short career in Nuremberg before he was executed by the sword in Leipzig for publishing a utopian treatise, *On the New Way of Conducting the Christian Life*. The Nuremberg city council rejected his wife's request to intervene for him in Leipzig on the grounds that such an intervention would have been more of a hindrance to his cause than a help, perhaps indicating tensions between evangelical Nuremberg and the duke of Saxony and ruler of Leipzig, Duke Georg. Hergot had extended credit to two Wittenberg printers, Hans Weiss and Jörg Plöchinger, in 1526, demonstrating the network that connected printers at the time. Nearly a third of the titles traceable to his press, thirty-two, including the German New Testament, stemmed from Martin Luther's pen.

Hergot's wife, ***Kunigunde* (d. 1548)**, married Georg Wachter within a matter of months of Hergot's death, and the two of them continued Hergot's printing operation, with Luther's works among their chief products, along with hymns by Luther and others.

Bavaria

In the lands of the duchy of Bavaria, Wittenberg plans for reform commanded the attention and enthusiasm of noble leaders and the common people but made few inroads into the official life of the church. Within that sphere, however, a noblewoman stands out as an example of the defiance of those at the edge of power or beyond its responsibilities who followed Luther with dedication and zeal. ***Argula von Grumbach* (1492–1554/68)** received a German Bible from her father, Bernhard von Stauff, when she was ten years old. At fifteen, she became a lady-in-waiting to Duchess Kunigunde of Bavaria, the sister of EMPEROR MAXIMILIAN I, two years before the death of both parents. In 1516 she married Friedrich von Grumbach, who exercised an administrative post in Dietfurt in Franconia and opposed Argula's turn to the gospel as proclaimed in Wittenberg. Indeed, Duke Wilhelm of Bavaria deprived him of his position because he had not bridled his wife's support for Luther's teaching. Argula's brother Bernhard called an evangelical preacher to his lands in 1522. The next year when a student and arts instructor at the University of Ingolstadt, Arsacius Seehofer, was forced to renounce his commitment to Luther's and Melanchthon's Reform publicly, Argula sent a protest to Duke Wilhelm of Bavaria and published an open appeal on Seehofer's behalf to the town council of Ingolstadt. In late 1523 she made contact with FREDERICK THE WISE. Her literary activity in support of Luther's Reform continued; her treatises demonstrated her thorough command of Scripture. She began corresponding with the Reformer as well as MELANCHTHON, GEORG SPALATIN, PAUL SPERATUS, and ANDREAS OSIANDER. She urged Luther to marry. During the imperial diet in Augsburg in 1530, she visited Luther at the Castle Coburg to encourage him and gave him suggestions for his wife on how to ween the baby Magdalena. In that year her husband died, and two years later she married into the von Schlick family, leading nobility in Bohemia, who supported the Reformation, but this second husband also died after two years. Argula attempted to mediate in the differences over the Lord's Supper between Strassburg and Wittenberg. In addition to the loss of two husbands, she suffered the loss of two sons, who were murdered. Yet, she remained strong in her faith, confessing her adherence to Luther's teaching and supporting its spread until her death, the exact date of which is unclear due to a lack of documentation regarding her later years.

Wye ein Christliche fraw des adels / in
Beyern durch iren / in Gotlicher schrifft / wolgegrund
tenn Sendbrieffe / die hohenschul zu Ingoldstat /
vmb das sie eynen Euangelischen Jungling / zu
widersprechung des wort Gottes / betrangt
haben / straffet.

Auch volgent hernach die artickel / so Magister Arsacius
Sehoffer von München durch die hohenschul zcu In-
gelstat beredt am abent vnser frawē geburt nechst
verschinen widerruffen vnnd verworffen hat.
Actum Ingelstat. M D XXiij.

Title page of Argula von Grumbach's broadsheet "Letter to the University of Ingolstadt" (1524)

The Wittenberg Reform in Augsburg

On the western edge of Bavaria and south of Nuremberg some one hundred miles, its rival in both economic and political influence, Augsburg, reflected in its civic profile the full range of religious options, with Roman Catholics, Lutherans, and Zwinglians contending with each other and Anabaptists and spiritualists throughout the first half of the sixteenth century. Both its preachers and its printers took prominent roles in the spread of Luther's way of thought.

Among the earliest proponents of Luther's theology in the city was ***Urbanus Rhegius* (Rieger, König) (1489–1541)**, son of a priest and his mistress, who encountered criticism from Roman Catholic opponents because of his illegitimate birth. This encouraged Rhegius to oppose clerical celibacy. His studies at the universities of Freiburg, Ingolstadt, and Basel directed him toward the new learning of biblical humanism. While at Freiburg, he became acquainted with two later foes, JOHANN FABRI and JOHANN ECK, whom he followed to Ingolstadt when Eck accepted a professorship there. As a student in Ingolstadt, he won the poet laureate's crown from EMPEROR MAXIMILIAN. His proficiency in Greek and Hebrew propelled him early on into a career of publication of works, initially on the priesthood and pastoral care. Ordained in 1519, he became cathedral preacher in Augsburg and soon thereafter announced from the pulpit the papal threat to excommunicate Luther. This aroused Rhegius's anger, and he affirmed the benefits of reading Luther's works. His criticism of indulgences and his proclamation of justification by grace through faith in Christ earned him dismissal from his post at the cathedral in 1522. In 1523, the city council of Augsburg called him to a pastorate in the city. On Christmas Day 1525 he celebrated the Lord's Supper in both kinds. He tried to mediate the dispute between Luther and ZWINGLI over Christ's presence in the Lord's Supper but opposed the Anabaptists in Augsburg in public disputations. Publications continued to pour from his pen, defending Wittenberg theology and demonstrating its strength for pastoral care. In June 1525 he married Anna Weissbrucker, from a prominent Augsburg family, with whom he fathered eleven children. When the imperial diet met in Augsburg in 1530, Rhegius played a significant role in support of MELANCHTHON and the other Wittenberg theologians. While at the diet, DUKE ERNST OF BRAUNSCHWEIG-LÜNEBURG requested that Rhegius move to his court in Celle to direct the introduction of Wittenberg theology and practice into the congregations of his lands. Rhegius complied. He dedicated the last decade of his life to transforming the medieval priests there into evangelical pastors. In response to the frequently asked questions of those priests, he composed a treatise, *How to Speak Properly and without Offense about* *the Chief Articles of Christian Teaching*, in 1535 in Latin; in 1536 the German translation appeared. This work became a standard for public teaching in several territories and towns as well as a widely used tool for pastoral guidance and instruction. Rhegius introduced new ecclesiastical ordinances for the towns of Lüneburg and Hannover within the duke's domains, and his correspondence reinforced the influence he exercised through his printed works. In the city of Braunschweig, he advised toleration for the local Jewish community. He attended the meeting of the Smalcald League in Smalcald in 1537 and was among the initial subscribers of Luther's Smalcald Articles. His posthumously published collected

Woodcut of Urbanus Rhegius, dated 1524

works made his exposition of Scripture available after 1562, and it continued to spread his influence.

In addition to Rhegius, one of the priests who introduced Luther's Reforms in the city was ***Stephan Agricola the Elder* (1491–1547)**. He became an Augustinian friar in his youth and left his cloister in Regensburg to attend the University of Vienna, where he earned his doctorate in theology in 1519. While serving as a confessor at the Habsburg court, he began reading Luther's treatises. By 1522 his appreciation of the Wittenberg Reformer became obvious enough for his archbishop and former patron, Matthäus Lang, to order his arrest. He used his incarceration as the occasion to compose a defense that pledged his faithfulness to the church but insisted that his ultimate authority was Scripture. Massive pressure from influential churchmen secured his release in 1524, and he found refuge and employment in Augsburg. His tenure in a parish in Augsburg witnessed his marriage and a battle against Zwinglians in the city. In 1531, he assumed the pastorate in Hof in Brandenburg-Ansbach. His role on the larger stage of the German Reformation included participation in the Marburg Colloquy (1529), the Diet of Augsburg (1530), the diet of the Smalcald League in Smalcald (1537), and the visitation of Neuburg and Sulzbach (1542–43). In 1546, Count Albrecht of Mansfeld called him to Eisleben as his court preacher. His translation of several of Luther's Latin writings into German aided the spread of the Reformer's ideas.

His son ***Stephan Agricola the Younger* (1526–1562)** studied theology in Leipzig (1544–47). While serving as parish pastor in Mansfeld county, he translated Latin works by CASPAR CRUCIGER, JOHANNES BRENZ, and Luther into German. His defense of GEORG MAJOR's proposition "good works are necessary for salvation" led him into controversy with other pastors in Mansfeld. After brief service in Augsburg and a return to Mansfeld (1553–56), he went to Wittenberg for further studies. Following service as a preacher in Merseburg and Naumburg, he turned to Roman obedience in 1560. He died in 1562 on a trip to Italy.

Augsburg became a center for printing quite early, in the last quarter of the fifteenth century, and some of its established printers were among the first to spread Luther's message. Among the first to seize upon Luther as a brand that was marketable was ***Jörg Nadler* (d. ca. 1525)**, who published Luther's comments on the *Seven Penitential Psalms* in 1517 and his *Sermon on Indulgences and Grace* in 1518 (along with printers in other towns). By that time, he had established himself through a decade of production as a leading printer in the city. He continued to issue works of Luther into the mid-1520s, some eighty different printings. ***Johann Froschauer* (d. 1523)** found Luther's name salable and printed his first work from Wittenberg, the Reformer's *Sermon on the Preparation for the Holy Sacrament* in 1518. Study in Ingolstadt apparently prepared him for the print business, and he had produced his first piece of devotional literature in 1494 in Augsburg. He specialized in almanacs, medical help books, and other popular literature and then took up the publication of works on reform.

Silvan Otmar* (1495–1539)** also began to take advantage of Luther's "bestseller" image in 1518, with the printing of his exposition of the Ten Commandments. Otmar had studied in Tübingen and then worked in the printing operation of his father, Johann, who had established his press in 1502 in Augsburg. Silvan began printing under his own name in 1513 and produced religious literature as well as other popular products. In 1516 he assumed control of his father's shop; within a decade he had become a prosperous citizen of the city. He earned an admonition from the city council in 1522 for printing Luther's *Against the Falsely-Designated "Spiritual" Estate of the Pope and the Bishops* but was also serving as the anonymous publisher for the council. From 1522 to 1535, the Swabian League employed him as its official printer. Among his employees for a short time (1525–26) were proofreaders Ludwig Hätzer, a professed antitrinitarian, and the Anabaptist leader Hans Denck. Otmar's presses produced books and pamphlets for a number of other publishers in other towns. He was able to print works in Hebrew type in the 1530s, providing printing services for the Jewish publisher Cjahim Schachor (Ben David Schwarz), 1533–36. Otmar engaged several prominent illustrators, including Hans Burgkmair. By the time of his death, over five hundred editions had flowed from his presses. His widow, ***Anna, took over his firm, and his son ***Valentin* (ca. 1515–1566)** continued the business until the year before his own death. Unlike his father, Valentin did not know Latin, but he was able to publish popular devotional literature as well as political pamphlets, although he did not serve the city council as its anonymous printer.

***Heinrich Steiner* (before 1500–1548)** learned the printing trade from Johann Schönsperger the Elder, who had pioneered the industry in Augsburg in the late 1470s. Steiner's first independent publication appeared in 1517, *An Exposition of Daniel's Dreams*, followed shortly thereafter by Luther's commentary *Seven Penitential Psalms*. Not only Luther but also the local Reformer Urbanus Rhegius provided Steiner with materials to publish. Translations of classical works, medical handbooks, and illustrated works on various subjects also commanded his presses. His techniques with illustrated works made him a leader in this field at the time. Unable to join the guild of printers because of his illegitimate birth, he nonetheless married into the citizenry. Despite his own bookselling business and keeping an inn in addition to his presses, he amassed serious debt and declared bankruptcy shortly before his death.

***Melchior Ramminger* (d. 1543)** worked in Augsburg as a bookbinder from 1508 until 1520 when he began to publish books from his own presses. Luther's *The Freedom of a Christian* was among his first publications, one of nearly seventy-five he produced, chiefly in the years 1522–25, earning him estimation as "the most significant distributor of Luther's writings in southern Germany." He took part in the revolt within the city in 1524. After 1526, financial difficulties brought about a decline in his publishing activities, and he concentrated on bookbinding.

***Philipp Ulhart the Elder* (ca. 1500–1567)** printed the first of his nearly seventy editions of works by Luther in 1522, while just beginning to establish his own press after working as an apprentice with Johann Schönsperger the Younger, who had begun to publish in Augsburg in 1510. Ulhart's commitment to Luther's Reform seems to have been quite secondary to interest in radical and Sacramentarian theologians; he printed the works of ANDREAS KARLSTADT as well as the spiritualists Sebastian Franck and KASPAR SCHWENKFELD. Toward the end of his life he also printed for the apostate Wittenberg student Friedrich Staphylus, who had returned to the Roman obedience. His roughly one thousand printed works point to his success as a publisher, who in Luther and authors across the religious spectrum recognized a source of profit easy to tap.

The Lonely Reformer of Cologne

To the west of Augsburg, cities along the Rhine river present a varied picture of the ways in which Luther's thought and Reform spread or, in some cases, did not spread. The city of Cologne proved most resistant to Luther's way of thinking, despite the attempt of ***Hermann von Wied* (1477–1552)**, its archbishop, to bring his domains into the Wittenberg movement. As fourth son of Count Frederick of Wied-Runkel and his wife, Agnes, Hermann was destined for service in the church and, at age six, received his first benefice in the cathedral chapter of nearby Cologne. Although he had not completed a degree, he became a member of the faculty of law at the University of Cologne in 1493. His colleagues in the chapter elected him archbishop in 1515, and in 1518 he was ordained a bishop. His support of CHARLES OF HABSBURG for the imperial crown in 1519 earned him the emperor's favor, and he enforced the Edict of Worms, suppressing Lutheran teaching and teachers

Portrait of Hermann von Wied, Archbishop of Cologne (sixteenth century)

to the extent possible in the years following 1521. By the early 1530s, he recognized the need for extensive reform of the church. With the aid of Johannes Gropper, he began the elimination of abuses within the framework of existing papal and imperial law. Reform measures published in 1538 had limited impact because support for Luther's theology was growing among nobles within the archbishopric and even at Hermann's own court. After conversations at the diets in Hagenau and Regensburg in 1540 and 1541, the archbishop engaged Martin Bucer to meet the demands of his own nobility to introduce Reformation. Bucer, with Melanchthon's aid, composed a set of ordinances for the life of the church in the archdiocese, derived in part from the Nuremberg-Brandenburg church ordinances of 1533. Scripture was to serve as the only norm for public teaching and practice while the traditions of the church were not ignored. With Hermann's support, efforts began in 1543 to introduce these changes, against the opposition of a majority of the cathedral chapter, the Cologne city council, the university faculty, and Jesuits, who began working in the archdiocese in 1544. Excommunicated in 1546, Hermann lost the support of the nobility, who felt the threat of military pressure from EMPEROR CHARLES, and he abdicated in January 1547.

The Reformation of Strassburg

Upriver from Cologne, the city of Strassburg played a key role in the early spread of Luther's ideas in the southwestern German lands. From the beginning in the 1520s, pastors and their wives had taken strong leadership in cultivating evangelical reform in the city. Its theological leadership strove initially to find a middle position that might bring together Reformers of Wittenberg and Zurich, but by 1550 the city was moving into a kind of "second Reformation," under the leadership of JOHANN MARBACH, Luther's and Melanchthon's student.

***Matthäus Zell* (1477–1548)** left his home in Kaysersberg, Alsace, to study at the Universities of Mainz, Erfurt, and finally Freiburg, where he enrolled in 1502. Before leaving the university he served as rector (1517–18). In 1518, he accepted a call to become cathedral preacher and priest in Strassburg and also served as the bishop's assistant for dispensing absolution. His discontent with the behavior of many priests propelled him in the direction of Luther's call for reform, and he integrated what he was learning from Luther's treatises into his sermons in 1521. He avoided removal from office, the fate of three earlier evangelical preachers in the town, because of

Portrait of Matthäus Zell, in 1590 publication

popular support and the uncertainty of the cathedral chapter over a decision to comply with the bishop's insistence on his ouster. Zell alone led the proclamation of Luther's theology and the gradual institution of corresponding changes in ecclesiastical life until 1523, when Wolfgang Capito joined him, as did Martin Bucer and Kaspar Hedio soon thereafter. Zell's marriage to Katharina Schütz in 1523 and her support for his efforts in behalf of reform also strengthened his ability to work for the cultivation of the Christian life in the manner set forth in Luther's writings. He himself defended Wittenberg teaching in a published address to the bishop of Strassburg in 1523. In 1525, his catechism appeared in print for the education of the children of the city. Zell only slowly came to oppose the Anabaptists who had found refuge in Strassburg. Similarly, he was intrigued by the spiritualizing theology of Kaspar Schwenckfeld, who had won Zell's wife's allegiance. Zell committed himself, however, to affirmation of the true presence of Christ's body and blood in the language of the Wittenberg Concord. The Zells visited Wittenberg and met Luther for the first time in 1538; he made a most favorable impression upon them. As the city's leading clergyman after Bucer's departure, he opposed compromise with the emperor regarding the introduction of the Augsburg Interim in 1548 but died in the midst of the resulting tensions.

***Katharina Schütz Zell* (1497/98–1562)**, orphaned at an early age, represented the Strassburg elite, and her marriage to Matthäus Zell in 1523 helped cement the relationship between the reforming clergy of the city and its traditional establishment. Attacks on their marriage provoked her to publish a sharp critique of clerical celibacy, praising marriage as God's creation and gift and blasting the abuses of celibacy in the bastard tax on priests' families and other similar practices. Her only two children died in infancy, but her household was lively, with frequent guests. She regularly visited the sick, expectant and new mothers, and those in prison. At the end of the Peasants Revolt of 1524–25, she aided in organizing relief for refugees that poured into Strassburg. She continued to publish short treatises on theological topics, edited a hymnal, spoke at funeral services for her husband and the follower of Schwenkfeld, Felicitas Scher, and worked for the improvement of health care provisions in the city. When Martin Bucer and Paul Fagius were banned from Strassburg because of their outspoken criticism of the Augsburg Interim in 1549, she hid them in her home until they could depart for England. The next year she was thrown out of her home to make place for a Roman Catholic priest who moved into the city under the provisions of the introduction of the Interim. Her defense of Anabaptists and particularly Kaspar Schwenckfeld and his spiritualist theology won her the criticism of her friend LUDWIG RABUS, who had lived with the Zells and worked closely as assistant to her husband.

Martin Bucer (Butzer) **(1491–1551)**, a native of Schlettstadt in Alsace, entered the Dominican cloister in his hometown. His superiors sent him to the University of Heidelberg after his secondary education. There he read and absorbed ERASMUS's writings. His attendance at the Heidelberg Disputation of the Augustinian Eremites in 1518 attracted him to Luther through his theses on his "theology of the cross." In 1521, Bucer became a secular priest and joined the cause of the knights led by FRANZ VON SICKINGEN and ULRICH VON HUTTEN. In 1522, he and his bride, the former nun Elisabeth Silbereisen, moved to Weissenberg in Alsace to introduce reform, and in May 1523 he came to Strassburg, where he rose rapidly to leadership of the ministerium there. His efforts to bridge the differences on the understanding of Christ's presence or non-presence in the Lord's Supper between ZWINGLI and Luther initially aroused deep suspicions in Wittenberg because his own realist orientation from his instruction in the theology of Thomas Aquinas while he was still a Dominican continued to shape his expression of his doctrine. By the late 1520s, he found in Luther's definition of the "sacramental union of bread and wine with Christ's body and blood" a suitable articulation that avoided the medieval superstitions that led to a magical view of the sacrament and at the same time assured that Christ is present to convey his benefits to those who receive the Supper in faith. After his participation in the Colloquy in Marburg in 1529, Bucer conducted negotiations on the issue with MELANCHTHON in the early 1530s. This led to the conversations in Wittenberg between Bucer and Luther and their associates in 1536 that produced the "Wittenberg Concord," which became a part of Lutheran teaching in the *Formula of Concord*. Bucer opposed the teaching of Anabaptists and spiritualists, including KASPAR SCHWENCKFELD, who found refuge in the city. He welcomed JOHN CALVIN, however, and placed the young French Reformer as pastor of Strassburg's French-speaking congregation (1538–41). Bucer's influence on Calvin was considerable. Bucer's attempts to persuade Roman Catholic theologians of the truth of evangelical teaching led him into extensive conversations with these theologians and into participation alongside MELANCHTHON in the negotiations set in place by EMPEROR CHARLES V in 1540–41 in Hagenau, Worms, and Regensburg. Particularly Bucer's relationship with Johannes Gropper provided important material for these discussions although they finally came to naught. The efforts of Melanchthon and Bucer to produce church ordinances for ARCHBISHOP HERMANN VON WIED of Cologne in 1543 also came to naught when CHARLES V ended Hermann's attempts to introduce

Engraving of Martin Bucer by Jan Veenhuisen (seventeenth century)

Reformation to his archdiocese through military action (1546). Luther expressed his discomfort with certain elements in the ordinances and returned to older suspicions of Bucer due to formulations regarding the Lord's Supper in the Cologne church ordinances. Emperor Charles wished to have Bucer as a member of the commission charged with formulating imperial religious policy after the defeat of the armies of the Smalcald League in 1547, but Bucer refused, and he opposed the commission's final product, dubbed the Augsburg Interim. This made it advisable for him to leave Strassburg—by that time under occupation by imperial troops—for Cambridge in 1549, where he taught until his death two years later. Despite continuing tensions with Luther, Bucer sent students from Strassburg to Wittenberg to study in the 1540s and placed them in key positions in the churches of Strassburg upon completion of their studies. Particularly his exegetical commentaries and his writings on ecclesiastical order made a lasting contribution to subsequent generations.

Martin Bucer's second wife, ***Wibrandis Rosenblatt* (1504–1564)**, illustrates dramatically the challenges of family life in the period of the Reformation. Her mother gave up trying to follow her husband, a soldier who advanced steadily to the rank of knight in the service of EMPEROR CHARLES V, and returned to her native Basel to raise Wibrandis and her brother. In 1524 Wibrandis married Ludwig Keller (Cellarius), a member of the Basel circle of biblical humanists, who died two years later. After two years of widowhood, she was the choice of the Reformer of Basel, JOHANN OECOLAMPADIUS, when he decided to marry at age forty-six after the death of his mother. He died three years later, in 1531, after Wibrandis had borne him three children, who joined their older Keller sibling in the household. About the time of Oecolampadius's death, Agnes Röttel, the wife of Strassburg pastor and friend of the Oecolampadius family WOLFGANG CAPITO, died after eight years of marriage. Wibrandis became Capito's second wife. She opened their home in Strassburg to a stream of guests and refugees. With Capito she had her fifth, sixth, seventh, eighth, and ninth children. In 1541, plague struck Strassburg and over three thousand died, among them Capito and the wife of MARTIN BUCER, Elisabeth Silbereisen, whom he had married in 1522 after she had left the convent. The Bucers lost five children in the plague, and only their handicapped son Nathanael joined his new siblings from Wibrandis's first three marriages. Elisabeth had learned of Capito's death as she lay dying and commended her husband and surviving son to Wibrandis, who was attending her. They married in early 1542. When Bucer was exiled in 1549, she followed him to England and to the challenges of climate and food in Cambridge. She returned to Strassburg to bring her mother to England, but in 1551, when Bucer died, she took her mother and four remaining children back to Strassburg. In 1553 the plague drove her to the city of her birth, Basel, where in 1564 she was among seven thousand victims of the plague.

***Wolfgang Capito (Köpfel)* (ca. 1478–1541)**, left his native Hagenau to go to school in Pforzheim, and then studied at Freiburg and Basel, earning doctorates in theology, canon law, and civil law. He became preacher at a Benedictine foundation in Bruchsal and advanced his Hebrew competence through study with MATTHÄUS ADRIAN, a Spanish Jewish Christian. The spiritualist definition of Christ's presence in the Lord's Supper advanced by John Wyclif attracted him. In 1515, he was called to a professorship in Basel and to the office of cathedral preacher. His association with ERASMUS firmly planted him into

Engraving of Wolfgang Capito by M. Markworth (ca. 1750)

the wider circle of biblical humanists, in which he had already begun to make contacts. His enthusiasm for Luther's ideas led to his translating some of Luther's first publications in German into Latin. In 1521, Capito accepted the appointment of Archbishop Albrecht of Mainz to the office of cathedral preacher and, later, Albrecht's confessor and theological advisor. His influence at Albrecht's court helped limit the extent of the opposition to the Wittenberg Reform movement at this point. His desire to establish good relationships with Luther and Melanchthon led to two visits to Wittenberg in 1521 and 1522. In those conversations, Capito began to abandon his insistence on the freedom of the will in spiritual matters and to understand Luther's arguments for the clarity of Scripture. This brought about his open espousal of Luther's cause. His efforts to persuade Erasmus to do the same came to naught, and by 1524 he made clear his opposition to Erasmus's defense of the freedom of the will. In 1523 the city council in Strassburg appointed him to lead the foundation of Saint Thomas there. He quickly won the adherence of Martin Bucer, Kaspar Hedio, and Matthäus Zell for reform. The presence of Anabaptists in Strassburg caused Capito to consider their views seriously, but he rejected them. His support for Bucer's policies of reform and for his teaching led to his participation in the preparation of the Tetrapolitan Confession of 1530, with its attempt to find a formulation of the presence of Christ in the Lord's Supper that could provide a bridge between Zwingli's and Luther's views, but he also took part in the meetings in Wittenberg in 1536 that produced the Wittenberg Concord, bringing Strassburg and Wittenberg together in a common, if potentially ambiguous, expression of the doctrine of Christ's true presence in the sacrament. Capito and Luther remained in correspondence until the former's death.

***Kaspar Hedio* (1494–1553)** attended school in Pforzheim, not far from his home in Ettlingen, and began university studies in Freiburg in 1513. He later transferred to Basel, where he became a friend of WOLFGANG CAPITO, made contact with Ulrich ZWINGLI before Zwingli moved to Zurich, and became a devoted fan of Luther, writing to him in mid-1520. Hedio succeeded Capito as court preacher and counselor of ELECTOR ALBRECHT OF MAINZ in 1520 but aroused opposition with his open support for Luther's thought. His call to Strassburg in late 1523 brought him to the cathedral chapter there. He married a gardener's daughter in 1524. With BUCER, CAPITO, and ZELL, he actively promoted reform throughout Alsace and beyond. He lectured at the Strassburg Academy from 1538 on, on New Testament, patristics, and history. He came with the Strassburg delegation to Marburg in 1529 for the colloquy between Luther and ZWINGLI with their supporters. In 1540 and 1541 he stood at Bucer's side in Worms and Regensburg. He succeeded BUCER as president of the Company of Pastors in Strassburg when the latter had to flee to England after the establishment of the Augsburg Interim. In 1551, Hedio met with theologians from

Portrait of Kaspar Hedio (sixteenth century)

Württemberg to formulate a confession for the presentation of their theology at the Council of Trent. He died of the plague in 1552.

Engraving of Johann Marbach by Theodor de Bry (sixteenth century)

Johann Marbach **(1521–1581)** was born to a furrier family in Lindau and was sent to Strassburg for his preparation for university. He then proceeded to Wittenberg to study, attaining the doctorate in 1543. He returned to Lindau as a pastor, but the Strassburg ministerium and council called him back to the city to serve as pastor at Saint Nicholas church and instructor of theology at the academy. As Strassburg prepared to attend the Council of Trent in 1551, Marbach took part in the composition of its confession of faith, which was to be presented in Trent. The outbreak of war in the German Empire prevented meaningful participation by the Strassburg delegation in the council. When Kaspar Hedio died in 1553, Marbach succeeded him as presiding pastor of the Company of Pastors. Throughout his career he remained faithful to the teachings he had imbibed during his years in Wittenberg. His writings focused on the issues of the day and presented Wittenberg teaching, for instance, on the true presence of Christ's body and blood in the Lord's Supper and on ecclesiastical organization and practice. He fell into controversy in the early 1560s with another instructor at the theological faculty, Hieronymus Zanchi. The commission that the city council constituted to settle their disputes over the issues of the perseverance of the saints or limited atonement and over the Lord's Supper favored Marbach's position, affirming the Wittenberg Concord's position on the latter question, with a decidedly Lutheran interpretation of the document. It reaffirmed Marbach's insistence that questions related to the predestination of God's faithful people be determined on the basis of the proper distinction of Law and Gospel, ready to apply condemning judgment to unrepentant sinners in the church while assuring the repentant of God's unfailing faithfulness to those he has chosen, as they experienced his choosing through the word in its oral, written, and sacramental forms. In 1569, Marbach had a dispute with JOHANN STURM over the relationship of the theological faculty and the liberal arts faculty; the city council affirmed Sturm's governance of the entire academy program.

After Marbach's death, ***Johann Pappus* (1549–1610)** reclaimed the right of the dean of the theological faculty to govern that faculty without interference from the rector of the academy. Pappus, Marbach's successor as the presiding officer of the Strassburg Company of Pastors, also came from a furrier family in Lindau and received his education there and in Tübingen. In 1564 he joined the faculty of the Strassburg Academy, and in 1574 became professor of theology there. In 1581, he succeeded Marbach in the midst of a controversy with JOHANN STURM over the *Formula of Concord*. Although the city did not adopt the *Book of Concord* until 1598, Sturm's argument elicited critical reactions from the government of Württemberg, and the city council dismissed him. Pappus's learning and his commitment to the humanistic program of Sturm and others at the academy is reflected in his six-thousand-volume personal library and his publications on the history of the church, especially patristics, and on biblical teaching.

MARBACH's contemporary and colleague ***Ludwig Rabus* (1524–1592)** followed a career path similar to Marbach's, though he may have left Strassburg because Marbach became the president of the Company of Pastors in 1553. The two, who had shared many experiences in the previous decade, did keep in correspondence until Marbach's death. Rabus had come to Strassburg from his home in Memmingen to attend school and lodged with MATTHÄUS ZELL and his wife, KATHARINA. In 1538, Rabus departed for study at the University of Tübingen and then heard Luther and MELANCHTHON at the University of Wittenberg in the early 1540s. With a master's degree from Wittenberg, Rabus returned to Memmingen in 1543, but the next year the Strassburg council called him to assist Zell at the Münster. When Zell died in 1548, Rabus assumed his post; he had already won a large following among the population of the city. The imposition of the Augsburg Interim ended his brief career as preacher at the Münster, but the council appointed him pastor and director of the Collegium Wilhelmitanum, a foundation in the city, and he began to teach at the academy. In 1553 he returned to Tübingen and gained his doctorate, at the same time as JAKOB ANDREAE. In 1556 the council of Ulm called Rabus to become superintendent of its churches. Negotiations with Ulm had been conducted secretly; this alienated him for a time from the Strassburg leadership. In Ulm he led the church until 1590. He followed Marbach's path in introducing a "second Reformation" in Ulm, leading the city into a firm commitment to Luther's teaching from its earlier mediating position between Zwingli and Wittenberg. Rabus worked to counter Zwinglian, Anabaptist, and Schwenckfeldian teaching. This led him into conflict with Katharina Zell, who was defending Kaspar Schwenckfeld, who had also lived with the Zell family. Rabus supported the campaign for Lutheran concord of his friend Jakob Andreae. He helped improve the school system in Ulm and took other measures to deepen the piety of its people. Among his fourteen children, one, Johann Jakob, caused Rabus much pain by becoming a Roman Catholic; he became a fierce critic of Luther's teaching. During his internal exile in Strassburg during the imposition of the Interim, Rabus began a massive project, the composition of a martyrology that brought together accounts of biblical martyrs and those of the ancient church with the reports he gleaned from a variety of publications of evangelicals who had died at the hands of church officials or their secular arms in the sixteenth century. Defining "martyr" as any witness to the faith who had suffered as he testified to Christ, Rabus included Luther in the fourth of his eight volumes of martyr stories, supplying an early glimpse into the Reformer's life through summaries of his published writings.

Strong lay leadership also contributed mightily to the shaping of the evangelical church life of Strassburg. Within this group of civic leaders was ***Nikolaus Gerbel* (ca. 1485–1560)**, who, like Melanchthon, attended school in his native Pforzheim before studying at the universities of Vienna and Cologne. He returned to teach in Pforzheim before continuing his education at the University of Tübingen. He returned to Vienna to study law in 1514 and then received doctorates in both canon and civil law that year in Bologna. He assumed duties in the municipal government of Strassburg in 1515, and in addition worked as proofreader and editor for printers there. Johann Sturm engaged him as an instructor in history at the Strassburg Academy (1541–43). Gerbel's relationship with Luther led to his serving as baptismal sponsor for the Reformer's first child, Hans. His contacts with other Wittenberg theologians, especially Melanchthon and Bugenhagen, and his close relationship with Bucer and the other Strassburg preachers, made him a significant lay contributor to the Wittenberg movement. His strict adherence to Luther's understanding of the presence of Christ's body and blood in the Lord's Supper strengthened the tendencies of Jakob Sturm to guide the Strassburg churches in Wittenberg's direction. He engaged Thomas Murner with three satires critical of Murner's attacks on Luther's teaching.

***Johannes Sleidanus* (1506–1556)**, a native of Schleiden, in the duchy of Luxemburg, was a schoolboy in Lüttich when he first fell under the influence of the Brethren of the Common Life and began to develop his interest in history and texts from instructors

Johannes Sleidanus as depicted in 1854 publication Zweihundert deutsche Männer in Bildnissen und Lebensbeschreibungen

appreciative of biblical humanism. He spent 1524–33 as a tutor and then traveled to Paris and Orléans to study law before entering the service of a leading French cardinal, Jean du Bellay, who was interested in forging connections between Wittenberg, the Smalcald League, and the French royal court. In 1542, the worsening atmosphere for those working for reform within France and his father's death brought Sleidanus back to Schleiden. His friendship with MARTIN BUCER and other clergymen in Strassburg as well as with JOHANN STURM and JAKOB STURM brought him to that city, where he pursued his historical research and served the municipal government as a diplomat and bureaucrat. In 1551 the city sent him, with theologians and other civil servants, to represent its interests at the second session of the Council of Trent; five other towns in southwestern German lands—Biberach, Esslingen, Lindau, Ravensburg, and Reutlingen—also authorized him to represent their interests there. He published his *On the State of Religion and Civil Government of Charles V, Emperor* in 1555; it remains a key source of contemporary views of the Reformation.

***Jakob Sturm* (1489–1553)** was born to an influential patrician family that had supplied leadership to the city of Strassburg for a century. He studied in Heidelberg and Freiburg, with the intention of ordination and service in the church. He returned to Strassburg and immersed himself in humanist literature. In his years as secretary to Count Palatine Heinrich (1517–23), he was attracted to Luther's writings, in his mind following the trajectory upon which his mentor, the humanist Jakob Wimpfeling, had set him. After being chosen as a member of the Strassburg Senate and its large council, the Twenty-One, in 1524, he quickly gained the confidence of his peers and assumed several offices, including member of the privy council of the Thirteen, in charge of relations with other governments. His wife, a member of the prominent Bock family, whom he married in 1523, died in 1529, and he did not marry again. Sturm's convictions regarding reform led him to pursue alliances for the city with Landgrave Philip of Hesse and Elector Johann of Saxony. He joined the "*Protestatio*" of the evangelical princes at the imperial diet of Speyer in April 1529, and accompanied the Strassburg pastors to the colloquy in Marburg in September 1529. At the imperial diet in Augsburg in 1530 he represented the *Confessio Tetrapolitana* of the south German cities but led efforts to bring Strassburg into the Smalcald League through the city accepting the Augsburg Confession authored by Melanchthon. His leadership furthered the expulsion of Anabaptists and other spiritualizing groups. He successfully established lay control of the church in Strassburg but worked closely with Bucer and the other pastors to cultivate piety. He did, however, reject the idea that a truly Christian society is possible in a sinful world. In Strassburg's internal affairs, he promoted the educational system and its academy that were founded in 1538. His efforts to strengthen the Smalcald League came to naught. His attempts to work out a reconciliation with Emperor Charles V after the end of the Smalcald War aroused opposition within the city.

Portrait of Johann Sturm engraved by Hendrik Hondius (1602)

***Johann Sturm* (1507–1589)**, born in Schleiden in the duchy of Luxemburg, studied in Lüttich, Leuven, and Paris before accepting the post as founding rector of the first Latin secondary school in Strassburg, for which he developed his own system of pedagogy, shaped by the biblical humanism, particularly that of Rudolf Agricola, in which he had been steeped as a student. His efforts led to the establishment of the Strassburg Academy in 1538, which offered university-level education in the liberal arts and theology. He exercised influence over many educators and governmental leaders in the German lands, France, England, and beyond. The municipal government of Strassburg used him as a diplomat on many occasions, especially for contacts with French leaders, royal and noble. After the departure of MARTIN BUCER as leader of the city's ministerium, Sturm fell into increasing tensions with its new leadership, first JOHANN MARBACH and then JOHANN PAPPUS. Sturm's criticism of the *Formula of Concord* led to his dismissal by the municipal government in 1581. The program that he had instituted at the Latin school continued to be used into the early seventeenth century.

***Otto Brunfels* (ca. 1488–1534)**, son of a cooper, grew up in Mainz and studied at its university before entering the Carthusian monastery there, receiving ordination and then moving to the cloister in Strassburg. He left the cloister and became a chaplain for ULRICH VON HUTTEN and then a parish pastor in the upper Rhine Valley before perhaps spending a brief time in Wittenberg. Among his many humanist contacts at this time was NIKOLAUS GERBEL. He traveled then to Zurich before again assuming a pastorate. He gathered writings of Jan Hus, edited them, and dedicated his book to Luther; it appeared in 1524. In the disputes over the Lord's Supper, Brunfels favored Zwingli. He taught secondary school in Strassburg and finally, after attaining a doctorate in medicine, became municipal physician in Bern. His pioneering studies in botany exercised significant influence in medicine. His several aids to Bible study, including a *Catalog of Illustrious Men of the Old and New Testaments*, a similar work on the laws contained in the Bible, and a collection of prayers from Scripture and the church fathers, appeared in print in 1527 and 1528.

Strassburg was situated some 120 miles up the Rhine from Johannes Gutenberg's hometown, Mainz. Strassburg attracted printers in the latter half of the fifteenth century and served as an important hub for distribution of treatises from the pens of the Wittenberg Reformers. Strassburg printers contributed to the spread of their message throughout the sixteenth century.

***Matthias Schürer* (ca. 1470–1519)** had attended the Latin school in his native Schlettstadt and then journeyed to Cracow in 1491 to study there, attaining his bachelor of arts and his master of arts degrees there. His cousin Martin Flach the Younger employed him as a proofreader in his printing shop in Strassburg; he later proofread for Johann Prüss the elder and Johann Knobloch the elder. In 1508 the first works appeared from Schürer's own press. The humanist members of the Strassburg *sodalitas litteraria* welcomed him to their company; ERASMUS and Beatus Rhenanus, among others, sang his praises. His products consisted largely of classical texts and humanist discourses, but before he died, he printed

Luther's *Ninety-Five Theses on Indulgences.* His widow, Katharina, managed the printing business with the aid of her manager, Jakob Frölich, until 1530, and they dedicated their efforts almost exclusively to furthering the Reformation, printing over fifty titles by Luther himself, Melanchthon, Bugenhagen, Karlstadt, Andreas Osiander, Urbanus Rhegius, and others.

***Johann Herwagen the Elder* (1497–1557)** recognized the potential of Luther sales in the early 1520s, and between 1521 and 1528 he published thirty editions by the Reformer as well as works by Melanchthon, Bugenhagen, Jonas and the Strassburg pastors. Herwagen married the eldest daughter of the bookseller and publisher Wolfgang Lachner, when Johann Froben, her first husband, died, and this brought him to Basel in 1528. An affair with Katharina, the wife of his stepson, Johann Erasmus Froben, in 1542 earned him a stiff fine. His wife and Johann Erasmus, along with her son-in-law, the printer Nikolaus Episcopius, requested that the city council ban him from Basel. Eventually he won a pardon from Landgrave Philip of Hesse, and after Duke Christoph of Württemberg and the University of Basel intervened with the city council, he was able to return to Basel and work with a series of other printers, including his son Johann the Younger.

The printer's device of Wolfgang Köpfel shows the Holy Spirit in the form of a dove above two serpents grasping a stone block, perhaps serving as the headstone (cornerstone) of a building, and so serving as a wordplay on the printer's name (Kopf = head)

***Wolfgang Köpfel* (ca. 1500–1554)**, son of a smith and nephew of Wolfgang Capito, worked in the printing operation of Thomas Wolf in

Basel before he opened his press in Strassburg in 1522. The first of his nearly fifty titles by Luther, *On Confession and Absolution, Whether the Pope Has Control of It*, and three of the Reformer's other treatises appeared in that year. MATTHÄUS ZELL also published with Köpfel the next year; works by MARTIN BUCER, CAPITO, and ANTON CORVINUS followed. PETER BRAUBACH began his career as a printer as apprentice and proofreader in his shop. In 1526, Köpfel rented and took over management of the municipal paper mill and was also arrested by municipal officials for printing the report on the disputation in Baden between JOHANN FABRI, JOHANN ECK, "and their mighty gang," and the Reformer JOHANN OECOLAMPADIUS. Since his wife was expecting a child, he won freedom by paying a fine. His purchase of the printing operation of Franz Rhode in Marburg in 1529 expanded his business. Among his illustrators was Hans Baldung Grien. Köpfel's stock included hymnals, church ordinances, the Bible, and ancient classical texts. His sons Paul and Philipp inherited the press and in 1557 moved it to Worms, where they together with Philipp's son Wolfgang printed works by theologians from the Wittenberg circle until 1563.

***Johann Prüss the Younger* (ca. 1490–1555)** inherited the printing establishment of his father, Johann Prüss the Elder (1446/47–1510) upon his death and continued his line of printing, including a breviary and a psalter. Between 1520 and 1542, he published nearly thirty works by Luther as well as some by MELANCHTHON and BUCER.

***Wendelin Rihel* (ca. 1490–1555)** established himself as a printer in Strassburg in 1535 after four years of running a bookstore there. His edition of Luther's Bible in 1535 helped establish his business. He provided important publishing support to BUCER, JOHANN STURM, SLEIDANUS, and also to CALVIN. His publications included a number of humanistic works, including the Latin Dictionary of Peter Dasypodius. After the death of her first husband, Rihel's daughter Sarah married the printer Samuel Emmel, who also produced works for authors from the Wittenberg circle, including LUDWIG RABUS and CYRIAKUS SPANGENBERG. When Emmel was forced into bankruptcy in 1569, he moved to Cologne, where he did some printing. His shop was taken over by two of Sarah's brothers, ***Josias* (1525–1609)** and ***Theodosius* (ca. 1526–1608)**. Josias had cooperated with Emmel in issuing an edition of the New Testament in Erasmus's translation and other works. His presses produced works by JOHANNES SLEIDANUS, JOHANN STURM, and others. He and Theodosius worked together until 1558 when a disagreement caused them to separate their operations. Theodosius also published works by MELANCHTHON, SLEIDANUS, CASPAR PEUCER, and CYRIAKUS SPANGENBERG.

Hagenau, an imperial city some thirty miles northwest of Strassburg, attracted printers as early as 1489 when Henrich Gran established his shop there. The writings of Luther became a marketable product for the town's printers although his message did not elicit much positive response among the populace in general. The small community of his followers was easily driven out of the city in 1624 by Counter-Reformation forces.

***Thomas Anshelm* (d. 1523)**, who had come to Hagenau after publishing in Pforzheim, where Johannes Reuchlin was among his authors, printed a half dozen titles by Luther before his death along with missals and a number of humanist and classical works. The third of Hagenau's printers, ***Johann Setzer* (ca. 1478–1532)**, married Anshelm's daughter, and their daughter Anna in turn married the printer Peter Braubach, who worked for his future father-in-law in Tübingen as proofreader before Setzer moved their operation to Hagenau in 1523. In 1522 Setzer had begun studying medicine in Wittenberg and there formed a relationship with Melanchthon and Luther. He soon began to print works by Melanchthon, some authorized, some from lecture notes purchased from students. Apparently, the relationship between Setzer and Melanchthon was strong enough to survive the ensuing tensions that are reflected in Melanchthon's correspondence with the printer. Luther regarded him as a *diligens typographus* (hard-working printer); Eobanus Hessus found the quality of his product wanting. In 1524, Setzer was cited by local officials for not presenting all his projects for censorship, but he seems to have had a relatively good relationship with the municipal government in general.

Setzer's son-in-law ***Peter Braubach* (ca. 1500–1567)** assumed management of the family business and carried it on until 1536, when he was drawn by the local pastor Johannes Brenz to Schwäbisch Hall. He had already begun to print Brenz's commentary on Acts in that year. His first work published in Schwäbisch Hall, Urbanus Rhegius's catechism, appeared later in 1536. After his departure for Frankfurt in 1540, his brother-in-law ***Pancratius Queck***, husband of Setzer's daughter Margarethe, who had also worked in Setzer's shop in Hagenau, took over the press, printing the local church ordinances, Brenz's catechisms, and other works in the service of the Luther's and Brenz's Reform. When Queck died in 1543, his widow married an employee of Braubach's in Frankfurt, Peter Rump. ***Peter Frentz* (d. 1553)**, who had been an apprentice and then supervisor in Braubach's operation, took over the press and continued to print works for Brenz and other Reformers, including the Slovenian Reformer Primus Truber the Elder, until Frentz died in 1553.

The Printers of Basel

The Rhine river facilitated the spread of the printing industry from its birthplace in Mainz and nursery in Strassburg to Basel, where Johann Amerbach began a tradition of publishing works by and for humanists from the time he set up his press there in 1478. Basel's clerical leadership offers no prominent follower of Luther for our discussion apart from OECOLAMPADIUS (chapter 8). However, among its printers were several who had followed Amerbach to Basel in the 1480s and then looked to Luther for works to publish in the early 1520s and subsequent years. ***Johann Froben* (ca. 1460–1527)** joined the printing establishment in Basel as it was forming in 1491. He had worked for Anton Koberger in Nuremberg before coming to Strassburg, where he published a Bible in that year. He entered into joint ventures with Johannes Petri in printing and bookselling beginning in 1493, and with Johann Amerbach from 1500. Froben developed a close relationship with DESIDERIUS ERASMUS, first entertaining him as a guest in his home and then motivating him to produce his *Novum Instrumentum*, the first printed edition of the Greek text of the New Testament, in 1516. At the autumn book fair in Frankfurt am Main, Froben collected a number of Luther's treatises that were offered for sale. He commissioned WOLFGANG CAPITO, at the time cathedral preacher and professor of theology in Basel, to edit these works and gather them into a "collected works" in 1518, the first such of this genre for a living author in the brief history of post-Gutenberg printing. Froben had managed to gather all the printed Latin works of the Wittenberg professor to that time. Orders from book dealers across the German lands and in France, the Iberian Peninsula, Italy, the Netherlands, and England made Froben's gamble on this project

Portrait of Johann Froben by artist Hans Holbein (ca. 1522)

profitable. Erasmus, however, reacted with displeasure, perhaps jealous that this younger German, whose quick rise to prominence and more daring criticism of the old order seemed to spell trouble in the Dutch humanist's eyes, was receiving a publisher's compliment that his own works had not earned. Though the five-hundred-page volume quickly sold out, Froben abandoned the project and avoided losing Erasmus's friendship. Publication of this "collected works" was taken up, however, by others, including Froben's Basel colleagues Andreas Cratander and Adam Petri, and Strassburg printer Matthias Schürer. After Froben's death his widow, Gertrud, daughter of the bookdealer and publisher Wolfgang Lachner, married Johann Herwagen the Elder, and with their son Hieronymus Froben the Elder continued to publish titles from Wittenberg authors.

***Adam Petri* (1454–1527)** came to Basel around 1480, had begun to print by 1505, and in 1507 married Anna Selber, daughter of a notary of the city, the same year in which he assumed management of the printing establishment of his uncle, Johannes Petri, who had been printing in Basel since 1502. He specialized in devotional works; with the emergence of the Wittenberg authors group, he sprang to the service of Luther, Melanchthon, Bugenhagen, and Spalatin. Among those with whom he worked was Hans Holbein the Younger, who prepared illustrations for his works. When his business associate Johann Froben discontinued publication of Luther's collected works, Petri took up the project in 1520 and had a local Franciscan of reforming propensities, Konrad Pellikan, revise Froben's work for his own publication. His widow married Sebastian Münster, the Basel professor, whose work in Christian Hebraica and cosmography pioneered in both these fields.

The Petris' son ***Heinrich Petri* (1508–1579)** carried on his father's practice of close cooperation with the Wittenberg Reformers. He had studied in Wittenberg from 1523 to October 1527, when his father's illness caused him to return and assume responsibility for the family business. He married ***Dorothea Hütschy* (1509–1564)**, who had left the penitential order of Saint Mary Magdalene. Their eldest daughter, Anna, and her husband, the printer Hieronymus Curio, along with Dorothea, all died during an outbreak of the plague in 1564. Another of their eleven children, ***Heinrich Adam* (1543–1586),** studied law and became municipal secretary in Basel. In 1565 Petri remarried, this time ***Barbara Brand* (1520–1591)**, daughter of a mayor of Basel and widow of another printer, Hieronymus Froben. In 1534/35 Heinrich Petri combined forces with a colleague in Basel, Michael Isengrin, to publish the Hebrew-Latin Bible edited by Sebastian Münster, his stepfather. Petri published Münster's *Cosmography* as well. Among other authors on his list of publication were Ptolemy, Copernicus, and Nikolaus of Kues. Petri served as a member of the city council and held other elected offices in Basel. His son ***Sebastian* (1546–1627)** inherited control of the family printing operation.

***Andreas Cratander* (ca. 1485–ca. 1540)** left his native Strassburg to study at Heidelberg, where he attained the bachelor of arts degree in 1503. By 1505 he was working as a printer's apprentice in Basel, became a typesetter for MATTHIAS SCHÜRER by 1513, and entered ADAM PETRI's employ in 1515 as typesetter and proofreader. He and another employee of Petri, Servas Kruffter, began their own printing operation in 1518 with a work on Greek literature by JOHANN OECOLAMPADIUS. By the end of the year, Kruffter left Basel for Cologne, and Cratander pursued the business alone. Oecolampadius lived with Cratander's family and worked for him as a proofreader. In 1519, Cratander resigned his citizenship in Strassburg to become a citizen of Basel. His reputation for careful work and wise decisions strengthened his regard among scholars. Particularly his production of works in Greek won respect and admiration. His contacts extended beyond humanistic circles to those interested in reform, among them ULRICH ZWINGLI and Strassburg Reformers KASPAR HEDIO and WOLFGANG CAPITO. But the introduction of the Reformation in Basel in 1529 coincided with the decline of his business, and in 1536 he sold it to a combine of other Basel printers.

***Johann Oporinus* (1507–1568)**, son of a painter in Basel, Hans Herbster, went to school in Strassburg and became a teacher at the monastery of Saint Urban in the canton of Lucerne and then at the school of Saint Leonhard in Basel. He worked as an editor of the Greek church fathers for JOHANN FROBEN, studied Hebrew and jurisprudence at the university, and then became the personal secretary of Paracelsus, briefly leaving Basel with him when the physician was exiled in 1528. Oporinus returned quickly, however, and became an adherent of the Reformation. He accepted a position as a school rector and continued to attend lectures at the university. Around 1535, he entered a printing firm with his brother-in-law, Robert Winter, and two others; they produced Greek and Latin classics, textbooks, and commentaries on standard texts used at the university. Oporinus began instructing in the arts faculty of the university in 1536 as teacher of Greek and Latin, but finally fled from academic bickering in the midst of building sufficient personal capital to open his own printing operation, he later reported. His own press began operating in 1542. Among his first published works, in 1543, was a Latin translation of the Qur'an, which was immediately confiscated by the city council. Only with the intervention of Luther and Joachim Vadian did the council relent, and then only on the condition that the work not be sold in the city. Later that year, Oporinus published Andreas Vesalius's *De* *humani corporis fabrica*, with woodcuts by Johannes von Calcar. His business prospered but not without the frequent crises of debt that the printing industry often encountered. His third wife, Elisabeth Holtzbach, the widow of the printer Johann Herwagen the Younger, brought him control of Herwagen's press in 1565; when she died some four months after their wedding, he married Faustina Amerbach, the widow of a law professor, Ulrich Iselin. Faustina, daughter of Bonifacius and sister of Basilius Amerbach, brought him a good deal of wealth, but Oporinus assured her brother that he did not marry her for her money but rather because of her reputation; she should not worry about his debts since he was in the process of paying them off and reducing his operation. Thereafter he worked together with other Basel printers, including Nikolaus Brylinger, Johann Herwagen the Elder and

The printer's device of Johann Oporinus was designed by Heinrich Vogtherr the Elder. The device depicts the myth of Arion, the musician, who was rescued by a dolphin.

his son Johann, Heinrich Petri, Eusebius and Nikolaus Episcopius and the latter's sons Eusebius and Nikolaus the Younger, Polykarp Gemusaeus, and Peter Perna, among others. Oporinus published materials from a wide variety of authors. Those from the Wittenberg circle included reprints of Luther and Melanchthon, Joachim Camerarius, Nikolaus Selnecker, Johann and Cyriakus Spangenberg, Matthias Flacius, and Johannes Wigand.

Frankfurt am Main

Like Basel, Frankfurt am Main enjoyed competent pastoral leadership in the early days of the Reformation, but its pastors did not become prominent on the larger scene as in cities like Nuremberg and Strassburg. Though an important commercial and political center, Frankfurt did not become the publishing powerhouse it was later in the sixteenth century until after 1530. Its second printer, ***Christian Egenolff the Elder* (1502–1555)**, established his firm there, coming from Strassburg, which he may well have judged to have sufficient printers, to Frankfurt. He had studied at the University of Mainz (1516–19) and had begun to publish a wide range of works, on topics ranging from classical philology, jurisprudence, and medicine to astronomy, history, theology, and contemporary events. Cookbooks also appeared in his offerings. He specialized in illustrations and cultivated relationships with a number of artists. His wife, Margarethe Karpff, accompanied him from Strassburg to Frankfurt. Their children included Christian the Younger, who became a bookdealer and pastor in Frankfurt, and several others. The elder Egenolff established subsidiary presses in Marburg (1538–45) and very briefly in Hohensolms for the local counts (1547). Landgrave Philip of Hesse had asked him to come to Marburg to replace the printer Eucharius Cervicornus, whose work was inadequate in the landgrave's opinion. Egenolff became the official printer of the university. After his business manager, Andreas Kolbe, assumed direction of the Marburg operation in 1545, Egenolff continued to cooperate with him on occasion. He also purchased a paper mill in the Black Forest to supply his presses with raw material. His widow, ***Margarethe* (d. 1577)**, involved her brother-in-law Lorenz in the management of the publishing firm after her husband's death. As she grew older, she placed the firm in the hands of several of her children and grandchildren. A foundry for pouring type became the property of Judith, the oldest daughter of Christian the Younger, and her husband, Jakob Sabon, from Lyon in France. Lorenz continued in the management of the press, and his son spent some time as an apprentice by the Antwerp publisher Christoph

Woodcut depicting Christian Egenolff (before 1555)

Plantin, perhaps the most prominent of the printers of the Low Countries at the time. Throughout this period, works from Wittenberg theologians continued to appear from time to time on the sales lists of the firm.

Wittenberg Reform in Swabia

In the Swabian region of southwestern Germany, east of the Rhine, several important centers of Wittenberg Reform came into existence in the 1520s and 1530s. The imperial city of Schwäbisch Hall experienced the introduction of the Reformation under the local preacher ***Johannes Brenz* (1499–1570)**, who left his native Weil der Stadt to study in Heidelberg in 1514. There he encountered Luther at the defense of his theological framework in the Heidelberg Disputation in 1518. This experience set the direction for Brenz's developing theology, which was already grounded in the biblical humanism of instructors in Heidelberg, including Johann Oecolampadius. In 1522, the town council of the imperial city of Schwäbisch Hall named Brenz to be the town preacher, and he began to introduce Luther's teaching from the pulpit and to develop its implications for liturgical practice. By late 1526 a thoroughgoing Wittenberg way of church life had permeated the rhythm of municipal activities. Brenz led the struggle against the influence of noble patrons over the villages around Hall and slowly brought them to corresponding teaching and practice. By 1525 Brenz had begun to exercise his influence, particularly through publications, beyond the town. He called for princely moderation in suppression of the revolting peasants in 1525, and he began a lifelong critique of spiritualizing views of the Lord's Supper, differing sharply with his former instructor OECOLAMPADIUS, by this time in not-too-distant Basel. MARGRAVE GEORG OF BRANDENBURG-ANSBACH looked to Brenz for counsel in introducing the Reformation to his lands, and this created a lasting connection that extended to

Johannes Brenz, seventeenth-century etching

Georg's neighbor, the imperial city of Nuremberg. Brenz accompanied the margrave to the Diet of Augsburg and, with Andreas Osiander of Nuremberg, created the church ordinances that governed church life in Brandenburg-Ansbach and Nuremberg and that provided a model for other south German evangelical church ordinances. Brenz advised these two governments to remain out of the Smalcald League, arguing that violence in defense of the faith was wrong, for reasons related to his opposition to the death penalty for heresy. When Landgrave Philip of Hesse aided Duke Ulrich of Württemberg in regaining lands that the Habsburg family had seized from him in 1534, Brenz began a lifelong relationship with the duchy's government, extending over the reigns of Ulrich, his son Christoph, and into that of his son, Ludwig. Brenz composed the church ordinances for Württemberg in 1536 and in 1537–38 aided the reorganization of the University of Tübingen for Ulrich. In 1548 the new Habsburg invasion of Württemberg and surrounding territories, including Schwäbisch Hall, brought with it the imposition of the Augsburg Interim. With a price on his head, Brenz went into hiding for nearly four years, but during this period began working for Duke Ulrich and planning the reorganization of the church of Württemberg. He completed that work in the "Large Church Ordinances" of 1559 (initial version 1553). When the Truce of Passau made it possible to bring Brenz out of hiding, he became Duke Christoph's administrator of ecclesiastical matters in Württemberg as provost of the Foundation Church in Stuttgart. In the 1550s, the controversy over the true presence of Christ's body and blood flared up again within the church of Württemberg, and he led the ministerium of the church to a bold affirmation of Luther's position. With his new right-hand man, Jakob Andreae, Brenz defended the christological teaching that the sharing of the characteristics of Christ's divine and human natures meant that the human nature shared the divine characteristic of omnipresence, a view not shared by all of Luther's supporters. Brenz's some forty commentaries on biblical books, published from 1525 to his last years, along with his catechism (1553) and his postils (1550–56), became his most lasting influence on Lutheran church life.

The church of Württemberg found its form not only under the influence of Brenz but through the leadership of others, including the ducal counselor, Pietro Paulo Vergerio, and theologians, chiefly in Tübingen.

***Pietro Paulo Vergerio* (1498–1565)** came from a prominent family in Capodistria, in the Venetian domains across the Adriatic from the city. He studied law, earning his doctorate in Padua, and became a judge there and in Verona. In 1524 he settled in Venice as an attorney. His brother Aurel, an official at the papal court in Rome, obtained

Portrait of Pietro Paolo Vergerio engraved by Hendrik Hondius (b. 1573), whose monogram is at the upper right

a position for him there after his wife died. POPE CLEMENT VII named him to the delegation that attended the imperial diet in Augsburg in 1530 and appointed him his nuncio to KING FERDINAND. Several years service in papal diplomacy in Germany included his efforts to attract evangelical princes and towns to the council that POPE PAUL III formally called in 1537. These efforts also brought him to Wittenberg, where his visit with Luther made a special impression on him. Upon his return to Italy in 1536, he was named bishop of Modrus, near Capodistria, and also of Capodistria a few months later. In 1540 and 1541, the pope sent him to France and then to observe the negotiations at Worms and Regensburg between Roman Catholic and evangelical theologians. By 1546 he had fallen under suspicion as one inclined toward evangelical teaching. After his brother Giovanni Battista, bishop of Pola, died, perhaps by being poisoned, Vergerio fled north. He ministered to Italian-speaking congregations in the Swiss cantons and made contacts with a number of Swiss and south German theologians. In 1553, his contacts with the ducal court of Württemberg earned him a post there, and he declared his adherence to the Augsburg Confession. He supported the endeavors of PRIMUS TRUBER to bring the Wittenberg message to the Slovenian- and Croatian-speaking people of their common native area. He cultivated contacts with Strassburg, particularly with JOHANNES SLEIDANUS, and with the court of DUKE ALBRECHT of Prussia. His last years were spent in visits to various areas, from Prussia to Croatia. Truber was among those who attended him as he died, and JAKOB ANDREAE preached his funeral sermon.

***Erhard Schnepf* (1495–1558)** left his native Heilbron, where his artisan family lived, for the University of Erfurt in 1509, where JUSTUS JONAS and EOBANUS HESSUS were among his instructors. He then went to the University of Heidelberg in 1511. There, his instructors led him into the skills with language and rhetoric cultivated by the movement of biblical humanism, and there he heard Luther at the presentation of his theses on the theology of the cross in April 1518. He took Luther's ideas into the pulpit in three south German parishes. In Wimpfen he married the mayor's daughter, Margarethe Wurzelmann, but that did not spare him from the wrath of local defenders of the old faith, who ousted him from office. His support for JOHANNES BRENZ's *Swabian Syngramma*, which defended Luther's insistence that Christ's body and blood is truly present in the bread and wine of the Lord's Supper, attracted LANDGRAVE PHILIP OF HESSE, who called Schnepf to introduce Reform into the Hessian town of Weilburg. Schnepf participated in the Hessian church's synod at Homburg in 1526, which furthered the reform of Philip's lands. Schnepf assumed a professorship of theology at the new University of Marburg the same year. Philip took Schnepf with him to the imperial diets in Speyer in 1529 and Augsburg in 1530. When Philip aided DUKE ULRICH OF WÜRTTEMBERG in regaining his duchy from Habsburg control in 1534, he commissioned Schnepf to join Ambrosius Blarer of Constance, whose theology followed that of MARTIN BUCER, in guiding the theology of the duchy in a Lutheran direction while making more radical changes in liturgy and other practices than was the case in some Lutheran lands. Schnepf subscribed the Smalcald

Portrait of Erhard Schnepf
(seventeenth century)

Articles in 1537. Blarer left the duchy in 1538, and Schnepf guided its reform more firmly in a distinctly Lutheran direction. In 1544, Duke Ulrich called him to the University of Tübingen, and he represented Württemberg at the colloquies of Regensburg in 1541 and 1546. In 1548, he had to flee Württemberg in the face of its occupation by imperial troops intent on introducing the Augsburg Interim, which Schnepf sharply rejected. DUKE JOHANN FRIEDRICH THE MIDDLER of ducal Saxony called him to teach at his new academy, later university, in Jena, where he supported the Gnesio-Lutheran policies of the duke while challenging some of the measures proposed by MATTHIAS FLACIUS and his allies in the duchy.

***Matthäus Alber* (1495–1570)** came from a middle-class family in Reutlingen and attended school there and in several other towns before beginning studies at the University of Tübingen in 1513, where he and MELANCHTHON became friends. Alber continued his academic preparation at Freiburg. Ordained to the priesthood in 1521, he became a priest in the imperial city of Reutlingen and served there until 1548. In 1524, the imperial court summoned him to account for his introduction of reforms in the town, but he was not arrested. In Reutlingen, he introduced Luther's teaching but strove to be reconciliatory toward ZWINGLI. His liturgy was extremely simple, and his organization of the church based on governance by the elders. His leadership resulted in Reutlingen subscribing to the Augsburg Confession at the diet in 1530. In 1536, he accompanied BUCER and the Strassburg delegation to Wittenberg and signed the Wittenberg Concord. In 1539, the University of Tübingen awarded him the doctorate of theology. Despite popular support from the citizens of Reutlingen, he could not maintain his position against the occupation forces of the Habsburg, which had seized the land from DUKE ULRICH OF WÜRTTEMBERG in the Smalcald War. Alber went into hiding but in July 1549 accepted a call to serve as superintendent and pastor in Stuttgart. He worked closely with JOHANNES BRENZ in the subsequent years, for example in composing the Württemberg Confession of 1559 and the duchy's church ordinances in 1553. He participated in the colloquy in Worms in 1557 and in 1562 became abbot of Blaubeuren. His repudiation of Anabaptist teachings took a gentle form, and he opposed persecution of witches.

Tübingen's printers also contributed to the cultivation of Wittenberg Reform in southwestern German lands. ***Ulrich Morhart* (ca. 1490–1554)** began printing in Strassburg in 1519 and issued seven titles by Luther before moving to Tübingen in 1523. There he published an occasional work by Luther along with treatises by MELANCHTHON, including his commentaries on Matthew and John in 1522. Morhart also served as a leading publisher of the works of Johannes Brenz. During the Habsburg occupation of Württemberg, Morhart published works by Roman Catholic authors opposing the Wittenberg Reformers and other reform movements, but at its end in 1534, he used his presses to spread the message of Brenz and his Wittenberg compatriots. Pietro Paulo Vergerio used Morhart, too, as his publisher. Morhart's widow, Magdalena nee Kirsenmann (d. 1574), widow of the municipal secretary in Dornstetten, Jakob Gruppenbach, assumed control of the Morhart presses at her husband's death and ran them with her sons Oswald and Georg Gruppenbach until her death. She also worked together with her stepson, Ulrich Morhart the Younger, in publishing works by Brenz and the Slovenian Reformer Primus Truber, although stepmother and stepson had a strained relationship, which caused him to establish his own press and to work for other printers.

***Georg Gruppenbach* (ca. 1540–1610)** aided his mother in the printing business established by his stepfather, Ulrich Morhart, after the latter's death. He had studied briefly at the University of Tübingen. The death of his brother Oswald in 1571 or 1572 left him and his mother in control of the printing operation. In addition to serving the university as its printer, he published the works of theologians Martin Crusius, his brother-in-law, Jakob Heerbrand, Lucas Osiander, and Jakob Andreae. His cooperation with Hans Ungnad, Baron of Sonnegg, who was promoting mission to the south Slavs, the Croatians and Slovenians, made him the leading publisher of works for that mission led by Primus Truber. Gruppenbach amassed large debts and declared bankruptcy in 1606.

The lines between the individuals discussed in this chapter and the succeeding generation are also difficult to draw. Chapter 5 continues the description of the spread of Luther's and Melanchthon's way of thinking and the cultivation of the life and faith it was intended to produce.

CHAPTER 5

GERMAN STUDENTS: WITTENBERG EDUCATES A GENERATION

Wittenberg students and those attracted to Luther's message but who never attended a lecture in Wittenberg spread out throughout the German-speaking lands. Many were sent by their governments, territorial or municipal, to study with Luther and Melanchthon. However, others came from places where ecclesiastical leaders, often in concert with local civil authorities, sent a number of early students or followers of Luther to the stake on charges of heresy. The Augustinian Eremite cloister in Antwerp belonged to the reform movement initiated by JOHANNES VON STAUPITZ. By 1519 its prior, Jakob Spreng, was propagating Luther's understanding of the gospel. Because Antwerp lay in the Burgundian realm that CHARLES V had inherited from his paternal grandmother and place under the governance of his aunt, Margaret of Savoy, the enforcement of the Edict of Worms came decisively and quickly.

The Early Martyrs for Luther's Cause

Under the tutelage of their prior in the cloister in Antwerp, ***Heinrich Voes* (d. 1523)** and ***Johann Esch* (d. 1523)** were among those who had visited Wittenberg and gotten to know Luther personally. In 1523, they were arrested along with Spreng and his successor as prior, HEINRICH VON ZÜTPHEN. Their execution by fire in Brussels on July 1, 1523, provoked

Luther to compose his first "hymn," a recounting of their trial and death and a refutation of the claim that they had recanted on the pyre. Their deaths inspired many as they considered Luther's interpretation of Scripture.

Spreng and ***Heinrich von Zütphen* (ca. 1488–1524)**, were threatened with execution upon their arrest, although this did nothing to stem the preaching of Luther's teachings

Woodcut of martyrs Heinrich Voes and Johann Esch being burned at the stake in Brussels. From volume published in 1641.

among the other friars of the cloister. Von Zütphen had studied in Wittenberg at the time of Luther's arrival there in 1508. After serving as subprior of the Augustinian cloister in Cologne and as prior in Dordrecht, he returned to Wittenberg to study (1520–22). Supporters engineered von Zütphen's escape from prison in 1523, whereupon he was persuaded, as he passed through Bremen, to assume preaching responsibilities there. He commanded the respect of the populace but aroused the enmity of the bishop and the local Dominicans. Two years later, he followed a request to come to Meldorf, northwest of Hamburg, to preach. Dominicans in the town aroused peasants from the area, who in a drunken spree then lynched him in December 1524.

Others in this period also died for their adherence to Luther's teaching if they lived in parts of the German Empire outside the rule of evangelically minded governments. ***Caspar Tauber* (d. 1524)** was a leading merchant in Vienna, the center of Habsburg rule, who adhered to Luther's teachings. Priests and pamphlets had been spreading Luther's message within the domains of the Habsburgs, and in Vienna the faculties of the liberal arts, law, and medicine harbored numerous supporters of the Wittenberg professor's theology. Leading political figures and much of the citizenry found his call for reform attractive as well. While little is known about the earlier life of this prominent patrician, apart from the fact that he was married and had several children, a record of his trial exists. It was determined that he possessed publications by Luther and had himself written a defense of his teaching. Tauber was clothed in the garb of the heretic and brought before the cathedral congregation, where he refused to abjure his convictions, which included rejection of the veneration of the saints, purgatory, and the superior spiritual status of the clergy. His views also embraced some positions that Luther did not hold, including a rejection of the true presence of Christ's body and blood in the Lord's Supper. Tauber was beheaded on September 12, 1524. Rumors that he had attempted suicide in his cell were countered by the accounts of those who knew him and had visited him prison.

Such executions also took place in other regions of Austria, often those under Habsburg auspices. ***Leonhard Kaiser* (ca. 1480–1527)** came from a middle-class family in Raab on the border between Upper Austria and Bavaria, and enrolled at the University of Leipzig as a young man. He was serving as a vicar in a village near Raab in 1524 when his bishop had him examined and demanded that he recant his support for Luther's thought. Kaiser departed for Wittenberg in 1525 and from there sent books and letters to his home area, urging acceptance of the Wittenberg theology. When he returned to Raab in 1527 to visit his father, who lay on his deathbed, Kaiser was arrested on charges of teaching

Die recht warhafft vñ
Gründtlich Hystori oder geschicht Von brůder Hainrich inn
Diethmar verprent/durch Martinum Luther be-
schriben sampt dem Zehenden Psalmen auß-
gelegt zů Wittemberg: M. D. XXV.

Title page to Luther's book about the Protestant Reformer Heinrich von Zütphen published in Augsburg, 1525 justification through faith alone and rejecting the mass, along with purgatory, freedom of the will, veneration of the saints, and papal authority. Intervention on his behalf from Elector Johann of Saxony and Margrave Casimir of Brandenburg-Ansbach did not win his release, and Kaiser was burned at the stake in August 1527. Luther and Johann Eck exchanged polemical treatises over his execution.

***Georg Winckler* (d. 1527)** abandoned his zeal for medieval theology and practice after his friend Archbishop Albrecht of Mainz called him to a newly erected foundation in Albrecht's administrative center in Halle. By 1523, Winckler had introduced communion in both kinds and was reading Luther's treatises avidly. He visited Wittenberg although he did not study there, but he did make Luther's acquaintance. When fellow priests brought charges against him to the archbishop and he was summoned to Albrecht's residence in Aschaffenburg, Winckler also conceded that he had married as well. As he returned to Halle after being released by Albrecht, he was ambushed and murdered on April 23, 1527. Luther joined a chorus of voices accusing the archbishop of complicity in the murder, and that seemed confirmed when the archiepiscopal counselor Dr. Johannes Krause committed suicide after being publicly associated with the crime. The Reformer published his chagrin over the possibility of Albrecht's resorting to an assassination of his old friend. His treatise, *Comfort for the Christians in Halle* (1527), concentrated, however, on the propriety of communing the laity with both the Lord's body and his blood. Roman Catholic responses, led by Johannes Cochlaeus, also focused on this issue rather than asserting the innocence of the archbishop.

The Wittenberg Circle in Electoral Saxony after 1547

Most of the followers of Luther in the next generation exercised their ministries or lived their lives in areas where friendly governments gave them protection, before and after the adherents of the Augsburg Confession were granted legal, though inferior, status in the German Empire by the Religious Peace of Augsburg of 1555. The years after Luther's death in 1546 were wracked by sharp disputes within the Wittenberg circle that ended to a large extent with the adoption of the *Formula of Concord*, composed in 1577, and the *Book of Concord*, published in 1580. This book gathered the *Formula of Concord* and other confessional texts together in a *corpus doctrinae*, or summary of public teaching, on which two-thirds of the German evangelical churches could agree. Despite the fierce polemic exchange in attempts to precisely define the legacy of Luther and Melanchthon, the theologians of the third quarter of the sixteenth century shared many points of view and the method of practicing theology they had learned from their mentors in Wittenberg. Some of them avoided involvement in the polemical exchanges altogether. Therefore, it seems best to group the figures presented in this chapter with a rough geographical outline, although to a certain extent that does place them together in their camps, as Gnesio-Lutherans and Philippists, in many cases. With the transfer of the electoral title and electoral lands from the Ernstine branch of the Wettin family to the Albertine branch in 1547, electoral Saxony became the heart of Philippist interpretations of the Wittenberg legacy, centered in the universities of Wittenberg and Leipzig, while the University of Jena in ducal, Ernestine, Saxony assumed leadership of the much more geographically extended Gnesio-Lutheran party.

With Luther's death, Melanchthon remained the core of electoral Saxon thinking and ecclesiastical life, and upon his death in 1560, their student Paul Eber graduated into this role of leadership, although Melanchthon's son-in-law Caspar Peucer, a member of the medical faculty, played a significant role in the life of the Saxon church. Georg Major continued to command the respect of the church and of his colleagues although he was increasingly sidelined as he grew older by his younger colleagues. All three of these men were part of the teaching corps of the university before Luther's death; Major and Eber are presented in chapter 3 above. Within the Philippist party in Wittenberg and Leipzig, two wings developed. The one believed that Melanchthon continued to represent Luther's teaching faithfully, including his view of the Lord's Supper, while the other somewhat surreptitiously attempted to introduce a spiritualizing interpretation of Christ's presence in the Lord's Supper into the public teaching of the Saxon church because they believed that represented Melanchthon's mature view of the sacrament. The latter were labeled "crypto-Calvinists" by their opponents, although they might more accurately be labeled "crypto-Philippists." Theologians in the crypto-Philippist camp, supported and indeed led by Caspar Peucer, included Caspar Cruciger the Younger and Christoph Pezel, who never experienced Luther and studied in Wittenberg only one semester while Melanchthon still lived.

***Caspar Peucer* (1525–1602)** received his secondary education in Bautzen and in Goldberg under the famous educator Valentin Trotzendorf. Peucer's study in Wittenberg began in 1540 with the completion of his secondary preparation for the university, and he was drawn into the circle of students close to Melanchthon. Reception of his master's degree in 1543 paved the way for him to teach in the liberal arts faculty. His interests joined with those of Georg Joachim Rheticus and Erasmus Reinhold in the pursuit of new research in astronomy, and their interest in Copernicus's work fascinated Peucer as well.

By 1550 he occupied the chair for basic mathematics; in 1554 he assumed the professorship for higher mathematics. Six years later he received his doctor's degree in medicine and was appointed professor of medicine. In 1550 Peucer married Magdalena, daughter of Philip and Katharina (Krapp) Melanchthon. Their relationship with Peucer's mentor, Magdalena's father, provided the elder man with psychological and intellectual support, particularly in his last days. Peucer continued and completed his father-in-law's work on the *Chronicon Carionis*, a textbook for world history. His edition of Melanchthon's collected works in four volumes (1562–64) and his correspondence (1565, 1570, 1574) determined in large part the image of Melanchthon in subsequent years. After Melanchthon's death, no one commanded more respect and power at the university than Peucer exercised. He became the personal physician of Elector August and his family in 1570 and was counted among the elector's most influential advisors. Peucer also determined the direction

Caspar Peucer

of the theological faculty with the promotion of his friend Christoph Pezel, who became Wittenberg's leading theologian after the death of Paul Eber in 1569. Pezel and Peucer shared a spiritualizing view of the Lord's Supper and secretly worked together, with some colleagues in the university and the Saxon ministerium, to move the electorate's official teaching toward a view similar to that of JOHN CALVIN, though derived from their own interpretation of Melanchthon's thought. (Others, such as MARTIN CHEMNITZ and DAVID CHYTRAEUS, disagreed with this interpretation of their common preceptor's doctrine of the Lord's Supper and contended that Melanchthon had remained in agreement with Luther's position). The position formulated by Peucer and Pezel invited the label crypto-Calvinist for their views even though they protested against the label. When Elector August and his wife, ANNA OF DENMARK, found that they had been deceived by this party within their domains, they reacted sharply, fearing exclusion from the Religious Peace of Augsburg, and resenting the deception visited upon them. Peucer was jailed in 1574 and released only in 1586 when August married the daughter of Joachim Ernst of Anhalt after Anna's death and granted his new father-in-law his plea for Peucer's release. Peucer spent his last sixteen years in the service of the princes of Anhalt in Zerbst and Dessau. His wife had died soon after his imprisonment, and in 1587 he married a fellow native of Bautzen, Christine Schild (1563–1618), the widow of a mayor of the town.

Crypto-Philippist polices found support from some officials in the government of ELECTOR AUGUST and his wife, ANNA. The best example of these is ***Georg Cracow* (1525–1575)**, who left his home in Stettin in 1538 to study at the University of Rostock. In 1547, he became an instructor in mathematics and Greek at the University of Greifswald. Two years later, after his marriage to JOHANNES BUGENHAGEN's daughter Sara, he received an appointment to lecture on Latin literature in Wittenberg and received his doctorate in civil and canon law in 1554. Elector August named him professor of Roman law the same year and, in 1557, engaged him as a counselor of the electoral government. Cracow represented the elector at the religious colloquy in Worms in 1557 and at the imperial diet in Augsburg in 1559. In 1565, he succeeded Ulrich Mordeisen as the chancellor of the electorate. August trusted him completely and depended on his judgment. However, Cracow's support for his Wittenberg colleagues CASPAR PEUCER and Christoph Pezel in their attempts to introduce a spiritualizing sacramental theology to the electorate, and particularly a letter written in Greek in his hand that criticized the "feminine domination" of the elector by his wife, Anna, destroyed August's confidence in Cracow. The elector jailed his chancellor, along with Peucer and two others who led the promotion of this theology against

Luther's interpretation of Christ's presence in the Lord's Supper. Cracow died some nine months later in confinement.

Georg Sabinus (sixteenth century)

Although he avoided involvement in the controversies of the period, Melanchthon's other son-in-law, who had left Saxony to teach in Prussia and Brandenburg, reveals other aspects of life in this period. ***Georg Sabinus* (1508–1560)** came to Wittenberg to study in 1523 and quickly endeared himself to Melanchthon as a gifted young man with a talent for writing. His linguistic abilities made him a popular author of neo-Latin poetry. Melanchthon's daughter Anna married Sabinus in 1536; although their marriage was filled with strife and caused Melanchthon to deeply regret his false estimation of Sabinus, the couple reconciled before Anna's death at the birth of their sixth child, in 1547. In 1538 Elector Joachim II of Brandenburg called Sabinus to his university, Frankfurt an der Oder, as professor of rhetoric and poetry. Sabinus and his family left Frankfurt when Duke Albrecht of Prussia asked him to come Königsberg in 1544 to serve as first rector of the duke's new university. The perpetual turmoil among the instructors at the university drove Sabinus back to Frankfurt an der Oder in 1555. Elector Joachim II sent him on a number of diplomatic missions during his last five years.

Representative of the more moderate Philippists were Johannes Bugenhagen the Younger and ***Paul Crell* (1531–1579)**, a native of Eisleben. Crell attended secondary school in his hometown and enrolled in the University of Wittenberg in 1548. After completing his master's degree and his study of theology, he was appointed to be preacher at the castle church in Wittenberg and earned his doctorate in theology in 1559. He began lecturing as a professor the following January and married Anna, the daughter of Georg Major, soon thereafter. Elector August transferred him from the university to the consistory in the town of Meissen in 1569. When August discovered the crypto-Philippist establishment's plans to move electoral Saxon theology and practice in a spiritualizing direction in 1574, August recalled Crell to the university. He took a leading role in the reassertion of an interpretation of the work of Luther and Melanchthon that represented their views as one theology. He composed the "Torgau Articles" of 1574, which initiated the restitution of Luther's views while preserving Melanchthonian accents in the teaching on the Lord's Supper.

A critical figure in the electoral Saxon rejection of the crypto-Philippist point of view, ***Nikolaus Selnecker* (1530–1592)**, demonstrated his musical talents at the organ in his native Hersbruck, near Nuremberg, before he began studies in Wittenberg in 1549. He quickly was drawn into Melanchthon's orbit and was appointed a court preacher at the electoral court in Dresden in 1558. His criticism of the hunting practices of the nobility contributed to his removal from that office in 1565, but he did not lose the favor of

Copperplate engraving of Nikolaus Selnecker

Elector August completely. August advised his cousin Johann Friedrich the Middler to appoint Selnecker to the theology faculty in Jena as the duke turned against his Gnesio-Lutheran theologians. Johann Friedrich's brother Johann Wilhelm restored the Gnesio-Lutheran control of the faculty in 1568, and Selnecker became pastor of Saint Thomas congregation and superintendent of the churches in Leipzig. He lectured at the university as well. There he served until ousted by the crypto-Calvinist son of August, Christian I, when he assumed the throne at his father's death in 1586. During his tenure in Leipzig, Selnecker continued to publish biblical commentaries and composed a massive overview of Christian teaching in loci form, his *Institutes of the Christian Religion* (1573). He gradually edged away from his early "Philippist" positions and actively opposed the advance of crypto-Philippist spiritualizing views of the Lord's Supper in the 1570s, eliciting sharp attacks from some of his colleagues in Wittenberg and Leipzig. When August became aware of the plan to betray his confidence and introduce deviations from Luther's understanding of the Lord's Supper to his lands, he called on Selnecker as one of those who were to restore genuine Lutheran teaching. August had loaned Selnecker to Duke Julius of Braunschweig-Wolfenbüttel to work with Jakob Andreae and Martin Chemnitz in the reform of his lands in 1570. Though some personal tensions with Andreae had arisen at that time, Selnecker worked effectively with the two of them and the other colleagues tapped for the effort to formulate a settlement of disputes among the adherents of the Augsburg Confession. His theology came ever more into line with that of Chemnitz, and in 1576 and 1577 their cooperative efforts produced the *Formula of Concord*. Selnecker died days after his return to Leipzig from his last parish service in Hildesheim, where he had been called after his deposition by Elector Christian.

The Wittenberg Circle in Ducal Saxony

Counterpoint to the tones issuing from Wittenberg came the interpretation of the Wittenberg legacy at the University of Jena, founded in 1548 as an academy by Johann Friedrich the Middler and his brothers. Its first theologian represented the policies of his princes in support of the Gnesio-Lutheran understanding of Luther's teaching but remained in contact with the critics of that position in Wittenberg and Leipzig. ***Viktorin Strigel* (1524–1569),** born in the imperial town of Kaufbeuren, situated between Bavaria and Swabia, began his preparation for university studies in Augsburg and then went to the University of Freiburg. His teacher Johannes Zinck advised him to seek out

Philip Melanchthon in Wittenberg, who had known Strigel's deceased father while both studied in Heidelberg. Strigel instead chose the University of Leipzig, where Melanchthon's friend Joachim Camerarius taught, alongside other followers of the Preceptor, Johannes Pfeffinger and Bernhard Ziegler. He stayed there less than a year and then, at the end of 1542, proceeded to Wittenberg. Within two years Melanchthon had entrusted instruction in his *Loci communes* to Strigel, who also sometimes conducted the Sunday morning lectures that Melanchthon offered to non-German students with his mentor. Melanchthon nominated him for the theological professorship at the academy in Jena founded by the sons of Elector Johann Friedrich the Magnanimous when their family lost the University of Wittenberg after the Smalcald War. Strigel won wide respect for his command of Aristotelian philosophy. He served Dukes Johann Friedrich the Middler and Johann Wilhelm faithfully for fourteen years, articulating their criticism of the Augsburg Interim and the Leipzig Proposal of 1548, Andreas Osiander's doctrine of justification, and Georg Major's proposition that good works are necessary for salvation. Strigel welcomed the addition of Erhard Schnepf, who was fleeing from Spanish occupation forces in Württemberg, to his side, but he opposed the addition of another Wittenberg wunderkind, Matthias Flacius, to the theological faculty in 1557. Flacius's efforts to make peace with Strigel failed. Strigel continued to represent the dukes' policy of opposition to doctrinal compromise at the Colloquy of Worms called by Emperor Ferdinand in 1557 while at the same time trying to bridge the gap between that policy and Melanchthon and his colleagues from electoral Saxony. Strigel and Flacius fell into open conflict over the preparation of a confession for Johann Friedrich the Middler, the *Book of Confutation*. When Strigel and his allies, his colleague Schnepf and the local ecclesiastical superintendent Andreas Hügel, prepared a draft of the document on the condition that Flacius would not alter it and then the duke entrusted it to Flacius and a committee of his allies, open strife disrupted the university. Strigel's refusal to accept the alternative text proposed by Flacius' allies resulted in the duke's imprisoning him in March 1559. Released on probation, Strigel met Flacius in a disputation at the court in Weimar in August 1560. The death of Johann Friedrich's infant son and heir apparent ended the disputation, and tensions continued, but in the course of 1561 Flacius's resistance to the duke's plan for a lay-dominated consistory revived Strigel's standing at the ducal court. After the dismissal of Flacius and his allies, however, Strigel found no peace, and in October 1562 he accepted an instructor's position at the University of Leipzig. His spiritualizing definition of Christ's presence in the Lord's Supper alienated him from his friend Johannes Pfeffinger, dean of the theological faculty, so in 1567 Strigel left Leipzig for Heidelberg. For two years he taught ethics in the liberal arts faculty there, until his death.

Like Strigel, ***Justus Menius* (1499–1558)** remained personally loyal to Melanchthon while pursuing the policies of Duke Johann Friedrich the Middler as superintendent of the churches of Gotha, an office he had held since 1546, after serving as superintendent of the churches in Eisenach since 1529. He had studied in Erfurt before coming to Wittenberg and returned to Erfurt in 1525 to serve as pastor. He aided in church visitations in electoral Saxony in the late 1520s and in ducal Saxony in 1539. His literary work included devotional and sermonic materials; his translations, for example, of Luther's 1535 Galatians commentary into German, made the Reformer's vital interpretation of the epistle and other works available to a wide audience. The Wittenberg theologians brought him with them to the Marburg Colloquy, the negotiations leading to the Wittenberg Concord in 1536, the Smalcald League meeting in 1537, and the Colloquy of Regensburg in 1541. His defense of the right of the empire's princes to resist the emperor in 1547, which Melanchthon revised for publication, contributed to the support of the cause of the Smalcald League in the Smalcald War. He aided the sons of Elector Johann Friedrich in the preparation of a confession critical of the Augsburg Interim in 1549. His polemic against the Anabaptists appeared in print, and his activities as superintendent in Eisenach and Gotha opposed their advance into Saxony. His criticism of Andreas Osiander's doctrine of justification joined the many voices rejecting that position. In 1554 Menius teamed up with Nikolaus von Amsdorf in a visitation of the Ernstine Saxon lands; the two fell into sharp disagreement over the necessity of condemning Georg Major's proposition, "good works are necessary for salvation." Menius was concerned that the people practice the new obedience that flows from faith. Menius felt compelled to leave his posts in ducal Saxony and accepted a call to a congregation in Leipzig, where he died within a year.

Strigel's colleagues in Jena who differed from him were led by ***Matthias Flacius Illyricus* (1520–1575)**. He left his homeland in Istria or Croatia (Illyria) in 1539, fleeing the Inquisition, which executed his relative Baldo Lupetino. After brief periods in Basel and Tübingen, he arrived in Wittenberg in 1541. Luther's counsel uplifted and sustained him while he was suffering a severe spiritual crisis. Among the most intellectually gifted of all Luther's and Melanchthon's students, he won their respect and a position as Hebrew instructor in the university faculty. Melanchthon's supporting compromise with the papal party in the Leipzig Proposal or "Interim" of 1548 led to a severe breach between the two, marked by ever-increasing rancor and bitterness; both felt betrayed by the other. Flacius

Matthias Flacius (sixteenth century)

led the group later labeled Gnesio-Lutheran by scholars as it coalesced in Magdeburg and other centers after 1549. His intellectual gifts propelled him into leadership of the project to write the massive history of the church called the *Magdeburg Centuries*; the original concept of this history of the church stemmed from Flacius, but the actual composition lay in the hands of a team he helped assemble, led by JOHANNES WIGAND and Matthaeus Judex. Among his own works are the hermeneutical milestone, the *Clavis Scripturae sacrae* (Key to the Sacred Scripture), and his *Glossa* of the New Testament. DUKE JOHANN FRIEDRICH THE MIDDLER invited him to the faculty of his young University at Jena in 1557, but they broke in 1561. Flacius continued his vast literary efforts the rest of his life, finding abode in Regensburg, Antwerp, and Strassburg for shorter or longer periods of time, but always pursued by officials from the electoral Saxon government and always under attack, even from former friends, above all for his contention that original sin is the actual substance of the fallen human creature.

Among Flacius's closest supporters during their time in Jena was ***Johannes Wigand* (1523–1587)**, who had left his native Mansfeld for study at Wittenberg in 1538. He accepted a teaching position at the school of Saint Lorenz in Nuremberg in 1541 but returned in 1544 to Wittenberg for two more years of study. From 1546 to 1553 he served as pastor and teacher in Mansfeld and entered the lists against Roman Catholic opponents (in a critique of the catechism issued by Michael Helding in 1549). He also opposed the electoral Saxon positions taken in the Leipzig Proposal or Interim of 1548 and by Georg Major on the necessity of good works for salvation. In 1553, Wigand accepted a call to serve as pastor and superintendent of the ministerium in Magdeburg. During his seven-year pastorate there, he began coordination of Matthias Flacius's plan for a comprehensive history of the church, the *Magdeburg Centuries*, which he edited with his close friend Matthäus Judex. Their section on the doctrine found in the New Testament was published separately under the title *Syntagma* and was used as a textbook for Christian doctrine in the period. Wigand's literary campaign against Roman Catholics (Peter Canisius's catechism) and those who deviated from his understanding of Luther's theology—Andreas Osiander and also those in the Philippist camp—continued in this period. In 1560 Duke Johann Friedrich the Middler called him to Flacius's side at the University of Jena. As those gathered around Flacius opposed the duke's plans for a lay-dominated consistory to govern the church in his lands, they earned exile for themselves. After serving as superintendent in Wismar in Mecklenburg, Wigand returned to Jena (1568–73) but was again exiled when Elector August of Saxony took over control of the university at the death of his cousin Duke Johann Wilhelm. The University of Königsberg called Wigand to its theological faculty in 1573, and in the same year he became bishop of Pomesania. His cooperation with his colleague and friend Tilemann Heshusius, who had become bishop of neighboring Samland, fell apart over christological questions in 1575–77, resulting in Wigand consolidating ecclesiastical jurisdiction in the duchy of Prussia by assuming the Samland bishopric as well. Wigand and Heshusius had led their ministerium in offering constructive criticism of the Torgau Book, the draft of the Solid Declaration of the *Formula of Concord*, and his backing provided critical support for its acceptance by Gnesio-Lutherans.

Flacius's and Wigand's colleague ***Simon Musaeus (Meusel)* (1529–1582)** was born a peasant's son in Vetschau near Cottbus on March 25, 1529. After attending school in Cottbus, he moved to the electoral university of Frankfurt an der Oder in 1543 before transferring to Wittenberg in 1545. In 1547, MELANCHTHON recommended him as a teacher of Greek at the school of Saint Sebald in Nuremberg. In 1549, he was called as a pastor to Fürstenwald in Brandenburg. His marriage earned him dismissal from his post by the bishop of Lebus. His ministry in Crossen, in Silesia, propelled him into conflict with the town council when he defended the peasants on its lands. The town council exiled him. From his next pastorate, in Breslau, he returned to Wittenberg briefly, earning his doctorate in Wittenberg at municipal expense. However, local Roman Catholic clergy found his vehement attacks on the conservative liturgical practices of the city intolerable. They obtained a royal decree demanding his ouster in 1557. He found refuge in Ernstine Saxony, as pastor in Eisfeld, in Hildburghausen, and then in Jena as superintendent of the church and professor of theology, as a colleague of MATTHIAS FLACIUS, JOHANNES WIGAND, and Matthäus Judex. He assisted in the drafting of the Weimar *Book of Confutation* of 1558 and lent support to Flacius in the disputation held at the ducal court in Weimar in 1560. He later joined critics of Flacius's definition of original sin as the substance of the sinner. Because DUKE JOHANN FRIEDRICH THE MIDDLER was increasingly estranged from those around Flacius, Musaeus accepted a call to Bremen in September 1561, only weeks before the duke ousted other Gnesio-Lutheran leaders. In Bremen, with the support of the town's artisans, Musaeus opposed the supporters of the former Bremen pastor, Albert Hardenberg, but those who were continuing to hold to Hardenberg's spiritualizing view of the Lord's Supper, anchored in the merchant class, ousted him. In 1562, Musaeus accepted a call to serve as a ducal court preacher in Mecklenburg, and in 1566 he became superintendent of the church in Gera. The local princes commissioned him and a like-minded colleague, Georg Herbst (Autumnus), to compose a confession of the faith formulated in confutations of false teachings and organized according to the chief parts of Luther's catechisms. Musäus left Gera in 1568 to accept a call to a pastorate in Thorn. Pressure from the king of Poland compelled the town council to dismiss him in 1570. The electoral Saxon government took over the rule in Coburg, where he had served as superintendent from 1570 to 1574, when Duke Johann Ernst died. He retired to Soest and finally became pastor there until 1579, when his criticism of the municipal leadership brought an end to his ministry. The counts of Mansfeld called him to be superintendent of the churches in their domains, and he served until his death July 11, 1582. His publications provided pastoral helps in the form of a postil, devotional literature (including a treatise on melancholy), and a homiletical commentary on Genesis.

Printers played a vital role in Jena, not only in support of the professors at the university but also as an aid to the Ernstine government in its efforts to reclaim the place of the family as the leading representative of Lutheran political forces in the empire. ***Christian Rödinger the Elder* (d. 1557)** had begun to publish in Wittenberg in 1539 but quickly moved to Magdeburg, where he produced some two hundred works, including many by Luther, Melanchthon, and their Gnesio-Lutheran students. At the request of Elector Johann Friedrich, the elder Rödinger brought his presses to Jena in 1553 when the academy began to function there and accepted the elector's commission to publish the Jena edition of Luther's Works, which Gnesio-Lutheran students had fostered. Johann Friedrich placed the Carmelite monastery at the edge of Jena at Rödinger's disposal, and his first work produced in Jena saw the light of day in 1553, the prophet Joel in Luther's translation. In 1555, he began producing the Jena edition of Luther's collected works. When he died in 1557, his widow, Margarethe, supervised production until ***Thomas Rebart* (d. 1570)** married her daughter and took over the operation. When Rebart's wife died, he married Katharina Intze, the widow of the printer Weigand Han, and joined her in Frankfurt. He spent a brief time in Gotha at the time of the Grumbach revolt, but apparently he escaped the siege and went to Leipzig. Elector August had him arrested when he came to the Leipzig book fair in 1567, and he remained jailed for a half year and then returned to work with his first mother-in-law's second husband, Donat Richtzenhan.

After her first husband's death, Margarethe Rödinger married the family's apprentice, ***Donat Richtzenhan* (d. ca. 1605)**, in 1559, and they pursued production of some two hundred works by Wittenberg authors over the next forty years. His press printed official documents, devotional literature, music, and theological works.

Other Students of Wittenberg in the Greater Saxon Region

Two leading propagators of Luther's teaching who spread his message through their sermons and commentaries respectively lived in the greater Saxon region and cultivated contacts with both Gnesio-Lutherans and Philippists. ***Johannes Mathesius* (1504–1565)** was an orphan when he left his native Rochlitz to attend the University of Ingolstadt. During his service as tutor for a Bavarian noble family in Munich, he read Luther's *On Good Works* and proceeded to Wittenberg for the first of four brief opportunities to study there. He joined other students living in the Black Cloister and got to know Luther well. He recorded the Reformer's evening conversations. From a teaching position in Altenburg, Saxony, he was

Johannes Mathesius, later copper engraving

called to be a teacher and then preacher and pastor in Joachimsthal in Bohemia. In a single decade, that young mining town had gathered a large population, chiefly from neighboring Saxony. Mathesius's effective use of Luther's homiletical principles and model made his pulpit an instrument for cultivating a population that had absorbed Luther's understanding of reality. He cooperated with the local noble von Schlick family and resisted Habsburg pressure to reverse the Reformation. His influence spread through the printing of fifteen hundred of the roughly five thousand sermons he preached in Joachimsthal; many of them appeared posthumously. Their impact stemmed from their apt use of Luther's distinction of Law and Gospel, put into practice with sensitive and imaginative expositions of the biblical texts. His imaginative interpretation of the biblical text also captured Luther's narrative style and his rhetorical effectiveness. His sermons included his homiletical biography of Luther, his very popular *Postil* (1565); *Sarepta* (1562), sermons employing metaphors from mining that spoke to the Joachimsthal congregation; homiletical commentaries on Genesis 3:15 (1587), Psalm 130 (1565), Christ's life (1568), Christ's passion (1568, 1570, 1587), 1 and 2 Corinthians (1590), the flood (1587), and Jesus Sirach (1586); and collections of funeral sermons (1564), wedding sermons (1563, 1591), catechism sermons (1586), and sermons on Luther's Table of Christian Callings (1561).

***Hieronymus Weller* (1499–1572)** came to Wittenberg from his native Freiberg in the late 1510s and returned in 1527 for further study. The Luthers took him into the Black Cloister as the tutor of their children. When he returned to Freiberg in 1535, the town council created a professorship for him in its secondary school so that he could provide continuing education for pastors and teachers in the area. Often plagued by melancholy, Weller received letters of comfort and encouragement quite often from his mentor. His exegetical work continued despite the spiritual struggles; he produced commentaries on Job 1–20 in German and on 1 Samuel, Ephesians, Philippians, the Epistles to the Thessalonians, and Philemon in Latin. His brief overview of the Psalms included an introduction with instructions for good preaching for pastors. These works made him a favorite commentator among followers of Luther and Melanchthon in the last decades of the sixteenth century.

Within the Saxon sphere of influence, the counts of Mansfeld ruled their own county, often in fierce disagreement with each other. But in the 1550s and 1560s, they largely supported the Gnesio-Lutheran pastors they had inherited from the time of Johann Spangenberg's service as superintendent of the county's churches. ***Cyriakus Spangenberg* (1528–1604)** left his home in Nordhausen in 1542 for Wittenberg. Young Cyriakus's parents, the town's Reformer Johann Spangenberg and his wife, had raised their children in the faith expressed in Luther's Small Catechism and other writings. Cyriakus often visited the Black Cloister until he was called to be a teacher in Eisleben in 1547. He returned to study in Wittenberg in 1550 and was called soon thereafter to Eisleben as pastor. His attacks on the Augsburg Interim and the Leipzig Proposal of 1548 caused him to leave his post, but in 1553 he assumed the office of preacher for the town of Mansfeld and its adjoining castle. His close cooperation with superintendents Erasmus Sarcerius and Hieronymus Menzel secured the ministerium of the county of Mansfeld for Gnesio-Lutheran theology. Spangenberg steadfastly opposed Philippist positions on a series of issues. In 1566–67 he served as an advisor for the infant Lutheran congregation in Antwerp before its suppression by imperial and Spanish troops in 1567. Upon his return to Mansfeld, Spangenberg was faced with mounting attacks from both the electoral Saxon ecclesiastical establishment and Elector August himself. His support of Matthias Flacius's teaching that original sin becomes the substance of the fallen human creature led to his alienation from former associates, including Johannes Wigand and Tilemann Heshusius, as well as his colleague Hieronymus Menzel. The administrator of the nearby archbishopric of Magdeburg, Count Joachim Friedrich of Brandenburg, dispatched military forces to occupy Mansfeld and drove Spangenberg into exile in early 1575 as Brandenburg soldiers assaulted his pregnant wife. His mother was refused the Lord's Supper on her deathbed by his opponents, who had replaced him. Count Volrad of Mansfeld supported him but himself then reaped the wrath of Brandenburg and electoral Saxony by being exiled from his lands. Spangenberg found refuge in Strassburg, living as a private scholar, with an interruption from 1581 to 1591 for parish service in Schlitz in Hesse. Spangenberg's literary production is most impressive. His homiletical commentary on seven Pauline Epistles have been labeled by a modern scholar the most important commentaries of the time. His tabular outline of the Pentateuch and the Old Testament books from Joshua through Job is unique among biblical commentaries of the Wittenberg exegetical school. His wedding sermons and his editions of the funeral sermons of his father guided preaching at such occasional services throughout the later sixteenth century. His semiannual sermons (1562–71) on Luther's theological writings provide an early assessment of the Reformer's contributions. His application of MELANCHTHON's loci method to topics such as the nobility and music demonstrate how the Preceptor's influence shaped the method of even those who criticized some of his theological positions. Spangenberg's historical chronicles of Mansfeld, Saxony, Henneberg, Holstein, Querfurt, and the bishopric of Verden offer examples of the historical work of the Wittenberg circle.

Cyriakus Spangenberg (sixteenth century)

***Hieronymus Menzel* (1517–1590)** served as schoolteacher, pastor, and finally superintendent in Mansfeld county after studying in Wittenberg (1539–40) and Leipzig (1541–42). His Gnesio-Lutheran views continued Mansfeld policy as set in place by his predecessors, Johann Spangenberg and Erasmus Sarcerius; he opposed his friend Cyriakus Spangenberg on the issue of original sin since Menzel rejected Matthias Flacius's definition of it as the substance of the fallen sinner. His postils provided homiletical aids for hundreds of pastors. He also published more than twenty sermons individually or in small collections as well as a postil for the Sundays and festival days of the church year.

By the time of Luther's death, the church in Erfurt, divided into evangelical and Roman Catholic factions, had several of his former students in pastoral positions. ***Andreas Poach* (1516–1585)** studied in Wittenberg 1530–41. He served as deacon in Jena and Halle after leaving Wittenberg. In 1547 imperial occupation troops forced Poach and the Halle's superintendent, Justus Jonas, into exile; Poach moved to Nordhausen before becoming pastor of the Augustinian church in Erfurt in 1550. Georg Rörer bequeathed Poach notes on Luther's sermons and biblical lectures; Poach edited and published at least five volumes of this material and a second version of Luther's House Postil, which appeared in 1559. After serving as Senior of the Erfurt ministerium for two decades, he was forced from office in 1572 and ended his ministry as pastor at Utenbach northeast of Erfurt.

Luther's Disciples in Braunschweig

A majority of the leading theological minds who emerged in the Wittenberg circle in the period between Luther's death and the *Formula of Concord* adhered to what would later be called Gnesio-Lutheran positions, even though not all were closely associated with Flacius, Wigand, and Musaeus. In the city of Braunschweig two figures stood out, both of whom tried to maintain contact with Melanchthon while opposing at least some of the ideas that were being defended by those around him. The father of ***Joachim Mörlin* (1514–1571)** had taught in the liberal arts faculty in Wittenberg in the early 1510s but became priest in a parish near Coburg in the year of Joachim's birth. Originally destined for an artisanal craft, young Joachim managed to begin studies in Wittenberg in 1532 and received his doctorate in Bible in 1540. His close association with Luther shaped his theology and the course of his career as a critic of those who misrepresented the Reformer in Mörlin's eyes. At Luther's recommendation, he became superintendent of the church in the Saxon town of Arnstadt, but his lord, Count Günther of Schwarzburg, was displeased with his insistence on clerical independence. He was dismissed in 1544. Another term of four years awaited him in Göttingen. There he experienced another dismissal by Duke Erich of Braunschweig-Calenberg, whose introduction of the Augsburg Interim in his land raised fierce protest from ANTON CORVINUS and also Mörlin. In late 1548 he was living at the margins, but then accepted a call to Königsberg. There, he attempted to play a mediating role between ANDREAS OSIANDER, whom he liked because of their common suffering from the imposition of the Augsburg Interim, and his rivals. However, Mörlin quickly identified the great distance between Osiander's understanding of the justification of sinners and what he had heard from Luther, that justification is effected through the word of absolution based on Christ's death and resurrection. Osiander's rejection of this forensic teaching of justification and his espousal of a definition of the Christian's righteousness as the indwelling divine nature of Christ won Mörlin's finely tuned critique. DUKE ALBRECHT exiled Mörlin from Prussia in 1553 after he continued to adhere to his rejection of Osiandrism, even when what he saw as a totally inadequate compromise was attempted. Three calls came almost immediately his way, and he chose to become superintendent of Braunschweig. In Königsberg he had become a close friend of the ducal librarian MARTIN CHEMNITZ. Mörlin had the Braunschweig city council call Chemnitz as his assistant and coadjutor of the city's churches. The two of them formed a partnership that provided theological leadership based on Luther's teaching to the evangelical churches across northern Germany. They gathered a team to attempt to reconcile MATTHIAS FLACIUS and MELANCHTHON in early 1557. Despite Melanchthon's strong recommendations of Mörlin four years earlier and his fondness for Chemnitz, his feelings of betrayal by Flacius and his associates and his suspicions of their motives prevented him

Joachim Mörlin

from negotiating in good faith. Later in 1557, Mörlin was chosen as one of the representatives of the Wittenberg circle for the Colloquy of Worms, called by Emperor Ferdinand. He stood with the Gnesio-Lutheran delegation from ducal Saxony in insisting on clear statements of the evangelical doctrinal positions and further alienated Melanchthon by doing so. He then participated in the composition of the ducal Saxon *Book of Confutation* (1558). The intervention by Mörlin and Chemnitz in the controversy in Bremen over the Lord's Supper in the late 1550s and early 1560s resulted in the dismissal of Albert Hardenberg as pastor there because of his spiritualizing teaching on the presence of Christ in the Supper. Mörlin repeated his defense of the true presence of Christ's body and blood in the bread and wine of the sacrament in the controversy over this question of Christ's sacramental presence that was subject of sharp debate in the Palatinate about the same time. Duke Albrecht of Prussia was convinced to reverse the domination of his church by Osiandrians in 1567, and he called Mörlin and Chemnitz to aid in the return of his church to a firm Lutheran basis. The Braunschweig city council permitted both to travel to Königsberg, where they composed a doctrinal settlement, the *Corpus doctrinae Prutenicum*. The council refused, however, Albrecht's request for both to join his service permanently. The agreement between the two governments finally permitted Mörlin to remain in Prussia while the Braunschweig church retained Chemnitz. Mörlin's final years were dedicated to restoring Luther's teaching to the duchy.

Mörlin's friend and partner for a decade in Braunschweig, and then his successor, ***Martin Chemnitz* (1522–1586)**, emerged from the poverty imposed by the early death of his father, a weaver. Resisting the efforts of his older brother, who was charged with his care, to have him learn the trade of weaving, the young Martin embarked on an educational journey that carried him through secondary school in Wittenberg and Magdeburg to the universities of Frankfurt an der Oder and Wittenberg. At the Leucorea, his study was interrupted by periods of tutoring to earn funds for the next round of university work. His academic performance attracted the attention of Melanchthon. He did not formally study under Luther. Upon the recommendation of Melanchthon, he became librarian and astrologer for Duke Albrecht of Prussia in Königsberg. There, intensive study of Peter Lombard's *Sententiae*, the dogmatic textbook that governed medieval theological education, introduced Chemnitz to the church fathers through Lombard's extensive patristic citations, and he then began to read the recently published editions of their works. He also devoted much time to imbibing Luther's thought by reading his works, particularly his postils. In Königsberg he formed a fast friendship with Joachim Mörlin, a pastor there, and joined him in the critique of ANDREAS OSIANDER's misinterpretation of Luther's teaching of justification by faith. When Duke Albrecht sent Mörlin into exile for his critique of Osiander, Chemnitz soon followed, returning to Wittenberg, where Melanchthon commissioned him to hold lectures on the Preceptor's *Loci communes* as well as on several subjects in the arts faculty. Mörlin arranged for the city council of Braunschweig to call Chemnitz to the Braunschweig ministerium to serve as the coadjutor of Mörlin, the superintendent of the town's churches. The two of them led negotiations aimed at healing the breach between MATTHIAS FLACIUS and Melanchthon—and the disciples of these two—in the so-called "colloquy" of Coswig in 1557. Chemnitz and Mörlin played a leading role in the efforts of north German churches, especially those in the Hanseatic League, to maintain Luther's theology in the 1560s, rejecting the spiritualizing view of the Lord's Supper advanced by Albert Hardenberg in 1561, in Mörlin's *Lüneburg Articles.* In 1561, Chemnitz presented Luther's view of the Lord's Supper in his *Repetition of the Sound Doctrine of the True Presence of the Lord's Body and Blood in the Supper*; he added support for this teaching in his work on Christology, *On the Two Natures in Christ*, first published in 1570, revised in 1578. It provided a major response to the crypto-Philippist deviations from Luther's teaching on the Lord's Supper. Chemnitz began at this time to engage Roman Catholic theologians in polemic; in 1562 he examined the *Chief Elements of the Theology of the Jesuits*, and in 1565–73 four volumes of his *Examination of the Council of Trent* appeared, laying the foundations for Lutheran responses to Roman Catholic teaching for the next centuries. ELECTOR AUGUST OF SAXONY tapped Chemnitz for the committee that he

Portrait of Martin Chemnitz (sixteenth century)

and Jakob Andreae were forming in 1576 to attempt to reconcile the conflicting parties within the Lutheran churches. The two theologians had gotten personally acquainted when they, with Nikolaus Selnecker, worked on the introduction of Lutheran teaching and practice to Braunschweig-Wolfenbüttel in 1568–70. Despite personality conflicts, the three shared similar views on the major doctrinal issues of the day, and Chemnitz may well have shaped Andreae's and Selnecker's thinking at critical points. Chemnitz's work with them and others led to the production of the *Formula of Concord* (1577) and the *Book of Concord* (1580). With Selnecker and Timotheus Kirchener, representative of Elector Ludwig VI of the Palatinate, Chemnitz also helped compose the *Apology of the Book of Concord*, published in 1583. Although he had worked closely with Duke Julius of Braunschweig-Wolfenbüttel for a decade, Chemnitz sharply criticized the duke's attempts to gain territory by having two sons consecrated to minor orders in the Roman Catholic church so that the family could take over neighboring ecclesiastical territories. This led to a total break between the prince and the theologian. Chemnitz's successor, Polycarp Leyser, edited his commentary on Melanchthon's *Loci communes*, his postil, and his harmony of the Gospel accounts of Christ's life, leaving the Lutheran Church a rich treasure of theological reflection. This led Roman Catholic critics to say that had the second Martin (Chemnitz) not come along, the first Martin (Luther) would not have endured.

Luther's and Melanchthon's Disciples in Hamburg

Linked with Braunschweig in the informal league of north German ministeriums was the city of Hamburg, where ***Joachim Westphal* (1510–1574)** was born into an artisan family and spent his ministry. He studied in Wittenberg 1529–32 and 1534–35. With Melanchthon's recommendation, he was considered by several towns as pastor but chose to accept a call to Hamburg in 1541, where he stayed until his death. There, he worked closely with Johannes Aepinus and supported Aepinus in the controversy over Christ's descent into hell. In 1571 the city council appointed Westphal superintendent of its churches. Westphal had criticized the Leipzig Proposal or Interim of 1548 for its compromises with medieval practice. His critique of Calvin's teaching of the Lord's Supper deepened the divide between Calvin and most German Lutherans. Westphal responded to what he viewed as Calvin's abandonment of his earlier position, closer to that of Luther's, when the Genevan Reformer signed the Zurich Consensus of 1549. Its rejection of Calvin's earlier language on the presence of Christ in the Lord's Supper associated both Geneva and Zurich with

Joachim Westphal (seventeenth-century engraving)

a position closer to that of ZWINGLI. Thus, Westphal became a leading voice in the north German Lutheran circles in the 1550s and 1560s. Westphal was chosen by JAKOB ANDREAE to assess his "Swabian Concord" in 1574 but died before he could join CHEMNITZ and CHYTRAEUS in advancing this document in revised form as a basis for the *Formula of Concord*.

For a time, another son of the city, ***Paul von Eitzen*** **(1522–1598)**, served alongside WESTPHAL and AEPINUS in Hamburg. He returned to his home town, where his family belonged to the patricians who led the city, as pastor and later became ecclesiastical superintendent there after studying with Luther and MELANCHTHON in Wittenberg (1539–46) and then in Rostock (1546–48). His assumption of a pastorate in Hamburg in 1549 and later a succession of offices in Hamburg and neighboring Schleswig-Holstein may have prevented him from completing his only commentary, on Genesis. In Hamburg he supported his mentor, Johannes Aepinus, in a controversy over Christ's descent into hell, arguing against Melanchthon and Luther that it brought to completion the sufferings of Christ. In 1555 the city council appointed von Eitzen superintendent of the city's church. In 1556 the University of Wittenberg promoted him to the doctorate of theology. Von Eitzen preserved his friendship with and loyalty to Melanchthon personally despite his opposition to all spiritualizing tendencies in interpreting the Lord's Supper. He decisively rejected the views of Melanchthon's friend Albert Hardenberg in nearby Bremen, who argued that Christ is only spiritually present in the sacrament. In 1557, von Eitzen accompanied Joachim Mörlin and other pastors from the Lower Saxon ministeria to Coswig to conduct negotiations between Melanchthon and Flacius, an effort that failed to bring peace to the church. Also in 1557 von Eitzen took a leading role in composing a "Confession of the Preachers in Hamburg on the Holy Sacrament," which echoed von Eitzen's convictions. Duke Adolf of Schleswig-Holstein-Gottorp borrowed von Eitzen from Hamburg for a visitation of his churches in 1557, and he attended the meeting of the evangelical princes in Naumburg in 1561 at the duke's request. Adolf and von Eitzen joined Saxon Duke Johann Friedrich the Middler, Duke Ulrich of Mecklenburg, and Ulrich's theological advisor, David Chytraeus, in protesting the adaptation of the Variata of the Augsburg Confession as acceptable version of the Confession. In 1562, Adolf named him court preacher and superintendent of the churches in his lands. In 1564, von Eitzen assumed the office of general superintendent of all churches in the entire duchy of Schleswig-Holstein. His efforts to establish a university for the Danish government in Schleswig-Holstein in the years following 1556 ultimately failed. His opposition to the *Formula of Concord*, a sign of his loyalty to Melanchthon, whom he felt was being rejected in the document, prevented its adoption in Schleswig-Holstein. In his later years, failing health required the assistance of an adjunct administrator.

Luther's and Melanchthon's Disciples in Other Lands or Towns

In the nearby duchy of Braunschweig-Lüneburg, a former superintendent of the churches of the county of Henneberg provided leadership in the 1570s and 1580s. ***Christoph Fischer (Vischer)*** **(1518–1597/1600)** studied in Wittenberg 1537–43. He pastored parishes in Jüterbog and Bensen before beginning his service, at Melanchthon's recommendation, for the counts of Henneberg, Wilhelm and Georg Ernst, first as superintendent in Schmalkalden and, after 1571, in Meiningen. He served as court preacher for the dukes of

Braunschweig-Lüneburg in Celle (1574–77), then as pastor in Halberstadt (1577–83), and finally as general superintendent of the churches of Braunschweig-Lüneburg. His homiletical writings were widely used by pastors. Some scholars have labeled his theology as largely in line with that of the Gnesio-Lutherans, while others view his teaching as moderating between them and the Philippists.

Although he held himself aloof to a large extent from others who shared his points of view, ***Andreas Musculus*** **(1514–1581)** fits much of the pattern of those in the Gnesio-Lutheran group. This leading figure in the church of the electorate of Brandenburg was the scion of a middle-class family in Schneeberg, near Zwickau. He left the University of Leipzig after three years of study there and transferred to Wittenberg. He married the sister of the wife of JOHANN AGRICOLA and followed Agricola into the service of ELECTOR

Andreas Musculus (engraving ca. 1600)

Joachim II of Brandenburg in 1541. His appointment as professor of theology at Frankfurt's university the next year established him as a leading theologian in Brandenburg and beyond. He split from his brother-in-law over the Augsburg Interim and in subsequent years issued sharp critiques of three theologians in the service of Joachim's cousin, Duke Albrecht of Prussia: Andreas Osiander and Francesco Stancaro for their divergent views of Luther's teaching on justification and Friedrich Staphylus for his apostasy and return to the Roman obedience. Although not closely connected personally to leading Gnesio-Lutheran figures such as Matthias Flacius, he shared their theological convictions to a large extent. Musculus's rejection of Georg Major's proposal that "good works are necessary for salvation" brought him to reject the word "necessary" completely from any connection with good works, teaching instead that they flow spontaneously from the "free and merry spirit" created by faith in Christ. His colleague on the arts faculty, Abdias Praetorius, opposed Musculus, contending that good works are a necessary fruit of faith. Musculus continuously opposed the Frankfurt town council's attempts to limit the independence of the pastors in pursuit of their duties. In 1566 Joachim named him general superintendent of the church in his lands. Musculus's many polemical writings form only a part of his literary production. His patristic studies aimed at bringing the ancient church fathers into the usage of the church for catechesis and meditation. His ethical treatises in the genre of the "devil book," among them his *Pantsdevil*, an attack on provocative male attire favored by young noblemen, *Marriage Devil*, and *Curse Devil* did not feature the devil prominently but sharply criticized vices that were plaguing society. Elector Joachim appointed Musculus and his student and colleague Christoph Körner to the committee that the elector established in 1576 with August of Saxony to compose what became the *Formula of Concord*.

***David Chytraeus (Kochhafe)* (1531–1600)**, much like Musculus, did not actively participate in the controversies of the 1550s and 1560s but sided with Gnesio-Lutheran positions at many points. Chytraeus left his birthplace, Ingelfingen (near Schwäbisch Hall), at age eight for the University of Tübingen, where Joachim Camerarius and Erhard Schnepf, among his several instructors, recognized his gifts and recommended him to Melanchthon. In 1544, Chytraeus settled into Melanchthon's home and absorbed his teaching as well as Luther's. During the time when the University of Wittenberg closed in the midst of the Smalcald War, he studied briefly in Heidelberg and Tübingen, returning to the Leucorea in 1548. He began to lecture on Melanchthon's *Loci* as well as on rhetoric and astronomy. Melanchthon recommended him to the dukes of Mecklenburg as a professor of

David Chytraeus

the University of Rostock. During the brief service of TILEMANN HESHUSIUS in Rostock (1556–57), he and Chytraeus became close friends and shared a similar path of disillusionment with the direction of Melanchthon's thinking since the Leipzig Proposal of 1548. That led to Chytraeus's critique of the Frankfurt Recess of 1558 and his rejection of the Variata of the Augsburg Confession as a basis for giving legal standing under the Religious Peace of Augsburg to the Calvinist elector of the Palatinate, Friedrich III. Chytraeus regarded the Weimar *Book of Confutation* of 1558, an expression of the Gnesio-Lutheran views of the controversies of the time, as a proper formulation of Wittenberg theology. He also supported the rejection of the spiritualizing interpretation of the Lord's Supper held by Albert Hardenberg at the meeting of theologians of the Lower Saxon circle of the empire at Lüneburg in 1561. This placed him in close contact with JOACHIM MÖRLIN and MARTIN CHEMNITZ. Several universities attempted to lure him away from Rostock, but he remained there. Nonetheless, he accepted assignments to aid other churches as a trusted counselor of the dukes of Mecklenburg. From 1569 to 1572, he advised Austrian Lutheran nobles who had introduced Luther's Reforms to their churches on the formulation of church ordinances and liturgical forms. When JAKOB ANDREAE composed his "Swabian Concord" as a proposal for ending the controversies besetting the theologians of the Augsburg Confession in 1574, he asked Chytraeus and Chemnitz for their support. They solicited reactions from ministeria throughout northern German lands, and on the basis of Andreae's document they formulated the "Swabian-Saxon Concord." In 1576 ELECTOR AUGUST requested Chytraeus's participation in the commission that used this document, along with the Maulbronn Formula composed by representatives of Henneberg, Baden, and Württemberg, to compose the *Formula of Concord*, roughly one-quarter of which came from Chytraeus's pen. His commentaries, catechisms, and devotional treatises provided aids for pastors and instructional material for the next generation.

More openly supportive of Gnesio-Lutheran positions after 1560, ***Tilemann Heshusius (Hesshus)*** **(1527–1588)** had only slowly abandoned his attachment to Melanchthon. Heshusius had come to Wittenberg in 1546 after attending secondary school in Antwerp. His family belonged to the leadership of the town of Wesel on the Rhine. He interrupted his education in Wittenberg with periods of study at Oxford and Paris but returned by 1550. Melanchthon entrusted lectures on his *Loci* to Heshusius, an indication of the close relationship between the two. His preceptor sent him to Goslar as superintendent of the town's churches in 1553, where he married Hanna von Bert (1533–1564). The town council opposed his efforts to discipline the son of a Goslar mayor and removed him from office. Heshusius spent a brief time in Magdeburg, where he formed friendships with several Gnesio-Lutheran leaders, including Nikolaus Gallus and Johannes Wigand. The University of Rostock called him to teach there at Melanchthon's recommendation, but again questions of public morality arose and placed him in opposition to the town council, which sent him into exile. Melanchthon arranged for his call to Heidelberg, where Elector Ottheinrich was introducing reform patterned on Luther's theology. Ottheinrich's cousin and successor, Frederick III, leaned toward the theology of John Calvin, and Heshusius's faithfulness to Luther's teaching led to conflict with some fellow pastors and with the elector himself. In a memorandum that he believed would remain secret, requested by his niece's husband, a counselor at the electoral court, Melanchthon encouraged Frederick to remain on the course he had chosen and criticized Heshusius's use of some of Luther's language affirming the true presence of Christ's body and blood in the Lord's Supper. When the memorandum was published, it elicited severe criticism from Heshusius and his friends, but it also resulted in his dismissal. The city of Bremen then called him to serve as superintendent and to combat Calvinist sentiment among the laity, who had been influenced by their previous pastor, Albert Hardenberg. Heshusius had the support of the artisans of Bremen, but a leading merchant, Daniel von Büren, who had studied in Wittenberg, engineered his dismissal for his defense of Luther's teaching on the Lord's Supper. His return to the family home in Wesel brought little comfort since the pastors there also opposed his teaching on the sacrament. Duke Wolfgang of Zweibrücken in the Palatinate called him to be superintendent of the dukedom's churches, where he served until 1568, when Duke Johann Wilhelm of Saxony called him to the University of Jena, part of the group that restored the Gnesio-Lutheran theology of the faculty that had been set aside by the duke's older brother, JOHANN FRIEDRICH THE MIDDLER. Heshusius joined those who rejected MATTHIAS FLACIUS's definition of original sin as the substance of the sinner and also became a sharp critic of JAKOB ANDREAE's efforts at Concord. At Johann Wilhelm's death, Heshusius was removed from his professorship but with his friend JOHANNES WIGAND accepted an invitation to go to Prussia, where he assumed the position of bishop of Samland as part of the effort to deconstruct the Osiandrian direction of the church in the dukedom. He and Wigand fell into a dispute over christological definitions, and he moved to the University of Helmstedt and became a trusted counselor of Duke Julius of Braunschweig-Wolfenbüttel. He represented the duke's wish to scuttle the *Formula of Concord* in the late 1570s and early 1580s. In addition to publishing on the various controverted questions among the members of the Wittenberg circle throughout his career, Heshusius authored a number of biblical

Tilemann Heshusius (ca. 1589)

commentaries and provided model sermons for pastors and laity in his postils.

Nikolaus Gallus (16th century)

Also solidly in the Gnesio-Lutheran company of scholars and theologians, ***Nikolaus Gallus* (1516–1570)** studied in Wittenberg from 1530 to 1540 and enjoyed the tutelage especially of JUSTUS JONAS and MELANCHTHON. His career began as a school rector in Mansfeld; in 1543 the imperial city of Regensburg called him to a pastorate there. He played a key role in introducing Luther's Reforms to the city. With the imposition of the Augsburg Interim by imperial troops in 1548, Gallus fled north and finally settled in Magdeburg, where he led the city's clergy in its opposition to the Interim and to the new ecclesiastical establishment of Saxony under ELECTOR MORITZ. He was primarily responsible for the Magdeburg *Confession* of 1550, with its repetition of the teaching of the Augsburg Confession and its assertion of the right to resist the imperial government if it turned itself against the gospel of Christ. Gallus, together with his friend MATTHIAS FLACIUS, authored a flood of pamphlets against imperial policy and the writings of former friends and professors in Wittenberg who he felt had betrayed the gospel in the Leipzig Proposal and in their assertion of the necessity of good works for salvation, which that document asserted. In 1553, the city council of Regensburg requested that Gallus return, and he served again as the superintendent of its churches until his death. Gallus challenged Melanchthon's teaching on the freedom of the will, initially in private correspondence, and when that brought no solution, in print. His preceptor, deeply suspicious of Gallus for his attacks on the Leipzig Proposal, refused to discuss the topic with his student, in whom he had become bitterly disappointed. Gallus urged the Regensburg municipal government to give Flacius refuge, which it reluctantly conceded, in 1561. Gallus and Flacius then worked together to establish training for those from the Slavic areas to the south to bring the Wittenberg message to the Croatians, Slovenians, and

Primus Truber, woodcut by Jakob Lederlein (1578)

others. They supported this mission with plans for a printing operation for the production of literature for use among those people, but those plans came to naught.

In connection with these plans, however, Gallus worked with a nobleman, HANS UNGNAD, Baron of Sonnegg, and a pastor, ***Primus Truber* (1508–1586)**, a son of a miller in Rascia, near Slovenia. Truber received his education in nearby Fiume and then in Salzburg and Vienna. His voice earned him a place in the cathedral choir in Trieste, and later his superiors also appointed him as a preacher. His reputation spread, and he became cathedral preacher in Laibach. There, he soon ran afoul of his bishop for opposing clerical celibacy and advancing other proposals for reform. Because he could preach in his native Slovenian, however, he found other positions as a preacher in the ensuing years, finally in Laibach again. In 1547, he escaped arrest in a crackdown on those with evangelical tendencies in Laibach, because he was traveling at the time the evangelicals were being apprehended. He fled to Nuremberg, where Veit Dietrich received him and found him a position as a preacher in Rothenburg ob der Tauber. Already at this time, Truber was developing an orthography for the Slovenian language and subsequently published the first books ever published in that tongue, first a catechism that included the text of Luther's Small Catechism and subsequently other catechisms, hymnals, postils, and the New Testament. Duke Christoph of Württemberg drew Truber into his employ in 1552, calling him to a pastorate in Kempten, and in 1561 to Urach. There, working together with Hans Ungnad of Sonnegg, he established a printing operation that prepared materials for use in the Slovenian and Croatian areas under Habsburg and Venetian rule. Truber labored there in the early 1560s and was recognized by local evangelical pastors as their superintendent. He returned to Württemberg in 1565 and served there while continuing to prepare printed materials for his Slavic mission until his death.

***Hans Ungnad von Weissenwolff, Baron of Sonnegg* (1493–1564)** spent time at the court of Emperor Maximilian I as a youth. In 1519, he accompanied an Austrian delegation to Spain to negotiate with Charles V. He served King Louis of Hungary beginning in 1523, and in 1530 became administrator for the Habsburgs in Styria. In that year he attended the imperial diet in Augsburg as part of the Habsburg delegation. His victory over Turkish forces in 1532 helped win him a position as commander of military forces in the Habsburg family's Austrian domains and in the southern region that embraced Slovenian- and Croatian-speaking populations. His commitment to Luther's theology and his active pleading for toleration of adherents of the Augsburg Confession led to increasing tensions with King Ferdinand and others in his government. In 1555, he resigned his positions and moved to Wittenberg, where he developed close contacts with Melanchthon. Duke Christoph of Württemberg appointed him to his staff and gave him a residence in Urach, where he began to work closely with Primus Truber in his Slavic mission. The press that he helped create and that he funded produced some thirty titles in Croatian and others in Italian and Slovenian. When his own funds had been exhausted, he raised money with appeals to municipal and princely governments. This effort did not survive long after his death.

Sonnegg and Truber worked more directly with the court of Duke Christoph of Württemberg. Its leading theologian, ***Jakob Andreae* (1528–1590)**, sometimes called "Schmidty" by his foes because of his father's occupation, received ducal support for his secondary and university education. Apart from ERHARD SCHNEPF, Andreae's professors in his time at the University of Tübingen (1541–46) were not the strongest thinkers. In 1546, he was called to be deacon in Stuttgart and married Johanna Entringer, who became mother of his eighteen children. The enforcement of the Augsburg Interim drove him from his post. With ducal support, he returned to Tübingen and obtained his doctorate before assuming the superintendency of the church in the town of Göppingen in 1553. DUKE CHRISTOPH quickly began using him as an ecclesiastical diplomat and representative of his government. Andreae's attempts in 1557 to find a formula of agreement with the church in Geneva through contacts with Theodor Beza earned them opposition both in Geneva and Württemberg. Quickly, Andreae submitted to the criticism of JOHANNES BRENZ and became his ardent disciple. The two together represented Württemberg at the colloquy in Worms in 1557, where Andreae became acquainted with theologians from northern German Lutheran churches. He aided the introduction of the Reformation in Palatinate-Neuburg and Baden-Durlach in the 1550s and opposed the Anabaptists in a colloquy at Pfeddersheim in 1557 on behalf of Elector Ottheinrich of the Palatinate. He played a leading role in the composition of the Württemberg confession, which resolved a controversy on the presence of Christ in the Lord's Supper that endorsed Brenz's position in 1559. In 1561, Andreae represented Württemberg at a meeting of evangelical governments attempting to formulate a united reaction to the final session of the Council of Trent, and he also traveled to Poissy to take part in a colloquy between French Roman Catholics and Huguenots, but arrived after the conclusion of their talks. In 1562, Andreae led a reconciliation team in ducal Saxony that attempted to heal the breach between VIKTORIN STRIGEL and supporters of MATTHIAS FLACIUS. In 1568, Duke Christoph sent Andreae to the duke's cousin, Julius of Braunschweig-Wolfenbüttel, to aid in the introduction of the Reformation to Julius's lands, with an added commission to work once more for a solution to the disputes that were wracking the Wittenberg circle. Andreae's visits to various towns and princely courts ended with a colloquy at Zerbst in 1570, with token acceptance of Andreae's "Six Articles," a brief and general proposal for ending disputes. It was dismissed out of hand by Gnesio-Lutherans and taken very lightly by others. About this time, Andreae came to recognize the deep division between his and Brenz's position on the Lord's Supper and the person of Christ and that of the Wittenberg faculty. Andreae then composed his *Six Sermons on the Divisions among the Theologians of the Augsburg Confession*, published in 1573, with detailed examination of the chief issues under dispute, and with explicit condemnations of false teachers, chiefly the electoral Saxon theologians

Jakob Andreae

of the crypto-Calvinist stripe. MARTIN CHEMNITZ and others suggested that Andreae recast his ideas in another form rather than the homiletic genre and make his positions a proposal of the entire Tübingen faculty. Andreae took on the task himself and sent to select northern German colleagues his draft of what came to be known as "The Swabian Concord." Chemnitz and DAVID CHYTRAEUS led efforts to discuss it with north German ministeriums, producing "the Swabian-Saxon Concord." At about this time, in 1574, ELECTOR AUGUST OF SAXONY discovered the crypto-Philippist conspiracy to subtly import a spiritualizing view of the Lord's Supper into the electorate's public teaching. For the project of returning electoral Saxony to Luther's theology, he borrowed Andreae from the young Duke Ulrich of Württemberg for five years. Andreae and August resolved to use the formulation of a settlement for Saxony as an appeal for unity to all evangelical churches. August constituted a committee, with Andreae, Chemnitz, Chytraeus, his own NIKOLAUS SELNECKER, and two representatives of electoral Brandenburg, ANDREAS MUSCULUS and Christoph Körner. At meetings culminating in May 1576 in Torgau, they produced a formula for concord, circulated it to all evangelical ministeria, revised it in light of the critiques in May 1577 at Bergen Abbey near Magdeburg, and published it with other Lutheran confessions in *The Book of Concord* in 1580. For that volume Andreae prepared a preface, and he also composed an "epitome" of the Torgau Book for easier consumption by governmental leaders. Andreae worked tirelessly to bring churches into the Concordian settlement. With that task accomplished, he continued to serve the church in Württemberg, defending Lutheran theology against attacks from the Jesuits and the Reformed, the latter most famously in a colloquy in the Württemberg lands in France, Mömpelgaard (Montbéliard).

The variety of backgrounds, specific positions, political situations, and personalities did not always make for precise agreement among the disciples of Luther and Melanchthon, but their common commitment to the gospel as their mentors had taught it drove them to strive for proper proclamation of Law and Gospel in their pulpits, and for this common confession of the faith.

CHAPTER 6

INTERNATIONAL STUDENTS: WITTENBERG EDUCATES REFORMERS FROM AFAR

Late medieval academe knew no firm borders, neither geographically nor linguistically. Latin was the "lingua Franca" of the medieval university. Some students, for instance, from the kingdom of Hungary, came to Wittenberg and never learned German. Being unable to understand the vernacular formed a barrier on Sunday mornings when local worship services were in German, but in hearing professors and conducting disputations as part of the university's instructional program Latin ruled. Therefore, students from various parts of Europe visited Wittenberg for study. Just as William Shakespeare would later report of his fictitious Hamlet's study in Wittenberg, so already in the 1520s students from various parts of Europe began coming to Wittenberg to hear MELANCHTHON, Luther, and their colleagues lecture. Close ties bound those within the sphere of influence of the Hanseatic League, so by the early sixteenth century students from the kingdoms of Denmark-Norway-Iceland and Sweden-Finland were accustomed to coming to Rostock and Greifswald for higher education. Wittenberg soon became an intriguing option for them as well. Students from the east had the universities in Cracow, Prague, and Vienna closer at hand, and the great wave of those from the Hungarian lands came after Luther's death, although already in the 1540s Melanchthon was conducting a Sunday morning "Bible class" in Latin for Hungarians whose German was limited. Certainly, by the end of the century the few examples of international students in Wittenberg could be multiplied significantly. Those presented in this chapter serve to demonstrate an important aspect of the shape of the Wittenberg circle.

The Kingdom of Denmark-Norway-Iceland

***Hans Tausen* (1494–1561)** joined the monastery of the Order of Saint John of Jerusalem at Antvorskov around 1504. His study at the University of Rostock (1516–20) acquainted him with the work of biblical humanists. In 1521, at the University of Copenhagen, he studied with Paul Helie, a Carmelite committed to Erasmian reform, who led him deeper into the study of Scripture. After a brief time at the University of Leuven/Louvain, he moved on to Wittenberg in 1523 but was recalled to his monastery the following year and placed in limited confinement. His preaching made a positive impact on officials in his order and outside it, and he was called to Viborg in Jutland as a preacher. His decidedly Luther-like message led to his suspension in 1526 by ecclesiastical officials, but KING FREDERICK I appointed him a court preacher. In 1527 Wittenberg Reform was introduced in Viborg. In 1529 Tausen was called to the Church of Saint Nicolaus in Copenhagen and introduced reform to the city. He contributed significantly to the *Confessio Hafniensis* of 1530, a statement of Luther's followers prepared for a religious colloquy that did not take place. In 1533 Frederick died, and in the tensions that followed, those who favored a Danish church of medieval character but independent of Rome condemned Tausen. Popular support on his behalf spared him, and when Frederick's son, CHRISTIAN III, defeated his enemies and took the throne in 1536, Tausen worked at his right hand to introduce a national church ordinance in 1536–37. He assumed a post of lecturer in Hebrew at the University of Copenhagen and the office of cathedral preacher in Roskilde. In 1541, he began two decades of service as bishop of Ribe in Jutland. His writings and translations

Hans Tausen

brought Wittenberg theology to the popular level as he critiqued medieval theology and practice and cultivated the theology of Luther among the Danish populace.

In Viborg, Tausen had the help of ***Jørgen Jensen Sadolin* (ca. 1499–1559)**, whose early life is not clearly traced in the extant sources. He had studied at a university when he became associated with Hans Tausen's reform efforts in Viborg, where Tausen ordained him in 1529. After Tausen's departure, Sadolin continued introducing Wittenberg Reforms. In 1529 and 1530 he saw to the publication of his Danish translations of Luther's *On the Lord's Supper, Confession* and his *Parents Are Not to Force Their Children into Marriage* and Johannes Bugenhagen's *Summary of Salvation* and *Instruction of Those Who Lie Sick*, an "art of dying" in evangelical style. In the turbulence that beset the Danish kingdom in the early 1530s, he became an aide to the reform-inclined bishop of Odense, Knud Gyldenstjerne, assisting in efforts to introduce reform of the clergy. He translated Luther's Small Catechism and the Augsburg Confession into Danish. When Johannes Bugenhagen arrived from Wittenberg to aid in the reform of the Danish church, Sadolin assisted him as well and was ordained by Bugenhagen as bishop of Odense.

***Christian Pedersen* (ca. 1480–1554)** studied at Greifswald, Paris, and Leuven/Louvain before becoming a canon at the cathedral in Lund. In 1522 he assumed office as the chancellor for the archbishop of Lund and in 1526 went into exile with King Christian II. In the Netherlands he became a disciple of Luther. Returning to the Danish kingdom, he settled in Malmö in 1531 and opened a printing operation, which he placed in the service of Wittenberg Reform. During the civil war, he divested himself of his presses but continued to write and translate the rest of his life. He published an edition of the twelfth-century history of the Danish kingdom by Saxo Grammaticus. Before his commitment to Luther's Reform he published a number of popular devotional pieces. He translated the New Testament into Danish in 1529, using the Vulgate, Erasmus, and Luther. His prefaces to the biblical works offer a primer of evangelical theology.

***Peder Palladius* (1503–1560)**, son of a cobbler in Ribe, Jutland, was caught up in the spread of biblical humanism in Denmark from the time of his secondary education. He became rector of the secondary school in Odense, and in 1531 went to Wittenberg to study. He had previously read Luther, and he absorbed his theology during his six years at the Leucorea, where he also became a disciple of Melanchthon. He returned to Denmark in 1537 to occupy the post of bishop of Zealand, with residence no longer in Roskilde but now in Copenhagen; his was the most powerful position in the Danish church. He worked closely with Johannes Bugenhagen in composing the ordinances of the church and in its restructuring. He taught at the university, advised the kings on ecclesiastical affairs, and devoted himself to preparing printed materials for the populace. His policy of visitation of congregations furthered reform. Among his writings were an important theological treatise, *On Repentance and Justification* of 1558, and his *Introduction to the Prophetic and Apostolic Books* of 1557, which won wide readership in Germany as well as the Nordic lands.

***Niels Palladius* (ca. 1510–1560)**, Peder's brother, joined his brother in Wittenberg in 1534, where he studied for a decade before returning to a convent in southern Denmark as a teacher in 1544. He returned to Wittenberg but became a pastor in Copenhagen in 1550 and bishop of Lund in 1551. He wrote some twenty books in Latin, Danish, and Icelandic, conveying the theology he had learned from Luther and MELANCHTHON. His *Useful and Necessary Rules for Conducting Sermons* of 1556 provided guidance for Danish pastors in carrying out their office; his *Oration on the True and Catholic Church* of the same year was intended to guide the organization and practice of the church. His other works treated predestination, invocation of the saints and the use of images (which he rejected), and a number of moral issues, including excessive drinking, marriage, and preparation for death.

***Niels Hemmingsen* (1513–1600)** received his secondary education in Roskilde and Lund. He returned to his native Denmark after studying in Wittenberg 1537–42. There his attraction to MELANCHTHON and his method of interpreting Scripture molded Hemmingsen's thought and career. The University of Copenhagen engaged him first as professor of Greek, then of dialectics, and finally appointed him to a chair in theology in 1553. His *Handbook of Theology* (1555) served as a textbook far beyond Denmark's borders. Its treatment of ethics went beyond the contents of its model, Melanchthon's *Loci theologici*, which it also conveyed, and provided a model for evangelical instruction in the Christian life. His *Evangeliepostil* (1561) provided outlines and interpretation for preaching on the pericopes. His *Pastor* (1562) gave pastors a detailed treatment of the various aspects of the pastoral office. In addition, Hemmingsen published extensively, treating marriage and biblical hermeneutics, and composing commentaries on the Psalms and several New Testament books. His views of the Lord's Supper drifted in a decidedly spiritualist direction, and he must be counted among the leading crypto-Philippist thinkers, views that he expressed in a 1571 attack on those defending Luther's view of Christ's presence in the Lord's Supper. His dogmatics text, the *Syntagma* of 1574, expressed his position explicitly. Pressure from German governments regarding these views ended his career at the University of Copenhagen. In 1579 KING FREDERICK II relegated him to the abbey at Roskilde, where he continued to write until his death.

The Kingdom of Sweden-Finland

***Olaus Petri* (1493–1552)**, son of a blacksmith, had studied at the University of Uppsala before coming to Wittenberg in 1516. He spent two years under Luther's tutelage and then returned to the Swedish part of the Danish realm, becoming a deacon in Strängnås and secretary to his bishop. He quickly won a colleague, Laurentius Andreae, to Luther's convictions, and the two began preaching Luther's theology, though not without arousing opposition from defenders of the old faith. In 1520 Gustav Vasa led a revolt against the Danish monarchy, and in 1523 Gustav was acknowledged as king of an independent Sweden. Andreae became Gustav's chancellor, and within a year Petri had been called to a pastorate in Stockholm and was engaged as municipal secretary. In 1525 Petri married, heightening criticism of his position. During the following decade some sixteen of his books were published, bringing Wittenberg theology to the Swedish people, tripling the number of books printed in the vernacular. In 1526 his translation of the New Testament appeared. He became personal secretary of the king in 1527, and in this office he guided the decisions of the Diet of Västerås in 1527 to accept extensive reform measures for the church. A brief interim as chancellor of the kingdom ended with his return to parish service in 1531. Petri was condemned for treason by the king because he and his friend Laurentius Andreae had not betrayed the confessions of conspirators against Gustav, but the sentence of death was lifted. He continued to preach and cultivate Wittenberg piety until his death.

***Laurentius Petri* (1499–1573)** followed his brother's example in going to Wittenberg for study, returning in 1527. Following his return, King Gustav placed him in the office of archbishop of Uppsala in 1531, and he slowly worked toward completing the introduction of Lutheran Reform into the church of Sweden. That process lasted until 1571, concluding with the acceptance of a church ordinance. After Gustav's death in 1560, Laurentius guided the church through the reigns of Gustav's two older sons, Erik XIV, who supported and promoted the introduction of Calvinistic ideas into his realm and, after his death in 1568, Johann III, whose subtle efforts to return Sweden to the Roman obedience met resistance from the archbishop as well as from the nobility and populace.

***Laurentius Andreae* (ca. 1470–1552)** followed up his secondary education in Sweden with study at the University of Rostock. His acquaintance with Olaus Petri converted him to Luther's theology, and as archdeacon of the bishopric of Strängnås took over when his superior was executed in 1520. Andreae supported the efforts of Gustav Vasa to win independence from Danish control, and in 1524 became an advisor and member of

Gustav's council. He used his position to further the introduction of Wittenberg Reform in the new monarchy. He gradually lost favor and was accused of treason along with Olaus Petri in 1540. He supported the translation of the New Testament that Petri undertook in the 1520s and himself authored an exposition of the creeds and the Christian life that served as a catechism.

Luther's thought began to infiltrate the Finnish parts of GUSTAV VASA's domains through ***Pietari Särkilahti* (d. 1529)**, who never formally enrolled at the University of Wittenberg but who, as a disciple of ERASMUS, began reading Luther's treatises after he moved from the University of Rostock, where he had enrolled in 1516, to the University of Leuven/Louvain. Probably around 1522, he returned to his native Turku, where his father had served as mayor, and he was the first priest in the Swedish realm to break his vows of celibacy and marry. He became rector of the secondary school in Turku and spread the publications of Olaus Petri as well as Luther among the priests in the area. Many of them followed his example and married. His program of reform remained incomplete when he died in 1529.

Among those who absorbed Särkilahti's message was the bishop's secretary, ***Michael Agricola* (1510–1557)**, who had completed his secondary education in Viborg in eastern Finland before coming to Turku. His humanistic interests and skills attracted the attention of Bishop Martin Skytte of Turku, who appointed Agricola his personal secretary and later sent him to study in Wittenberg (1536–39), where he became acquainted with both Luther and MELANCHTHON. Upon his return to Turku, he became rector of its school and in 1554 bishop of Turku. His activities in reform extended beyond his administrative measures bringing Wittenberg theology and practice to the Finnish congregations. His writing promoted not only Luther's thought but also the use of the Finnish language. He worked ardently to deconstruct medieval piety and center the faith of the people on Christ's atoning death and resurrection. His first published work presented basics for the education of children, including initial catechetical instruction in the faith. His *Biblical Prayer Book* of 1544 cultivated devotions in the home and the education of the children in the basics of Christian belief and practice. His work on translating the New Testament into Finnish, begun while he was studying in Wittenberg, appeared in 1548. It followed Luther's translation closely, but Agricola also worked with the Greek text itself. He went on to initiate a translation of the Old Testament, most importantly of the Psalms. His manual for worship and his missal translated the Swedish liturgical works of OLAUS PETRI and shaped Finnish worship to this day. His annotated translation of Luther's postils helped transform pastoral practice and preaching in Finland.

Mikael Agricola, by Albert Edelfelt (nineteenth century)

***Paavali Juusten* (c. 1516–1575)**, son of a patrician family in Finnish Viborg, moved to Turku in 1536 for further education and was drawn into the circle around Bishop Martin Skytte that included MICHAEL AGRICOLA. Juusten studied in Wittenberg in 1543–46 and visited the universities of Rostock and Königsberg on his way back to Finland. He returned to assume the rector's position at the secondary school in Turku. He later moved back to his home town, Viborg, where GUSTAV VASA appointed him bishop. In 1563 King Erik XIV appointed him bishop of Turku. In 1569 King Johan III sent Juusten to Moscow as head of a delegation to negotiate with Czar Ivan the Terrible regarding a lasting peace between Sweden and Russia. After extended exchanges that produced little, Ivan arrested the Swedish delegation, and in the course of his imprisonment Juusten's health was broken. Freed in 1572, he did not fully regain his health and died three years later. His literary production includes a catechism, a postil, liturgical works, and the chronicle of the bishops of Turku.

Luther's and Melanchthon's Disciples in England and Scotland

Although the Lutheran confession of the faith never established itself in the kingdom of England or in neighboring kingdom of Scotland, Luther's treatises were read in London and Cambridge in the 1520s. Out of the roots of the protest against Rome of the fourteenth century, led by John Wyclif and furthered by those called the Lollards in the fifteenth century, and out of the influence exercised by ERASMUS and other humanists, interest in the study of Scripture and a sense of distance from the papacy flourished in intellectual circles, particularly in Cambridge, from the 1520s on. A few individuals reflected Luther's and MELANCHTHON'S influence more deeply than others.

***William Tyndale* (ca. 1494–1536)** studied at both Oxford and Cambridge and was drawn into the circle of the biblical humanists there. While a private tutor in 1522, he translated ERASMUS'S *Handbook of the Christian Soldier*. In 1523, he proposed a new translation of the Bible into English to the Erasmian bishop of London, Cuthbert Tunstall. Tunstall rejected his proposal, and Tyndale traveled to Germany, working in Hamburg and then in Antwerp. The accusation from the pens of Thomas More and JOHANNES COCHLAEUS that Tyndale had consulted the Wittenberg Reformers is not corroborated by other sixteenth-century evidence. It is clear, however, that Tyndale knew Luther's translation of the New Testament well and often followed its interpretations in his own translation. Although his own introductions to the New Testament do not slavishly follow Luther, influences from Luther's own prologues to the biblical books and his *Freedom of a Christian* seem to have shaped Tyndale's formulations frequently. When driven from Cologne, Tyndale found his way up the Rhine to Worms, where his translation was completed. In 1526 his translation of the New Testament was printed in

William Tyndale portrait from Foxe's Book of Martyrs *(first edition, 1563)*

Cologne and sent to England, where Tunstall, More, and others fiercely attacked it. Tyndale also translated the Pentateuch and Jonah. From the continent, Tyndale responded to attacks on his theology by Thomas More, King Henry VIII's chancellor in the early 1530s. The imperial government of Charles V arrested Tyndale in 1535 and had him burned in 1536. His translation, significantly dependent on Luther's translation, reflecting much of the Wittenberg theology, continued to shape the several subsequent translations of the New Testament and Pentateuch for a century.

Tyndale's friend ***John Frith*** **(ca. 1503–1533)** fell under the influence of biblical humanism during his secondary education at Eton and then at King's College in Cambridge. There he met Tyndale and was persuaded that Luther's understanding of biblical authority and justification by faith were true and that the distinction of Law and Gospel served to clarify and apply the message of Scripture. Tyndale sought Frith's advice as he began planning his translation work. Appointed a canon in Oxford, Frith was imprisoned on charges of heresy in 1528 but escaped, fleeing to Marburg. While in Germany, he worked further with Tyndale and composed a number of works arguing against medieval practice and promoting ideas he had gleaned from the writings of Luther and also from Zwingli. In his years on the continent, Frith authored several works that borrowed heavily from Luther's published treatises. In 1532 Frith returned to England, and the chancellor, Thomas More, had him arrested for denying that purgatory and transubstantiation were biblically based dogmas. More had him burned in 1533.

Robert Barnes **(ca. 1495–1540)** became an Augustinian friar while studying in Cambridge, perhaps as early as 1505. His reputation as a scholar grew, and he associated with other biblical humanists in Cambridge after studies in Leuven/Louvain in 1517–21. As Augustinian prior in Cambridge in the subsequent years, Barnes gathered like-minded scholars for conversation at the White Horse Inn. One of them, Thomas Bilney, convinced him of the truth found in Luther's writings, which, in all likelihood, Barnes had known through his order and his time in Leuven. Barnes publicly called for reform of a variety of ecclesiastical practices in 1525, although he did not embrace a doctrine of justification by faith at that time. Arrested in 1526 and subjected to an order of public submission, he was detained at the Augustinian house in London and then in Northampton, where he staged a suicide and escaped to Antwerp. He moved to Wittenberg in 1530 and began formal studies at the university in 1533, living in Bugenhagen's home and conversing frequently with Luther, Melanchthon, and their colleagues. He returned briefly in 1531 to England, arousing the antagonism of Thomas More, who attacked him on several counts.

Nonetheless, KING HENRY VIII regarded Barnes as a valuable contact with the Danish court and with several German princes who had introduced Wittenberg Reforms. In 1533 and 1534 Barnes enjoyed Henry's confidence. Barnes's *Supplications* of 1531 and 1534, addressed to the king, supported English royal policy in moving away from the Roman obedience and also presented key teachings of Luther. In 1536 he published his antipapal history of the papacy, *Lives of the Roman Pontiffs*, dedicating the work to King Henry and including in it a preface written by Luther. After the execution of Queen Anne Boleyn, Barnes was imprisoned briefly in the Tower of London, but Thomas Cromwell needed him to pursue plans for an alliance with the Smalcald League, and Barnes preached publicly in 1537 and 1538. He also served with an English delegation to the League, which attempted to negotiate a treaty of cooperation between Henry's government and the League. This effort failed, and Barnes fell from favor. Stephen Gardiner, bishop of Winchester, whom Barnes knew personally, attacked his doctrine of justification by faith, and had Barnes and others who supported his teaching arrested in early 1540. He was burned at the stake July 30, 1540. Luther issued a fresh attack against HENRY VIII and praised Barnes as a martyr in print.

One of the few Scots to endorse Luther's theology openly, ***Patrick Hamilton* (ca. 1504–1528)**, became abbot of Fern as a minor, at age thirteen. He studied in Paris and Leuven/Louvain before becoming an instructor at Saint Andrews in 1523. In each of these places he encountered Luther's writings. In 1526 his sympathies with Luther's theology became public; the next year he visited Luther and MELANCHTHON in Wittenberg and also went to Marburg. His *Patrick's Pleas* or *Places* appeared in 1527, propagating Wittenberg theology in a form similar to Melanchthon's *Loci communes*. JOHN FRITH translated this work from Latin into English. Upon Hamilton's return to Scotland he was

Portrait of Patrick Hamilton painted between ca. 1645 and 1730

arrested. Alexander Alesius was appointed by Archbishop James Beaton to convince him of his errors, but Hamilton convinced Alesius of the truth of Luther's way of thinking, and Alesius fled Scotland. Hamilton was burned at the stake in February 1528.

Luther's and Melanchthon's Disciples in the Kingdom of Hungary

Not long after the posting of his Ninety-Five Theses on Indulgences, Luther's name and his challenge to medieval teaching and practice made an impact among the followers of Jan Hus in Bohemia. Positive reactions to his performance at the Leipzig Disputation came from Jan Poduška (d. 1520), a priest in Prague, and Wenzel von Roždalowski (d. 1520), provost of the Emperor Charles College in Prague; Roždalowski had been present at the disputation. Luther's writings spread and attracted support, resulting in a trickle of students beginning to go to Wittenberg.

In 1539, ***Leonhard Stöckel*** **(1510–1560)** returned to his native Bardejov in the county Zips in Upper Hungary (modern Slovakia) after an extended stay in Wittenberg. He had gone there in 1530 after preparatory education in Bardejov, Košice, and Breslau. He spent one year teaching in Eisleben but fell into dispute with Johann Agricola because of the latter's antinomian teaching. He returned to Wittenberg as a private tutor but then accepted a call to head the Latin school in Bardejov. He introduced a three-class system of instruction, adapting elements from the programs developed both by Melanchthon and by Johann Sturm in Strassburg. He wrote a number of works for use in the school, including a commentary on Melanchthon's *Loci communes*. This commentary pioneered the efforts to use Melanchthon's work as the basis for further teaching of Christian doctrine, as is exhibited most famously in the similar commentary by Martin Chemnitz. Stöckel's influence on education spread throughout the kingdom of Hungary. He actively promoted Luther's and Melanchthon's teaching in Upper Hungary. In 1546 the five free cities of his area accepted the Augsburg Confession and the *Loci* as their doctrinal standard. In 1548 these cities accepted the *Confessio Pentapolitana*, possibly composed by Stöckel, as well. It argued for the catholicity of Lutheran teaching. Stöckel opposed those who undermined the doctrine of justification by grace through faith in Jesus Christ, the spiritualizing definition of Christ's presence in the Lord's Supper, and antitrinitarianism in the several forms in which it was developing in the Hungarian realms. Stöckel's promotion of music and other disciplines in the liberal arts as well as his confession of the faith exercised profound influence in those realms.

Matthias Dévai (Dévay) **(ca. 1500–1545)** became a Franciscan after study at the University of Cracow (1523–26). He came to Wittenberg in 1529 but by 1531 had returned to the Hungarian lands and began preaching in Buda. He was arrested for preaching evangelical interpretations of Scripture in Košice in Slovakia. After extensive interrogation, he escaped prison in 1533 and returned to Buda, where he was again arrested. Upon his release in 1537, he traveled to Wittenberg and to Nuremberg, visiting VEIT DIETRICH, whom he had gotten to know while studying with Luther and MELANCHTHON. After teaching in Uj-Sziget, where he published a guide to the Hungarian language, he became chaplain for a Hungarian nobleman, Péter Perény, who was introducing reforms in the ecclesiastical life of his lands. He fled the threat of persecution in 1541, traveling to Wittenberg, Ansbach, and Basel. In 1541 Dévai returned to Hungarian territory. His views of the Lord's Supper began to express a spiritualizing understanding of Christ's presence, and that earned the criticism of LEONARD STÖCKEL. His works aided the spread of what he had learned in Wittenberg among Hungarian pastors and people.

These two and a few other contemporaries anticipated a flood of Hungarian and Slovakian students who attended the university in the years after Luther's death. They, along with the examples from the Nordic and British lands, demonstrate the wider appeal of the Wittenberg message.

CHAPTER 7

Princes Friendly and Hostile: Wittenberg's Engagement with Political Leadership

The unfolding developments of the sixteenth-century Reformation movements—Lutheran, Reformed, Anglican, Roman Catholic—were all intertwined (as was the entire medieval history of the church in Europe) with the political authorities. Medieval governmental authorities had commandeered the Christian faith as their public ideology, and so the relationships of church and secular governance worked sometimes for the benefit and sometimes for the detriment of one institution or the other. Among those rulers who played significant roles in the Reformation were some very pious princes and some scalawags as well as some at least outwardly pious scalawags. Some made it clear that they feared public disorder as well as dishonor for God from a theology of "grace alone." Others found the liberating message of the free forgiveness of sins a source of comfort and hope in the midst of the problems of families and individuals with political power in their hands. Some combined the traits of Wittenberg Reform with the policies of their predecessors, who had strengthened their role and control of the church in their lands over the preceding few centuries. This chapter presents glimpses into the lives of some of the most prominent who took on importance as supporters or opponents of the Wittenberg theologians.

Ernstine Saxon Rulers

***Frederick III, the Wise, Elector of Saxony* (1463–1525)**, inherited his lands and title from his father, Ernst, who had received these lands and title from his father, Frederick II. Frederick II had divided the possessions of the house of Wettin between Ernst and his younger brother Albrecht in 1485. The younger Frederick had attended the monastery school at Grimma, where he learned Latin and absorbed the influence of some of the earliest German proponents of biblical humanistic studies. He also learned French while at the court of Elector Archbishop Dieter II von Isenburg of Mainz, whose successor, Elector Archbishop Berthold, later joined the Saxon prince in working for reform in

Portrait of Frederick III the Wise by artist Albrecht Dürer (1524)

the German Empire that strengthened the powers of regional princes while limiting the expansionist dreams of Emperor Maximilian I. Frederick cultivated ties with humanists, including Erasmus, and artists such as Albrecht Dürer. His piety, honesty, and straightforwardness commanded widespread respect in the German Empire and beyond. In 1502, he founded the University of Wittenberg to serve his lands by training teachers, priests, physicians, and especially legal experts. The Saxon university, Leipzig, had fallen to Albrecht's family in the division of the electorate. In contrast to many princely siblings, Frederick and his brother Johann ruled their lands in harmony. Their cousin Georg, heir to Albert's part of Saxony, on the other hand, was a frequent antagonist, and this strained relationship worsened when Frederick and Johann did not suppress Luther's heresy. They also experienced no little hostility from their neighbor to the north, Elector Joachim I of Brandenburg, who managed to replace two younger Wettin brothers with his own brother, Albrecht, as archbishop of Magdeburg, administrator of the diocese of Halberstadt, and archbishop of Mainz. Elector Frederick seldom saw Luther and did not meet him personally, in part because Frederick seldom visited his castle in Wittenberg, preferring his castles in Torgau, where he had grown up, and in Altenburg. Frederick's own piety had taken him on pilgrimage to Jerusalem in the 1490s and 1517 and had led him to assemble a massive collection of relics, which offered those who patronized the collection in the foundation church attached to his Wittenberg castle enormous relief from purgatory. Frederick forbade the sale of the indulgence peddled by Johann Tetzel for the benefit of Albrecht of Mainz's debt reduction program and the building of the cathedral of Saint Peter in Rome. Therefore, Luther's attack on Tetzel seemed welcome despite its implied threat to Frederick's own parallel enterprise. Through Luther's friend Georg Spalatin, Frederick's trusted advisor, the professor and the prince communicated through the difficult days of 1518–21, in which Frederick protected his professor from ecclesiastical and imperial attacks. Frederick had political leverage since Emperor Maximilian was ill and then died on January 12, 1518. Frederick himself was advanced as a candidate for the imperial throne, and the other candidates, King Francis I of France, and Maximilian's grandson Charles, maneuvered for his support, which he finally lent to Charles. Frederick placed Luther in protective custody after the Diet of Worms in 1521. Luther strove to accommodate Frederick with opposition to the outbreak of violence in Wittenberg under the leadership of his colleague Andreas Karlstadt, which he also personally found abhorrent. Frederick never publicly declared his acceptance of Luther's teaching, but he did receive the Lord's Supper in both kinds at his death. Luther preached his funeral sermon.

Portrait of Johann the Steadfast by artist Lukas Cranach the Elder (1526)

***Johann the Steadfast, Elector of Saxony* (1468–1532)**, the brother of FREDERICK THE WISE, had received his education at several princely courts within the German Empire, including that of the emperor, the Habsburg Frederick III, his great-uncle. Johann served with his cousin MAXIMILIAN in military ventures and in other activities of the empire, although relationships between the two were strained by Maximilian's interference in Saxony's relationships with its neighbors. Johann worked closely with his brother and shared the rule at his side, differing from him, however, in his open and avid support of Luther's call for reform. The duke showed himself to be more rigorous in demanding strict adherence to the new piety than Luther himself at times. When Johann assumed the government of electoral Saxony at Frederick's death, he began to plan with his counselors and theologians at the university to visit the parishes of his domains to make certain that they were reforming practice and preaching according to Luther's direction. MELANCHTHON and Luther composed the "Saxon Visitation Articles" in 1528 to aid in the accomplishment of these goals. Johann actively pursued alliance with other evangelical princes, particularly with PHILIP OF HESSE, but he did insist that any defense of the faith be undertaken only with those who shared the faith. Therefore, he promoted reaching a statement of agreement regarding key elements of public teaching on which principalities could unite. The first result came in October of 1529 with the "Schwabach Articles," drawn up by Luther and Melanchthon in consort with theologians from Hesse and Brandenburg-Ansbach. Johann participated in the "*Protestatio*" of evangelical princes, a formal appeal for toleration of their reforms, that was composed at the imperial diet of Speyer in 1529, and he also led in the formulation and the presentation of the Augsburg Confession at the imperial diet in Augsburg in 1530. Luther's relationship with the elector remained close to the end, and the Reformer admired the prince as much as the prince admired the Reformer. Melanchthon also worked closely with Johann and the relationship of trust that bound the two remained firm to the elector's death.

***Johann Friedrich the Magnanimous, Elector of Saxony* (1503–1554),** son of JOHANN THE STEADFAST and his wife, Sophia, Duchess of Mecklenburg, grew up at his father's court in the shadow of the developing Reformation centered in Wittenberg, led by Martin Luther and PHILIP MELANCHTHON. Therefore, he dedicated his life to the defense and propagation of the faith that he had absorbed from them. He had assimilated less of his education in the humanistic arts and in the Latin and French languages than he had of the training in the military arts, jousting, and the related consumption of alcohol, a characteristic that earned him Luther's not always so subtle critique. Their warm relationship permitted such admonitions and also Luther's very explicit criticism of the behavior of many of the courtiers who ran the administration of Johann Friedrich's lands. Johann Friedrich married Sibylle, daughter of Duke Johann III of Jülich-Cleves, in 1526, and she provided him support and encouragement even in his imprisonment at the hands of EMPEROR CHARLES V toward the end of his life. When Johann Friedrich succeeded his father in 1532, he pursued much the same policies, promoting the evangelical cause wherever he could and providing active leadership to the Smalcald League of evangelical principalities and towns. His attempts to reconcile with Emperor Charles V and Charles's brother FERDINAND did not succeed. Thus, the Saxon elector prepared for the defense of his lands while at the same time actively supporting plans to reach agreement with the Habsburg brothers and their ecclesiastical associates through negotiations. This policy and pursuit climaxed at the religious colloquy in Regensburg in 1541. In league with LANDGRAVE PHILIP OF HESSE, Johann Friedrich had skirted the edges of legality, particularly in laying siege to the castle of DUKE HEINRICH OF BRAUNSCHWEIG-WOLFENBÜTTEL and ousting the duke from his rule after Heinrich had burned the imperial free city of

Portrait of Johann Friedrich the Magnanimous by Lukas Cranach the Elder (1531)

Einbeck to the ground in his attempt to stamp out its commitment to Luther's Reform. Thus, CHARLES V had a basis for declaring war on Johann Friedrich and Philip (also because of Philip's bigamy in violation of Roman law) in June 1546. Not all the allies in the Smalcald League supported them. Johann Friedrich's cousin MORITZ OF SAXONY, Philip's son-in-law, sided with the emperor, whose forces defeated those of the Smalcald League at the battle of Mühlberg in Saxony on April 24, 1547, truly a day of infamy. Charles condemned his two evangelical foes to death and then commuted their sentences, depriving Johann Friedrich of his electoral office and of half of his territory, which was assigned to Moritz. Johann Friedrich was released from a rather harsh imprisonment in 1552 and died two years later. Many of Luther's followers hailed him as a martyr, for he had throughout his life given witness to the faith that Luther had taught him as a child.

***Johann Friedrich the Middler, Duke of Saxony* (1529–1595)**, the oldest son of JOHANN FRIEDRICH THE MAGNANIMOUS, assumed rule of the reduced duchy that remained after the transfer of the electoral title and lands to his cousin, DUKE MORITZ OF SAXONY, in 1547. After Moritz fell in battle in 1553, Johann Friedrich the Middler married his widow, Agnes, daughter of PHILIP OF HESSE. She died two years after their wedding in 1555, and he then embarked on an affection-filled and supportive marriage to Elisabeth of the Palatinate, daughter of Elector Frederick III. Johann Friedrich the Middler directed the government along with his brothers JOHANN WILHELM and Johann Friedrich the Younger (1538–1565), whose sickliness rendered him ineffective as a ruler. Johann Friedrich the Middler had grown up in the atmosphere of his father's court, which centered its policies and activities around the reform led by Luther and Melanchthon. From his tutor BASILIUS MONNER he learned Greek and Hebrew as a child and mastered Luther's theology with a firm commitment to it. After the war, he energetically pursued the reorganization of his lands, founding in 1548 an academy in Jena that attained university status in 1558. MELANCHTHON declined to come to Jena to lead the new university, wishing instead to preserve the University of Wittenberg, the existence of which was in doubt since Moritz, who had taken over control of Wittenberg, could well have decided that his university in Leipzig sufficed for his lands. Melanchthon did recommend VIKTORIN STRIGEL for the Jena theological faculty and Johann Stigel for the faculty of the liberal arts. Johann Friedrich embarked on a course of strong support for those later labeled "Gnesio-Lutherans." Strigel and his colleague, the Hebrew instructor ERHARD SCHNEPF, supported the duke's policies, Schnepf more warmly than Strigel, who never broke his relationship with Melanchthon despite pursuing policies contrary to his preceptor's desires in the early 1550s. In 1557 Johann Friedrich began

Portrait of Johann Friedrich the Middler by Lukas Cranach the Younger as part of an altar panel in Herder Church (1555) in Weimar, Thuringia

expanding the theological faculty with the addition of Gnesio-Lutherans, chief among them MATTHIAS FLACIUS, but also JOHANNES WIGAND, SIMON MUSAEUS, and others. Strigel and Flacius fell into conflict, two wunderkinder in a small university and a small town. The duke proposed to end Lutheran conflict over the definition of key elements of the Wittenberg theology with a *Book of Confutation*, which focused on ending controversy by examining false views in these disputes. Strigel and Schnepf received the assignment to compose such a document and agreed with the provision that Flacius would not be able to revise it. Johann Friedrich, however, asked Flacius, Wigand, and others, along with two theologians from outside ducal Saxony, JOACHIM MÖRLIN and ERASMUS SARCERIUS, to do just that. Strigel's refusal to subscribe to the new confessional *Confutation* that Flacius and his team produced landed him in jail and subsequently led to the Weimar Disputation of August 1560. It ended inconsequentially when the eldest child of Johann Friedrich died. However, Flacius and his associates opposed ducal plans for a consistory with a majority of laymen in its membership, and this led to their being sent into exile in 1560 and 1561. Johann Friedrich's personal policy, at odds with that of his brother Johann Wilhelm, veered then away from Gnesio-Lutheran personnel though not decisively from their positions. Throughout his rule, Johann Friedrich the Middler agitated for the return of the lands and title that had fallen to Moritz and then his brother AUGUST after the Smalcald War. In the mid-1560s, Johann Friedrich entangled himself, on the advice of his chancellor CHRISTIAN BRÜCK, in the plans of the rebellious Wilhelm von Grumbach, a nobleman from lands south of Johann Friedrich's. At imperial command Johann Friedrich was besieged in his fortress, Grimmenstein, in 1567. When his troops mutinied, he was captured and spent the rest of his life in imperial prison, largely in Wiener Neustadt, along with his wife Elisabeth. His sons, Johann Casimir and Johann Ernst, did later assume rule over parts of his territories.

***Johann Wilhelm, Duke of Saxony* (1530–1573)**, the second son of JOHANN FRIEDRICH THE MAGNANIMOUS, demonstrated a more practical and less adventuresome character than his elder brother. He married DOROTHEA SUSANNA of the Palatinate, the sister of his brother's wife, and they cooperated closely in promoting the prosperity and welfare of their lands. In 1557 Johann Wilhelm surrendered his co-regency to his elder brother and spent the next two years in rather unsuccessful military service to the French royal family. Upon his return to Saxony in 1559 the policies of his brother caused him no little consternation, and so he forced a new division of powers and assumed rule in the southern part of the Saxon duchy, residing in Coburg. In his pursuit of a policy opposing the Calvinist tendencies of his father-in-law, he again sided with the French crown in its war against the Huguenots in France, with little success. The imperial government forced him to surrender some of his lands to the sons of JOHANN FRIEDRICH THE MIDDLER. Upon his accession to the rule of the entire duchy in 1567, Johann Wilhelm immediately restored the University of Jena's theological faculty to Gnesio-Lutherans, calling JOHANNES WIGAND back to Jena along with TILEMANN HESHUSIUS and two other like-minded theologians. Shortly before his death, he and AUGUST OF SAXONY arranged for a colloquy at Altenburg in an attempt to reconcile their theologians, who at the colloquy fell ever deeper into disagreement.

***Dorothea Susanna, Duchess of Saxony* (1544–1592)**, met her future husband, JOHANN WILHELM, Duke of Saxony, when he accompanied his elder brother to the court of her father, Elector Frederick III of the Palatinate, to marry her older sister, Elisabeth. She fiercely opposed her father's efforts to find a husband for her with views closer to his own developing Calvinistic theology and prevailed in her own determination to follow her heart. The happy marriage of JOHANN WILHELM and Dorothea Susanna brought her into conflict with her father over doctrinal issues, for she followed the commitment to Wittenberg theology as taught by the Gnesio-Lutherans with zeal and with a rather deep understanding of the issues involved. She functioned well as a "mother of her lands" and was particularly engaged in promoting the church and education. When Johann Wilhelm died, she was drawn into fierce confrontations with ELECTOR AUGUST OF SAXONY, who assumed rule of ducal Saxony as well as his own territories and took over as the guardian of Dorothea Susanna's sons. August dismissed many of the pastors and all of the professors who represented her views, but she continued to rely on JOHANNES WIGAND and TILEMANN HESHUSIUS as they sought refuge elsewhere, and others, including Caspar Melissander,

Portrait of Dorothea Susanna, Duchess of Saxony, by artist Christoff Leutloff (1575)

her sons' tutor, served as advisors and supporters as August strove to restrict her influence. By 1576 she had reclaimed at least some of her ability to direct the religious life of her husband's territories. With Melissander as her penman, she had a confession of the faith composed, which JAKOB ANDREAE, MARTIN CHEMNITZ, and others found in agreement with the *Formula of Concord*, which they authored in 1577.

Albertine Saxon Rulers

The Wettin family had two branches. The Albertine branch strove to gain power over against the Ernstine branch from the division of Saxony in 1485, and the Reformation exacerbated the rivalry, initially because of the animosity of ***Georg, Duke of Saxony*** (1471–1539), toward his Ernstine cousins. Georg inherited the smaller half of the lands of his grandfather, Elector Frederick II, from his father Albrecht; from his mother, Sidonia, daughter of King Georg Podiebrad of Bohemia, he inherited a familiarity with the Bohemian reform movement that arose out of the preaching of Jan Hus. Georg wished at all costs to prevent the military action in which his father-in-law had participated in defense of the Hussite cause. Georg's wife, Barbara, daughter of King Casimir IV of Poland, and he enjoyed a close relationship. His piety also led him to oppose Luther; he feared that the populace would abandon proper behavior because of the message of salvation by grace through faith in Christ alone. In addition, he sincerely supported the practices and polity of the medieval church. His jealousy of his Wettin cousin, FREDERICK THE WISE, did nothing to dampen this opposition. He freely expressed his hatred for his cousin, Frederick's brother JOHANN THE STEADFAST. Georg decided to sponsor the disputation between JOHANN ECK and the Wittenberg faculty in 1519 because he believed that the church should not suppress public airing of the issues and so that people would not be deceived by the Wittenberg teaching. In subsequent years, his fear of the disorder that he believed Luther's rejection of papal authority would cause moved him to publish attacks on Wittenberg Reform under his own name. He also promoted the publication of anti-Lutheran polemic by his court preachers or advisors, JOHANNES COCHLAEUS, HIERONYMUS EMSER, and GEORG WITZEL. The duke and Luther exchanged sharp epistolary attacks on each other. Georg organized military alliances to oppose the Wittenberg movement and strove to prevent his brother HEINRICH from succeeding him since Heinrich had become an open follower of Wittenberg theology. However, Georg's two sons died before he did, and these efforts came to naught.

Portrait of Georg, Duke of Saxony, by Lukas Cranach the Elder (ca. 1534)

Elisabeth of Hesse, Duchess of Saxony (Elisabeth von Rochlitz) **(1502–1557)**, daughter of Landgrave Wilhem the Middler of Hesse and Elisabeth of Mecklenburg, was married to Duke Johann of Saxony, son of Duke Georg, in 1517 and lived from that year on at the ducal court in Dresden. She and Johann had no children. She followed her brother, Philip of Hesse, into the ranks of Luther's followers, however, and thus encountered the enraged hostility of her father-in-law. Her husband maintained that he staunchly defended the old faith as well, but his love for food and drink in excess diminished his influence at court. In the midst of continual tensions with Georg, Elisabeth strove to bring his theologians into a dialogue with those of electoral Saxony in Wittenberg. During this time, she avidly read Luther's writings and discussed his thought with her brother Philip in letters, despite Georg's threats that he would lock her up in the dungeon. Her troubled relationship with Duke Georg improved after the death of his wife, Barbara, and one of their daughters in 1534. She mediated a dispute between him and Elector Johann Friedrich in 1536. When Johann died in 1537, she left the court in Dresden and administered a small part of the duchy centered at Rochlitz, where she promptly introduced the Reformation. In 1546 Georg's nephew Moritz rejected her pleas and arguments for not entering into alliance with Emperor Charles against the Smalcald League, which she had joined. Moritz occupied her lands and deposed her, but two years later she was awarded an annual pension. She ended her life in the domains of her brother Philip, in contact with Wittenberg theologians as she had been for years.

After failing in his attempts to administer the family lands in Frisia, and therefore surrendering them to his elder brother in 1505, Duke Georg's younger brother, ***Heinrich, Duke of Saxony* (1473–1541)**, gained popularity among his subjects in the small area around the mining town of Freiberg that was granted him by Georg. In part because of his musical gifts, he won a reputation as a prince more interested in enjoying festivities than in exercising his administrative duties as ruler. He had grown up formed by typical medieval pious practices and made pilgrimages to Jerusalem and Compostella. Heinrich hesitantly and slowly became more and more interested in Luther's proclamation of faith in Christ under the influence of his wife, Katharina. In 1531, while visiting his cousin Elector Johann, he requested to hear Luther preach. A visit in 1534 to the court in Wittenberg turned Heinrich decisively to the Wittenberg Reformation. When his brother died in 1539, Heinrich quickly moved to introduce the Reformation in all of ducal Saxony, as he had already done in Freiberg and his other domains. A team of visitors that included Luther, Justus Jonas, Friedrich Myconius, and others led parishes into reforming the teaching and practice of the faith.

Portraits of Heinrich, Duke of Saxony, and his wife Katharina of Mecklenburg by artist Lukas Cranach the Elder (1514)

Heinrich's wife, ***Katharina of Mecklenburg, Duchess of Saxony*** **(1487–1561)**, the fourth daughter of Duke Magnus II of Mecklenburg and sister of Anna, the mother of LANDGRAVE PHILIP OF HESSE, and Sophia, the wife of ELECTOR JOHANN OF SAXONY and mother of ELECTOR JOHANN FRIEDRICH, married the younger brother of DUKE GEORG OF SAXONY in 1512. She bore him three daughters and then three sons. MORITZ succeeded his father, Severin died quite young, and AUGUST succeeded Moritz. After Heinrich removed three of her ladies-in-waiting for reading Luther's writings in 1523, Katharina apparently dedicated herself to examining the Reformer's ideas more carefully. By 1525, she was maneuvering in the treacherous waters of the politics surrounding her brother-in-law in order to defend some of the individuals whom he was trying to persecute for their commitment to Luther's Reform. As her husband committed himself to Luther's Reform, she was able to place the Wittenberg student Jacob Schenk as court preacher in Freiberg and worked with him to establish Luther's understanding of the teaching and practice of the church among the populace. The friction between Georg and his brother and sister-in-law over their promotion of Luther's theology ended with the former's death in 1539. Katharina actively supported Heinrich's introduction of the Reformation with the help of a visitation team from electoral Saxony in the following two years. Heinrich and Katharina considered arranging a marriage of their oldest son, Moritz, to Agnes, daughter of Landgrave Philip of Hesse and his wife, Christine of Saxony, but finally rejected the idea. Moritz secretly traveled to Philip's court to pursue the marriage himself, in defiance of his parents. After Heinrich's death, the relationship between Moritz and his mother was proper and respectful but not close. On the other hand, she developed a strong relationship with her son August and the wife she had helped find for him, Anna of Denmark. In the two decades she spent as a widow, she traveled often in promoting family interests and in furthering Luther's cause.

Duke Heinrich was succeeded by his older son, ***Moritz, Duke, then Elector of Saxony* (1521–1553)**, who married Agnes, daughter of Philip of Hesse and Moritz's cousin Christine, without the approval of his parents. He spent much of his youth at the courts of his uncle Duke Georg, electors Johann and Johann Friedrich, and Archbishop Albrecht of Mainz. His enjoyment of alcohol and his affairs with women suggest that he did not take the religious commitment of his parents seriously, although he showed no inclination toward a return of his lands to the Roman obedience. He did not continue his father's commitment to the Smalcald League but assisted his father-in-law and his cousin Elector Johann Friedrich of Saxony in the action that dethroned Duke Heinrich the Younger of Braunschweig-Wolfenbüttel. Moritz established a good relationship with Emperor Charles V by fighting against the Turks in 1542 and against France in 1543. He employed counselors who had advised his uncle Duke Georg, who had remained fiercely loyal to the papal obedience. Among these counselors whom Moritz inherited were Georg von Carlowitz and his nephew Christoph. They steered Moritz into a pro-Habsburg attitude that resulted in the alliance that produced a victory for Moritz and the emperor over Moritz's cousin Johann Friedrich and his father-in-law Philip in the Smalcald War. In 1547, Charles V awarded Moritz a large portion of Johann Friedrich's lands, including Wittenberg, and the title, duties, and privileges of the electoral office. Melanchthon and

Portrait of Duke Moritz by Lukas Cranach the elder

his colleagues in Wittenberg, who wished to preserve their university, supported Moritz in his search for a religious policy that would stave off imperial occupation of Saxony and the end of Lutheran preaching there. Moritz set loose a fiery storm of criticism with his "Proposal" for the Saxon diet that met in Leipzig in December 1548. The nobility and towns of the electorate rejected this proposal, labeled "the Leipzig Interim" when it was leaked by its opponents, and Moritz himself became ever more disappointed with and alienated from CHARLES and his brother FERDINAND. He managed to end the criticism pouring from the presses of Magdeburg through a peace agreement that ended his three-year siege. In 1552, he helped form an alliance that joined the French monarchy with several German princes to oppose the emperor. This alliance forced FERDINAND of Habsburg to grant the Truce of Passau in 1552, ending the imperial policies that aimed at the eradication of Lutheran Reform after the Smalcald War. His former friend and ally Margrave Albrecht Alcibiades of Brandenburg-Kulmbach led his troops into surrounding territories to expand his own domain, and Moritz went to battle against him in league with Ferdinand of Habsburg. Though his forces defeated the margrave, Moritz was fatally wounded at the battle at Sievershausen in July 1553.

Tensions between Moritz and his brother August over the younger brother's rights did not alienate the two, so ***August, Elector of Saxony*** **(1526–1586)**, assumed his office at Moritz's unexpected death in 1553 with some experience in administration but with significantly less daring and fewer dreams of creating his own empire in the central German lands than his brother had had. The debts accumulated by Moritz provided one of his first challenges as ruler. August carefully tended to commercial and mining interests in his lands, and the Saxon economy gained strength under his stewardship. August also revealed a much stronger commitment to Luther's theology and to his moral standards than had

Moritz. At age fifty, August's curiosity regarding cabalistic interpretation led him to study Hebrew. He sought reconciliation with his cousins, Johann Friedrich and his sons, who had been reduced through their defeat in the Smalcald War from elector to duke, concluding a treaty in Naumburg with them in 1554. Prominent in the negotiations that led to the Peace of Augsburg and its concession of a legal, if inferior, status for adherents of the Augsburg Confession (1555), August strove to provide leadership for the evangelical governments of the empire in the following years. The elector took interest in the theological debates of the time and defended his own theologians, particularly those in Wittenberg but also those in Leipzig, against charges that they were deserting Luther's teaching. August took action against critics of his theologians, including Cyriakus Spangenberg, whose arrest he ordered in vain because of the support of the counts of Mansfeld for their man. As proof mounted in the early 1570s that indeed the electoral Saxon theologians were divided by the tendency of some, led by Christoph Pezel and Caspar Peucer in Wittenberg, to lay Luther's teaching on the true presence of Christ's body and blood in the Lord's Supper aside, August and his wife, Anna of Denmark, reacted vehemently. They felt personally insulted and deceived by some of their most trusted advisees, including the chancellor of the electorate, Georg Cracow, some leading university instructors, and Peucer, who served as August and Anna's personal physician and was baptismal sponsor for one of their children. This spiritualizing movement threatened the status of the electorate under the Peace of Augsburg in addition to being a betrayal of the trust accorded them by the electoral pair. August imprisoned Cracow and Peucer, along with one of his court preachers, Christian Schütz, and a leading churchman, Johannes Stössel. Fourteen other prominent pastors or university professors went into exile when they refused to sign the new confession on the Lord's Supper

Portrait of August, Elector of Saxony, by Lukas Cranach the Younger (ca. 1564)

authored by others within the electoral Saxon ecclesiastical establishment. In order to reaffirm the electorate's commitment to Luther's theology, August borrowed JAKOB ANDREAE from DUKE CHRISTOPH OF WÜRTTEMBERG for five years. Andreae not only directed the reform of Saxony but also with the aid of August and other princes provided leadership that led to the composition of the *Formula of Concord* and the publication of the *Book of Concord.*

***Anna of Denmark, Electress of Saxony* (1532–1585)**, daughter of KING CHRISTIAN III OF DENMARK and sister of his successor, FREDERICK II, had been raised at the Danish court as it was establishing Wittenberg Reform throughout the kingdom. Married to AUGUST OF SAXONY in 1548, she gave birth to fifteen children, four of whom survived to adulthood. She experimented with medicinal formulas and promoted gardening in the "Danish-Dutch" style, especially the cultivation of fruit. She directed the electoral household in exemplary

Portrait of Anna of Denmark, Duchess of Saxony, by Lukas Cranach the Younger (after 1565)

manner and played an active role in August's rule, accompanying him on most of his journeys. Her encouragement for the development of Saxon textile production contributed much to Saxon economic development. Her collection of books, largely religious, gives evidence of her widespread interests and deep piety. She supported August in his religious policy. Upon learning that those trying to introduce a spiritualized view of the Lord's Supper had particularly targeted the woman in the ruling couple, she reacted sharply against this undermining of her own convictions and actively promoted the return to Luther's teaching.

Other Rulers Who Subscribed to the Augsburg Confession or Gave It Early Support

In addition to electors Johann of Saxony and Johann Friedrich, five other princes of the empire signed the Augsburg Confession in June 1530: Philip of Hesse, Ernst of Braunschweig-Lüneburg and his brother Franz, Georg of Brandenburg-Ansbach, and Wolfgang of Anhalt. Relatives of the latter two also deserve mention among Luther's most prominent supporters.

***Philip the Magnanimous, Landgrave of Hesse* (1504–1567)**, succeeded his father and his incapable uncle as ruler of the entire landgraviate of Hesse when he was five years old. His mother, Anna of Mecklenburg, guided him through a ten-year regency. He formed a close relationship with Duke Georg of Saxony, whose daughter Christine he married in 1524; Philip's sister Elisabeth married Georg's elder son Johann. Although his formal education seems to have been minimal, he became a devoted reader of the Bible at a young age. Emperor Maximilian proclaimed him capable of ruling at age fourteen. The first years of rule were disturbed by the forces under the command of Franz von Sickingen, whom he decisively defeated in 1523, in league with the electors of the Palatinate and Trier. Philip continued to offer military leadership to surrounding princes, including crucial and rapid suppression of revolting peasants in 1525. He had conferred with Luther at the Diet of Worms in 1521 and informed himself on the development of Wittenberg theology. His decision to support Luther's Reform in 1524 alienated him from his father-in-law but placed him alongside the Saxon electors at the forefront of the political leaders of the Wittenberg Reformation. In 1526, Philip gathered Reformers from his territories at a synod in Homberg, where the basis of a new order for church and social welfare was laid, although Luther's criticism of the multiplication of regulations contained in the ordinances of Homberg induced Philip to desist from full implementation. The following year he established the University of

Marburg and staffed it with sympathizers of Wittenberg Reform. His ardent efforts to bring Luther and ULRICH ZWINGLI together to enable a pan-Protestant political alliance against Roman Catholic forces culminated in the Marburg Colloquy of 1529, where these two Reformers and their close associates came to agreement on a series of issues but remained in disagreement on the Lord's Supper. Philip depended ever more on MARTIN BUCER of Strasburg to lead his efforts to bring together a wider spectrum of evangelicals. His hopes were partially fulfilled with the Wittenberg Concord of 1536. At the diet of Speyer in 1529 Philip helped construct the evangelical "*Protestatio*," and in 1530 he supported and signed the Augsburg Confession. He advanced the cause of the Reformation by lending military aid to Duke Ulrich of Württemberg in his efforts to reclaim his duchy from Habsburg occupation in 1534. Philip and his advisors played significant roles in Ulrich's introduction of the Reformation. His forces also contributed to the military defeat of the Anabaptist kingdom

Portrait of Philip, Landgrave of Hesse, by artist Hans Krell (ca. 1534)

in Münster in 1535. With ELECTOR JOHANN FRIEDRICH OF SAXONY, the Hessian landgrave went to war against DUKE HEINRICH OF BRAUNSCHWEIG-WOLFENBÜTTEL, his former friend, because of the latter's use of military force against reform in the town of Einbeck and threats of military action against other evangelical governments. In 1542 Philip and Johann Friedrich occupied Heinrich's lands. However, Philip's position was significantly weakened by his bigamous marriage to his mistress, Margarethe von der Saale. This played a role in the imperial defeat of Hesse and electoral Saxony in 1547 in the Smalcald War. Not all their allies in the Smalcald League supported them after EMPEROR CHARLES V outlawed the two leaders in 1546; Philip's own son-in-law MORITZ, Duke of Saxony, betrayed the alliance and, through support of Emperor Charles in the war, successfully sought to gain the title and lands of his cousin Johann Friedrich. Philip spent five years in often severe confinement. After his release, he concentrated his energies on rebuilding his own lands.

***Ernst the Confessor, Duke of Braunschweig-Lüneburg* (1497–1546)**, whose mother Margarethe was the sister of FREDERICK THE WISE OF SAXONY, was raised at his uncle's court in Torgau. He spent nearly six years at the University of Wittenberg early in Luther's career there (1512–18). After more than two years at the court of King Francis I of France, Ernst returned to assume rule alongside his father in their duchy. His father, Heinrich, abdicated in 1532 in favor of Ernst and his younger brothers Otto and Franz. Franz had joined Ernst in signing the "*Protestatio*" in Speyer in 1529 and the Augsburg Confession in 1530. Otto renounced his right to rule in 1539, Franz in 1542. Abuses and

Portrait of Ernst the Confessor by artist Lukas Cranach the Elder (sixteenth century)

mismanagement during their father's reign had brought the duchy unrest and economic crisis, and this situation remained a challenge throughout his own rule. Luther's understanding of the gospel and his plans for reform attracted Ernst early on, and the two formed a friendship. In 1526, Ernst began taking over the administration of cloisters in his lands. Out of a conversation with the Reformer during Ernst's visit to Saxony in 1527 came more concrete moves toward reform. At the diet in Augsburg in 1530 Ernst had gotten to know URBANUS RHEGIUS, pastor in Augsburg, and asked him to come to his court in Celle to implement reform. Rhegius complied, and the duke and the theologian formed a team that not only changed the shape of church and society in Braunschweig-Lüneburg but also diffused their influence to surrounding lands and towns.

***Georg the Pious or the Confessor, Margrave of Brandenburg-Ansbach* (1484–1543)**, spent time as the younger son of Friedrich the Elder of Brandenburg-Ansbach at the

Portrait of George the Pious by Lukas Cranach the Younger (dated 1571)

courts of Landgrave Wilhelm of Hesse and of his uncle King Wladyslaw of Bohemia and Hungary. He married Beatrix, widow of the son of Matthäus Corvinus of Hungary, and served as negotiator and mediator in several disputes in Poland and the Hungarian lands in the early 1520s. He assisted his brother ALBRECHT, who was serving as the master of the Teutonic Knights, in secularizing his lands and introducing the Reformation. After Beatrix's death, Georg married Duchess Hedwig of Münsterberg, and after her death, Aemilie, daughter of DUKE HEINRICH and DUCHESS KATHARINA OF SAXONY. When his elder brother Kasimir died in 1527, Georg assumed the rule over his heavily indebted lands and continued projects that he had begun earlier to rebuild their economic situation. He supported the introduction of Luther's Reform in his lands in the early 1520s and coordinated these efforts with neighboring Nuremberg, for instance, in the common church ordinances introduced in 1533. He joined in the evangelical "*Protestatio*" at the imperial diet of Speyer in 1529. His counselors cooperated with Saxon representatives in the preparation of the Schwabach Articles as a basis for an evangelical defensive league in October 1529, a document that served as a foundation for the text of the Augsburg Confession. At the diet of Augsburg, he knelt before EMPEROR CHARLES V and confessed that he would rather be beheaded than surrender his faith; he signed the Augsburg Confession at the diet. Although in his youth he had a reputation as one who partied too much, his personal piety set him apart as he assumed leadership in his margravate and inspired many.

Portrait of Albrecht, Margrave of Brandenburg-Ansbach, by Lukas Cranach the Elder (1528)

***Albrecht, Margrave of Brandenburg-Ansbach, Master of the Teutonic Knights, Duke in Prussia* (1490–1568)**, younger brother of GEORG OF BRANDENBURG-ANSBACH, became a canon in the cathedral foundation in Cologne in 1506, participated in military action under EMPEROR MAXIMILIAN I in Italy in 1508, and as a result of negotiations conducted by his oldest brother, Kasimir, became master of the Teutonic Knights and ruler of the order's extensive holdings on the southeast coast of the Baltic Sea in 1511. Hostilities with Poland and a widespread peasant revolt unsettled the early years of his rule, but he ended these conflicts and thereafter preserved peace for his principality. The influence of his brother Georg and the preaching of ANDREAS OSIANDER, whom he heard while visiting Nuremberg, brought him to accept Luther's proclamation of the gospel. In 1525, after consultation with Luther and others, he secularized the order's lands and assumed the title of duke under the feudal lordship of the king of Poland. CHARLES V placed him under imperial ban, but he moved freely about the empire despite his status as outlaw. His marriage to Dorothea, daughter of KING FREDERICK I OF DENMARK, cemented his ties to Lutheran rulers. His second wife was Anna Maria, the daughter of ELISABETH OF BRANDENBURG, Duchess of Braunschweig-Calenberg, and her husband, Duke Erich I. Albrecht took measures to strengthen the economy of his Prussian domains, and in 1544 he founded a university in Königsberg, his capital. GEORG SABINUS, MELANCHTHON's son-in-law, taught in its liberal arts faculty and served three years as its first rector. The duke cultivated a program of music and the arts at his court that culturally enriched his lands. When the Augsburg Interim forced Osiander from Nuremberg, Albrecht welcomed him to Königsberg and placed him on the university faculty. Osiander's personality and theology gave offense and enveloped him, the duke, and the dukedom in controversy. Albrecht exiled Osiander's opponents and promoted those who supported his theology. Osiander's supporter and Albrecht's court chaplain Johann Funcke and the visiting polymalth and mystic, the Croatian Paul Scalich (1534-1575),, who capitalized in Albrecht's interest in astrology and the occult, produced more conflict between the court and the nobles and towns of Prussia. After several years of tensions, Funcke was executed and Scalich fled Prussia. In 1567, shortly before his death, the duke recalled two of Osiander's opponents, JOACHIM MÖRLIN and MARTIN CHEMNITZ, to dismantle the Osiandrian teaching and practice.

Wolfgang, Prince of Anhalt **(1492–1566)**, studied at the University of Leipzig and assumed rule of his father's lands at his death in 1508. His sister Margarethe married Johann of Saxony and thus strengthened Wolfgang's connections to the electoral Saxon court, where he had become acquainted with Luther's call for reform and began to support it in the early 1520s. The Saxon electors named him a privy counselor. He worked hard to improve the conditions of the church and its pastors in the 1520s and 1530s and participated in the *"Protestatio"* at the imperial diet of Speyer as well as the Diet of Augsburg in 1530, where he signed the Augsburg Confession. His participation in the Smalcald League

Portrait of Wolfgang, Prince of Anhalt, by the Cranach school (sixteenth century)

ended in disaster after its defeat by imperial forces in 1547. Only at high financial cost and personal sacrifice was he able to regain rule of his lands. As ELECTOR MORITZ OF SAXONY lay siege to Magdeburg, Wolfgang took part in the mediation between the two sides in late 1550. His last years he dedicated to the restoration and strengthening of his own lands.

Wolfgang's cousin, ***Georg III, the Pious, Prince of Anhalt* (1507–1553)**, did not sign the Augsburg Confession, but as the only ordained member of a princely family among the Wittenberg Reformers and a gifted theologian, he, too, contributed much to the Wittenberg Reformation. Georg lost his father when he was eight years old; his mother, Margarethe, Duchess of Münsterberg, sister of URSULA OF MÜNSTERBERG, advocated reform of ecclesiastical life but fiercely opposed Luther's version of improving the church. Georg became a canon in the foundation at Merseburg in 1518 and its leader in 1524. ARCHBISHOP ALBRECHT named him to the cathedral chapter in Magdeburg in 1529. With his two older brothers, he became committed to Luther's movement, but the three waited until after the death of their mother in 1530 to confess their views publicly and to introduce the Reformation into their lands (1532). Georg began studies in canon law in 1519 and taught himself theology through extensive reading over the years. In 1544, DUKE AUGUST OF SAXONY became secular administrator of the bishopric of Merseburg, and Georg assumed the office of spiritual administrator, from which he was removed after the defeat of the Smalcald League in 1547. Luther had ordained him to the office. Georg's dedicated work of practical reform gave the church in Anhalt a conservative liturgy, a theological cast reflecting MELANCHTHON's views, and a good system of schools. His doctrine of the Lord's Supper included a strong defense of the true presence of Christ's body and blood in the sacramental elements. He aided and supported his colleagues in Wittenberg in formulating and defending the Leipzig "Interim." His assistance in the reform of the electorate of Brandenburg lent that same conservative cast to its church, preserving medieval liturgical elements and practices wherever possible while retaining Luther and Melanchthon's view of justification by faith.

The Hohenzollern Family of Brandenburg

Neighbors and rivals of the electors of Saxony, the cousins of GEORG OF BRANDENBURG-ANSBACH, the margraves of Brandenburg with their primary seat in Spandau on the Spree, provide an example of the complicated personal relationships within a family in the troubled time of the Reformation. ***Joachim I, Elector of Brandenburg* (1484–1535)**, son of Elector Johann Cicero and Margarethe, daughter of Wilhelm III, of a collateral line of the Saxon Wettin family, departed his parents' court as a boy for the court of his father's cousin in Franconia, Friedrich the Elder of Brandenburg-Ansbach. There he acquired a humanistic education that made him a convincing speaker and shrewd strategist. The early death of his father placed him in a critical position. He personally negotiated the marriage contract with King Johann of Denmark for the hand of his daughter Elisabeth. Against the provisions of the "Golden Bull" of 1356, the constitutional document guiding imperial governance, he brought his younger brother ALBRECHT into his government and engineered Albrecht's acquisition as a minor of the archbishopric of Magdeburg, the post of administrator of the foundation of Halberstadt, and the archbishopric of Mainz. The two were quite different in personality: the elder brother daring, shrewd, strong-willed, and ready to use power to his full advantage; the younger more interested in the arts, with a mild approach

Portrait of Joachim I by artist Lukas Cranach the Elder (1529)

to policy formulation and difficulty in coming to decisions. Joachim pursued a number of measures to strengthen his family, the Hohenzollerns, in addition to his promotion of his brother. He arranged for his four Franconian cousins to assume a variety of posts, including that of master of the Teutonic Knights, which Albrecht, son of Friedrich the Elder, became. Joachim furthered his domains and his own power through many measures, including the founding the University of Frankfurt an der Oder in 1506. He suppressed robber barons among the Brandenburg nobility, executing some seventy of them in an initial crackdown and more later. He diminished the powers exercised by their class in general. His persecution of Jews in 1510 was carried out with cruel decisiveness. His rejection of Luther led him to forbid all the Reformer's writings, including Luther's Bible translation, in his lands and to enter into a series of military alliances designed to suppress the Reformation. His strict position led his wife, Elisabeth, to flee to Wittenberg. His counselor Achatius Brandenburg was said to be his illegitimate son. His affair with the wife of a leading citizen of Berlin, Katharina Hornung, who bore him two other children, became a public scandal, to which Luther contributed published criticism. His astrological interests led him to employ Melanchthon's friend, Johann Carion, author of a chronicle of world history, as a member of his advisory circle. His attempt to obligate his sons Joachim and Johann to remain with the Roman church failed; both became warm supporters of Luther.

***Elisabeth of Denmark, Electress of Brandenburg* (1485–1555)**, daughter of King Johann of Denmark and his wife, Christina of Saxony, niece of Frederick the Wise and his brother Johann, married Joachim I, Elector of Brandenburg, in 1502. Her unpopular brother, Christian II, succeeded their father in 1513 and pursued a political course that led him to spend time with Luther in Wittenberg. His wife, Isabella, sister of Emperor Charles V, had become attached to Luther's interpretation of Scripture. Their association also won Elisabeth to Luther's understanding of the Christian faith, although she had earlier practiced her faith in a typical medieval manner, receiving with gratitude, for example, a piece of the holy cross from her brother-in-law Albrecht, archbishop of Mainz, in 1518. Her path to her strong commitment to Luther's teaching was not recorded, but by 1527 she was secretly receiving the Lord's Supper in both kinds, a sign of her commitment to Luther's teaching. As it became evident to her husband, he strove patiently to dissuade her and win her back to his equally strong faith in the medieval practices with which they had both been raised. But his temperament was, in principle, not tolerant of diverging opinions, and he increasingly made Elisabeth's life at the Brandenburg court difficult. In March 1528, she fled secretly and made her way to the Saxon court in Torgau. This

Elisabeth of Denmark by unknown artist

caused unwelcome political tensions for Elector Johann, but he and particularly his son JOHANN FRIEDRICH supported Elisabeth. Cut off from all her income by her husband, she was essentially impoverished, since her brother had been imprisoned in Denmark by their uncle, FREDERICK I, who only slowly revealed his inclination to Luther's theology. Elisabeth turned to Luther for counsel on many decisions. Oppressed by severe melancholy, the electress lived for a while in the Black Cloister with the Luther family, and KATHARINA VON BORA patiently nursed her during a long period of illness in 1537, in which Luther sadly noted her childishness. When Joachim I died in 1535, Elisabeth's sons, JOACHIM II and Johann, urged her to return to Brandenburg, but she refused unless she could introduce Wittenberg Reforms to the lands over which she would exercise jurisdiction. Joachim II was not yet willing to do that, having promised his father to remain faithful to the old faith, so Elisabeth did not leave Saxony until 1545. Her melancholy had receded, but physical ailments plagued the last decade of her life. Until her death in 1555 she continued to lend active support to the advance of the Wittenberg Reformation.

Electress Elisabeth's daughter, ***Elisabeth of Brandenburg, Duchess of Braunschweig-Calenberg-Göttingen* (1510–1558)**, enjoyed a thorough, humanistically shaped education as a child in the company of her brothers, Joachim II and Johann, and her sisters. At age fifteen she was married to the fifty-five-year-old Duke Erich I of the duchy of Braunschweig-Calenberg-Göttingen, a widower without children, who needed a male successor to ward off the claims of his nephew, Duke Heinrich of Braunschweig-Wolfenbüttel.

Portraits of Duke Erich I of Brunswick-Calenberg and Duchess Elisabeth, Princess of Brandenburg

Their second child became Duke Erich II; he had three sisters. Erich returned to an earlier mistress, causing Elisabeth no little distress, which was compounded by charges that she practiced black magic. The penitent Erich awarded her more territory as her personal fief, and she exercised there something close to complete sovereignty. While visiting her mother in Lichtenberg in 1534, Elisabeth met Luther and began exchanging letters with him. At the same time, her brother Johann was urging her to accept Luther's interpretation of Scripture. She called a disciple of Luther, ANTON CORVINUS, to her residence in Münden, and in 1538 introduced communion in both kinds. Unlike Elisabeth's father's treatment of her mother, Erich tolerated his wife's departure from the old faith. After his death in 1540 and with the aid of PHILIP OF HESSE, she led the reform of ecclesiastical life in her lands, against the protests of Heinrich. He was given responsibility for the raising of Elisabeth's son, the future Duke Erich II. She herself wrote a foreword for the church ordinances that Corvinus prepared for her church. She also prepared a lengthy work directing her son on how to rule in accord with God's will, a "mirror of the prince" that demonstrated how well she had learned the theology being propagated in Wittenberg. Her son paid little attention. In the Smalcald War he fought on the imperial side against the Smalcald League, and in 1549 declared himself a follower of the papacy. He separated himself from his wife, Sidonia of Saxony, daughter of HEINRICH OF SAXONY and his wife, KATHERINA. Erich's self-indulgence in wasteful spending made him a weak ruler. He did arrest Anton Corvinus and burned his library. The widowed Elisabeth married Count Poppo of Henneberg, a dedicated follower of Luther, and had her daughter Anna Maria married to DUKE ALBRECHT OF PRUSSIA. For them she wrote a book on marriage. She sided with Margrave Albert Alcibiades of Brandenburg-Kulmbach against dukes HEINRICH OF BRAUNSCHWEIG-WOLFENBÜTTEL and MORITZ OF SAXONY in a feud that culminated in the battle of Sievershausen in 1553. Heinrich lost his two older sons and Moritz his life in the battle, as did Albert Alcibiades, but Heinrich emerged the victor and deprived Elisabeth of all her possessions. She was reduced to poverty and fled to Ilmenau, in Poppo's lands. Her final years saw a brief reconciliation with her son, who then turned against her again. She remained faithful to Luther's Reform to the end.

***Joachim II, Elector of Brandenburg* (1505–1571)**, received his education at his parents' court. In 1519, he met Luther and carried favorable impressions away from that encounter. His cousin, ALBRECHT, who became duke of Prussia and introduced the Reformation to his lands, reinforced the influence of his mother, ELISABETH OF DENMARK, to open his way to the Wittenberg Reformation, in opposition to the insistence of his father that he remain faithful to the papacy. The paternal influence was buttressed by the equally strong allegiance of his father-in-law, Duke Georg of Saxony, whose daughter Magdalena Joachim married in 1524. When she died in 1535, leaving behind four of the seven children to whom she had given birth, Joachim married Hedwig, the daughter of King Sigismund I Jagiellonian of Poland. Sigismund also demanded an oath of loyalty to the Roman church from his son-in-law. In 1551 Hedwig was severely injured, and subsequently Anna Sydow functioned publicly in performing the duties of the electress. Joachim's successful leadership of an imperial army against the Turkish forces near Habsburg borders in 1532 won him a good relationship with Charles V, but the defeat of forces under his command by the Turk in 1542 tarnished his military reputation. Like his uncle, Albrecht, archbishop of Mainz, the younger Joachim enjoyed the good life, including the arts, and was

Portrait of Joachim II, Elector of Brandenburg, by Lukas Cranach the Younger (ca. 1570)

generous in his expenditures for enhancement of churches in Brandenburg. When MELANCHTHON demonstrated in 1539 that JOACHIM I's grounds for his suppression of the Jews in 1510 had as its foundation a false report regarding a desecration of the host, Joachim II responded positively to the request of JOSEL VON ROSHEIM to readmit Jews to his lands. Four years after assuming the electoral throne in 1535, Joachim II received the Lord's Supper in both kinds and began installing sympathizers of Luther as leaders of his church. He helped negotiate the "Frankfurt Armistice" of 1539, in which Charles V granted breathing room to the members of the Smalcald League in their practice of Luther's Reform. Joachim's general stance remained conservative in liturgical practice, influenced by PRINCE GEORG VON ANHALT, and he also remained loyal to Emperor Charles in the Smalcald War. He named JOHANN AGRICOLA court preacher after Agricola had fled Wittenberg in 1540. Agricola served on the imperial commission that drafted the Augsburg Interim in 1548, although Brandenburg's compliance with this policy was selective. Increasingly, Joachim relied on Agricola's brother-in-law, ANDREAS MUSCULUS, who had not alienated himself from his Wittenberg mentors as Agricola had, for leadership and counsel in administering the church in his lands. Joachim contributed significantly to attaining the legal status afforded adherents of the Augsburg Confession by the Truce of Passau (1552) and the Peace of Augsburg (1555).

Joachim II's uncle, ***Albrecht of Brandenburg, Elector and Archbishop of Mainz* (1490–1545)**, younger brother of JOACHIM I, lost his father when he was nine, his mother at eleven. Modern scholars contrast him with Joachim I, who was bold, calculating, and strong-willed, because Albrecht was dominated by his love of the arts and proved himself generally to be a gentle, indecisive person. His education took place at his father's and brother's courts, and there he absorbed humanistic interests that led him to patronize architects, painters, and sculptors, poets and musicians, as well as scholars such as ERASMUS. His interests did not extend to use of Erasmus's biblical scholarship, however. He demonstrated more piety than many princely ecclesiastical officials, regularly celebrating mass in private as well as in public, and participating as officiant at baptisms, confirmations, and ordinations. His veneration of relics was renowned. He cooperated with Joachim in plans to extend the power of the Hohenzollern family, as Joachim sought to use church offices to do so. He strove to win positions formerly held by the Saxon house of Wettin, and first as archbishop of Magdeburg and then of Mainz he replaced brothers of FREDERICK THE WISE. Albrecht's assumption of office in Mainz was marked by two failed attempts to introduce reform. His pluralistic acquisition of three higher offices in the church, in violation

Engraving of Albrecht of Brandenburg by artist Albrecht Dürer (1519)

of ecclesiastical rules governing pluralism and acquisition of office as a minor, required significant expenditures. To raise the money, he cooperated with Pope Leo X's efforts to gain funding for the construction of Saint Peter's basilica in Rome. Albrecht commissioned Johann Tetzel to preach and direct the sale of the indulgences that Leo offered, and this provoked Luther to compose his Ninety-Five Theses against indulgence practices. Despite his altercation with Luther over the indulgences and those theses, Albrecht sent Luther and his wife a generous wedding gift. He promoted reform-minded Erasmian theologians and their efforts at moderate reforms, though sometimes in a rather half-hearted manner. Melanchthon had indications that the archbishop intended to play a mediating role at the Diet of Augsburg in 1530 but was disappointed. Luther's uncompromising pressure on

Albrecht in 1521 to abandon his support for medieval practices proved to be futile, even as the archbishop persisted in them. The Reformer harshly condemned Albrecht's alleged involvement in the assassination of the evangelical preacher GEORG WINCKLER (1527), and he rebuked him for his alleged role in the execution of his own courtier, Hans von Schnitz, in 1535. At the time of his death, Albrecht was still active in the politics of the empire and was involved in the planning of Roman Catholic princes for military action against the Smalcald League.

The Dukes of Württemberg

The dukes of Württemberg also played a decisive role in the spread of the Wittenberg Reformation in the southwestern German lands. ***Ulrich, Duke of Württemberg* (1487–1550)**, lost his mother at birth and was kidnapped by a relative to free him from the control of his mentally ill father, Count Heinrich. Ulrich's fiery temperament and strong ego alienated him from the establishment in the duchy, but he succeeded his childless uncle, Duke Eberhard II, in 1498 with the aid of EMPEROR MAXIMILIAN I, who in 1511 imposed upon Ulrich as his wife Duchess Sabina of Bavaria. Ulrich despised Sabina and never reconciled with her. He had assumed personal rule in 1503 and entered into military service for the emperor, but his abandonment of the Swabian League and participation in a rival group of princes estranged him from the Habsburg emperor. In 1514, Ulrich's own peasant subjects rose in revolt because he had levied ever heavier taxes on them; his nobles and towns exacted significant concessions from the ducal government in return for their support, which ended the peasant revolt with a bloody slaughter. The duke wished to make the wife of one of his courtiers his mistress and asked the man, Ludwig von Hutten, for his approval. When von Hutten spread the story, Ulrich stabbed him to death on a hunt. Such antics heightened tensions within the duchy and with the neighboring powers, the Wittelsbach family of Bavaria and the Habsburgs, who also held territory adjoining Württemberg. Maximilian placed Ulrich under the ban. When one of his courtiers was murdered in the nearly free city of Reutlingen, Ulrich swept aside the city's offer of compensation, and seized it in order to incorporate it into his own territory. The Swabian League invaded Württemberg in retaliation, and Ulrich lost control of his duchy. The Habsburgs assumed control after assuming payment for the costs of the invasion. By 1524, Ulrich, then in exile, had announced his support for Luther. Although his duchy of Württemberg lay under Habsburg control, he was still exercising power in his nearby French duchy, Mömpelgaard/Montbéliard, where he began introducing reforms of ecclesiastical life. In the decade 1524–34 Ulrich cultivated the friendship of PHILIP OF HESSE and gathered supporters for an effort to reclaim his duchy. This policy succeeded in 1534. Subsequently, with aid from Philip and others, he introduced the Reformation in Württemberg as well. Leaders in his efforts were the disciple of Luther ERHARD SCHNEPF from Hesse, and Ambrosius Blarer, a follower of BUCER. In 1534 they reached an accord, the "Stuttgart Concord," and slowly the adherence to Luther's teaching under the influence of JOHANNES BRENZ, whom Ulrich borrowed as an advisor from the imperial city of Schwäbisch Hall, became dominant. Imperial troops again occupied Württemberg in the Smalcald War, and the Augsburg Interim was imposed upon the land. Over two hundred Lutheran pastors were deposed. The situation was in flux as Ulrich died, but his son Christoph led Württemberg back into the Wittenberg camp.

The mother of ***Christoph, Duke of Württemberg* (1515–1568)**, Sabina of Bavaria, fled from the court of her husband, the irascible ULRICH, when Christoph was a child, and he was raised in her absence. CHARLES V assumed guardianship of the child after driving Ulrich from his lands. After 1530, Christoph moved with the emperor as he journeyed through his widespread holdings until in 1532 he refused to go to Spain and joined the court of his uncle, Duke Wilhelm of Bavaria. Wilhelm wished to maneuver the young man, educated in the old faith, onto the throne of Württemberg, displacing the Habsburg occupiers of the duchy and securing it for the Roman party. In 1534, however, Ulrich was restored to his rule, and Christoph returned to his father's court, whence he was sent for further education to the court of King Francis I of France. He demonstrated his diplomatic skills on missions for the French king, although it was not diplomatic at all when he refused to kiss the feet of POPE PAUL III on a mission

Woodcut of Christoph, Duke of Württemberg (sixteenth century)

to Rome. In 1542, Ulrich and Christoph made an agreement guaranteeing that Württemberg would remain faithful to its Lutheran faith. Two years later Christoph married Anna Maria of Brandenburg-Ansbach, who was committed to the Lutheran confession of her father, Margrave Georg. Upon the occupation of Württemberg by imperial forces after the Smalcald War, Christoph supported Ulrich in his efforts to protect and provide for the Lutheran pastors who had been ousted from their pulpits. After Ulrich's death in 1550, Christoph dedicated personal energy and funding to rebuilding his church according to the teaching of Johannes Brenz, who had brought Luther's doctrine and practice to the area. In the 1550s and 1560s, Christoph's voice led the chorus of those seeking Lutheran unity. He repeatedly attempted to launch efforts at promoting concord among the parties disputing the interpretation of Luther's legacy. Under his leadership, efforts to promote a spiritualizing understanding of the Lord's Supper were defeated within the duchy. His church ordinance of 1559 reinforced the role of the prince in the governance of the church. Through his ecclesiastical advisors Johannes Brenz and Jakob Andreae, Christoph played a decisive role in the direction of the Lutheran churches until his death in 1568. He entrusted to Andreae the negotiations for attaining concord within the Wittenberg circle, which led indirectly to the *Formula of Concord*, in which Andreae played a major role.

Sketch portrait of Maximillian I by artist Albrecht Dürer (1518)

The Habsburg Emperors

The most powerful opponents of the Reformation among the German princes came from the Habsburg family, for they also were occupying the imperial throne of the Holy Roman Empire of the German Nation throughout Luther's lifetime. The son of the Habsburg duke of Austria, Emperor Frederick III, and his wife, Leonora of Portugal, ***Maximilian I, Duke of***

***Austria, German Emperor* (1459–1519)**, grew up in a turbulent and violent time. His father's ability to rule was weakened by his feud with his brother Albrecht. Maximilian was determined to rebuild the power of the throne and the strength of his family. Besieged by continual conflicts with several other European powers and with the nobilities subject to his rule, Maximilian restored Habsburg fortunes above all through his marriage to Mary of Burgundy, sole heir to the lands of her father, Charles the Bold (although King Louis XI seized control of the southern portions of the duchy of Burgundy at Charles's death). Mary brought to the marriage the prosperous lands of the Low Countries, which resisted Maximilian's rule before finally submitting to him. The emperor also extended the interests of the family into the kingdoms of Bohemia and Hungary through marriage, setting the stage for his son Ferdinand to assume both crowns. Maximilian presided at the Diet of Augsburg in 1518 but did not involve himself with CARDINAL CAJETAN's examination of Luther in its aftermath.

***Charles V, Duke of Austria, King of Spain, German Emperor* (1500–1558)**, ruled more European land than anyone between Charlemagne and Napoleon, a fact that perhaps contributed more to the weakness of his rule than its strength. The marriage policies of his Habsburg ancestors had bestowed this far-flung empire upon him. His paternal grandfather, MAXIMILIAN I of Austria, also German emperor, married Mary of Burgundy, heir to the duchy between the German Empire and France, which included the Netherlands, a late medieval industrial center. They matched their son Philip with Joanna, daughter of King Ferdinand I of Aragon and his wife Isabella, queen of Castile and Leon. Charles assumed at least nominal rule of his grandmother's lands in the Low Countries when his father died in 1506. With his mother consigned to a convent because of alleged mental instability, Charles became ruler of most of the Iberian peninsula at the death of Ferdinand of Aragon in 1516. His grandfather Maximilian died in 1519, and after a contested election the electors of the empire chose Charles as Maximilian's successor. The new emperor was educated with three sisters in the Netherlands. His tutor, Adrian Florensz, became his regent in the Iberian Peninsula before being elected pope as ADRIAN VI in 1522. With his wife, Isabella of Portugal, Charles sired three children who survived infancy. The oldest became King Philip II of Spain. Among Charles's early challenges was the revolt of the Iberian nobility, who were resisting the merger of the traditional kingdoms that had existed since the liberation of the land from Muslim control that began in the eleventh century. His possessions in the New World caused him little difficulties, but the perpetual threat of war with France, continuing tensions with the papacy over the Habsburg rule in Italy (Naples and Lombardy were part of his realm), pirates in the Mediterranean Sea, and, above all, the advance of Turkish forces on the eastern borders of his domains in Austria and Hungary diverted Charles's attention from his religious problems in the German Empire for much of his reign. Personally pious and committed to reform of religious life at the moral and institutional levels, he could not tolerate challenges to authority of any kind, particularly Luther contesting papal authority. Grudgingly he bowed to political pressure from influential princes and also some ecclesiastical officials to hear Luther at the imperial diet in Worms in 1521. But he acted swiftly after the formal close of the diet to marshal those sympathetic to his position to promulgate the Edict of Worms, which expressly called for the total eradication of Luther's ideas and his followers. Frustrated by the loose structure of his empire, he and his brother Ferdinand pursued a variety of policies to end the Wittenberg movement, including outright persecution in lands directly under his control (the duchy of Austria and the Netherlands witnessed a number of executions for the "Lutheran" heresy) and renewal of the Edict of Worms and its condemnation of the "Lutherans" at several imperial diets, as well as negotiations with evangelical rulers and theologians. Thus, his call for an explanation of their reform measures elicited the Augsburg Confession at the imperial diet in 1530. His rejection of the Confession included a threat of military force if the evangelicals had not returned to the Roman obedience by April 15, 1531. Pressures outside the German lands prevented his enforcement of the threat, and he concluded two armistices, that of Nuremberg in 1532 and that of Frankfurt in 1539, which permitted the exercise of their faith by adherents of the Augsburg Confession. Charles's advisors worked to bring about a religious colloquy at the diet in Regensburg in 1541. When it failed, he called for another colloquy at the diet in Regensburg in 1546, but at that time his plans for military action against the evangelical Smalcald League had developed so far that he showed little interest

Portrait of Charles V by artist Lukas Cranach the Elder (1533)

in a settlement. His forces defeated the League's armies at the Battle of Mühlberg April 24, 1547. Charles condemned ELECTOR JOHANN FRIEDRICH OF SAXONY and LANDGRAVE PHILIP OF HESSE, the leaders of the League, to death. He commuted their sentences and organized a commission that produced a settlement ordering all evangelical lands and towns to accept medieval teaching and practice with but two concessions, on clerical celibacy and communion on both kinds, measures that advocates of reform within the Roman camp had been calling for during the preceding decades. This policy, dubbed "the Augsburg Interim," was enforced in some areas but encountered severe opposition and critique from PHILIP MELANCHTHON and a host of other evangelical theologians. Charles had won the war because of the support of some evangelical princes, and when they turned against the Habsburgs in the early 1550s, Charles's brother FERDINAND was forced to agree to the toleration of the adherents of the Augsburg Confession in the Truce of Passau of 1552 and the Religious Peace of Augsburg of 1555, against Charles's strong opposition. In frustration, Charles abdicated in 1556 and spent his remaining two years in a Spanish monastery. He divided his realm, giving his lands in Spain, Italy, the Netherlands, and the New World to his son Philip, and his German lands to his brother Ferdinand, who succeeded him as emperor.

***Ferdinand I, Duke of Austria, King of Hungary and Bohemia, German Emperor* (1503–1564)** was born and educated in the Spanish holdings of his parents and settled in Vienna in 1521 when his brother Charles and he divided the family's holdings. Their grandfather had arranged the marriage of their sister Maria to King Louis II of Hungary, and when Louis fell in the battle of Mohács against invading Turkish forces in 1526, Ferdinand was

Portrait of Ferdinand I wearing mourning clothes, by Lukas Cranach the Elder (1548)

elected king of Hungary, and also of Bohemia. His support for moral and institutional reform of the church did not extend to the doctrinal reform that Luther was promulgating, so he supported his brother's policies of opposition to and persecution of followers of the Wittenberg Reformer. He did concede the right of the Utraquist wing of the Hussites in Bohemia to worship when he became king of their lands, but he suppressed the Bohemian Brethren and Anabaptists in Austria. He introduced the Jesuit order into the German Empire and promoted other Counter-Reformation measures. He compelled his son and successor, Maximilian, to remain faithful to Rome, although Maximilian made little secret of his inclinations toward Wittenberg practice. Nonetheless, Ferdinand recognized that the military threat to order in the empire required compromise, which he accomplished in the Truce of Passau of 1552 and the Religious Peace of Augsburg of 1555. In 1557, he organized a religious colloquy in Worms between representatives of the Wittenberg circle and Roman Catholic theologians, but this effort failed when Roman Catholic participants highlighted differences among the evangelicals at the table. The emperor continued to place pressure on the adherents of the Augsburg Confession to return to the Roman obedience.

Other Rulers for and against the Wittenberg Reforms

Among the inveterate opponents of the Wittenberg Reformation, ***Heinrich the Younger, Duke of Braunschweig-Wolfenbüttel* (1489–1568)**, stands out as a figure whose pursuits of his own goals added to the conflictive nature of the period. Heinrich assumed rule of his dukedom from his father, Heinrich the Elder, in 1514. His fiery temperament and zeal for power spread a reputation for ruthlessness throughout Europe, supported by his imprisonment of his brother Wilhelm for twelve years and his staging a burial for his mistress, Eva von Trott, to end public criticism while hiding her away in one of his castles. His military adventures included his participation in the suppression of the Peasants Revolt and feuds with the towns of Hildesheim and Einbeck (which he burned to the ground in an effort to incorporate it into his territory). His public insults of ELECTOR JOHANN FRIEDRICH OF SAXONY provoked Luther into a fierce polemic against his person and the view of the church he was defending in the Reformer's *Against Hans Sausage* (1541). In 1542, the forces of the Smalcald League intervened in Einbeck's behalf and successfully laid siege to Heinrich's castle in Wolfenbüttel. The League's occupation of his dukedom included efforts to introduce Wittenberg Reforms, which met with some success. Heinrich opened hostilities in 1545 and was taken prisoner by PHILIP OF HESSE, but he regained freedom and his territories after the defeat of the Smalcald League in 1547. His inclination to some reform in the church led him to permit communion in both kinds within his domains in his later years, and he counted followers of Luther among his advisors. His efforts to prevent his only surviving son, Julius—two elder brothers had been killed in the battle Sievershausen in 1553—from gaining the throne, since Julius had converted to the Lutheran movement, failed. Heinrich married Sophia, daughter of King Sigismund of Poland, after the death of his first wife, Maria of Württemberg, in 1556; Sophia also turned to Luther's confession of the faith.

A host of minor rulers throughout the German lands reformed their churches according to Luther's model. One example is ***Anna von Stolberg, abbess of Quedlinburg* (1504–1574)**, who was eleven years old when elected to be abbess of the cloister at Quedlinburg, which controlled extensive holdings at the edge of the Harz mountains between Saxony and Braunschweig-Wolfenbüttel. She had long expressed interest in Luther's theology but came out decisively for Wittenberg Reform only after the death of DUKE GEORG OF SAXONY, who exercised lordship over the cloister. She received support from her brother, Ludwig, who sent Tileman Platner from Stolberg to supervise the cultivation of the Lutheran faith in her lands. She promoted education and a lively piety in her subjects.

***Volrad IV, Count of Mansfeld* (1520–1578)**, was the son of Count Albrecht IV, one of the feuding counts whose dispute Luther calmed on his fatal journey to Mansfeld county in 1546, and his wife, Anna, Countess of Hohnstein. Volrad began studies at the University of Wittenberg in 1534. His military service in the imperial army of CHARLES V began a decade later. ELECTOR JOHANN FRIEDRICH employed him as counselor and administrator in his lands as well. During the Smalcald War, Volrad fought for Johann Friedrich and as a result lost control of his lands until the Truce of Passau restored them in 1552. His attempt to lead forces supported by the Hanseatic League to place JOHANN WILHELM, DUKE OF SAXONY, on the Swedish throne failed in 1556. He was part of the delegation that attempted to arrange a marriage between the duke and Queen Elizabeth I of England in 1559. His participation in the French Wars of Religion did not bring him success. Volrad formed a friendship with CYRIAKUS SPANGENBERG and supported the publication of his *Chronicle of Mansfeld* as well as his treatises on original sin. Electoral Saxony and the administration of the archbishopric of Magdeburg invaded his lands in 1575 to stamp out the Flacian position on original sin that Spangenberg and Volrad embraced. Volrad went into exile in the vicinity of Strassburg and died three years later.

Nordic Rulers

North of the German lands, in the kingdoms of Denmark-Norway-Iceland and of Sweden-Finland, Luther's concept of Christian teaching and practice won sympathizers by 1520 and in the following decades. In these two kingdoms, rulers played vital roles in the introduction and integration of the theology of Luther, MELANCHTHON, and their colleagues among the populace. ***Christian II, King of Denmark, Duke of Schleswig-Holstein* (1481–1559)**, married Isabella (Elisabeth), the sister of CHARLES V OF HABSBURG, later German emperor, in 1515, two years after his accession to the throne. His attempts to increase royal power by playing the middle class and peasantry off against the nobility and ecclesiastical leadership caused significant strife, which resulted in his voluntary exile in 1523. When he tried to regain his throne with an invasion in 1531, he was taken prisoner

Portrait of Christian II, King of Denmark, by artist Lukas Cranach the Elder (ca. 1523–30)

Portrait of King Frederick I of Denmark (artist unknown)

and spent the rest of his life in confinement. His manipulation of church offices contributed to the decline of the standing of the church with the populace. While in exile, he and his wife both became followers of Luther, whom they met personally. Although he renounced his support of the Wittenberg Reformation in 1531 in order to gain aid from his brother-in-law in reclaiming his crown, he seems to have never truly abandoned his understanding of Scripture gained from Luther's writings.

***Frederick I, King of Denmark, Duke of Schleswig-Holstein* (1471–1533)**, was serving as duke in Schleswig and Holstein when his nephew, Christian II, succeeded Frederick's brother Johann. When the Danish nobility revolted against Christian's attempt to limit their powers, they turned to the king's uncle to replace him. Although his coronation oath required him to oppose the heresies of Luther, Frederick rather openly supported the advance of the Reformer's teaching during his decade as king. He married his daughter

Dorothea to DUKE ALBRECHT OF PRUSSIA. His contacts with German evangelical governments also lent weight to the appeal of reform. In 1526 he asserted royal control over appointments to bishoprics, and in 1527 a diet of nobles meeting in Odense cut off all financial support for the Roman curia. Another diet in 1530 in Copenhagen mandated adherence to Scripture alone in preaching. Frederick had already extended royal protection to evangelical preachers, of whom his trusted advisor HANS TAUSEN was a prime example. Without formally rejecting the medieval church as such, Frederick left behind a land that had taken major steps toward reform in the Wittenberg manner.

***Christian III, King of Denmark, Duke of Schleswig-Holstein* (1503–1559)**, son of FREDERICK I, was brought to Luther's understanding of the gospel by his German tutors. Christian was present in Diet of Worms in 1521 and witnessed Luther's confession of his faith there. In 1525 he married Dorothea, daughter of Duke Magnus of Saxony-Lauenburg, and the next year introduced Lutheran teaching and practice to the lands directly under his control in Schleswig. In the turmoil following his father's death in 1533, Christian prevailed over other forces, imprisoned the bishops loyal to Rome, and confiscated all church property in his realm. He requested the aid of JOHANNES BUGENHAGEN in implementing reform at the parish level, and Luther's colleague came to spend over two years (1537–39) in Denmark. Bugenhagen's reforms reopened the University of Copenhagen, altered the structure of church governance, and mandated Lutheran teaching and preaching throughout the kingdom. Christian's own piety exhibited itself publicly, but his firm faith in Luther's teaching did not prevent him from a close relationship with EMPEROR CHARLES V, which held him apart from involvement in the Smalcald War and other political commitments to the Lutheran cause in the German Empire.

Portrait of Christian III, King of Denmark (artist unknown)

During the controversies within the Wittenberg circle in the 1550s, Christian expressed severe criticism of GEORG MAJOR's proposition, "good works are necessary for salvation." His daughter ANNA married ELECTOR AUGUST OF SAXONY, and she played a prominent role in his reign.

Christian's son and successor, ***Frederick II, King of Denmark, Duke of Schleswig-Holstein* (1534–1588)**, suffered from learning disabilities and did not display particularly sound judgment at times. He sought to regain control over Sweden in a war lasting from 1563 to 1570 that did no more than undermine the Danish economy, although his counselors managed to place it back on its feet. Frederick enjoyed the hunt, military activities, and Renaissance culture more than the rigors of political decision-making. His personal piety seems to have been faithful to the Lutheran faith of his parents. NIELS HEMMINGSEN, professor of theology at the University of Copenhagen and a devoted disciple of MELANCHTHON, influenced Frederick's thinking profoundly, although Hemmingsen's influence waned somewhat after accusations of "crypto-Calvinism" brought about his dismissal from his university post in 1579. Frederick's favor did not significantly diminish, however, and as a canon at the cathedral of Roskilde, Hemmingsen pursued his scholarly work. Frederick's sister ANNA, in contrast, consistently opposed spiritualizing tendencies in the teaching on the Lord's Supper as electress of Saxony. She enthusiastically supported the efforts of her husband, AUGUST, and his theological advisors to suppress ideas such as those Hemmingsen held, and warmly welcomed the affirmation of her convictions in the *Formula of Concord*. When Frederick received copies of the *Book of Concord* from his Saxon brother-in-law, he threw them into the fire and forbade importing of the book. He also sought to make common cause against Roman Catholic powers with Henry of Navarre in France and Elizabeth I in England.

***Gustav Vasa, King of Sweden* (1496–1560)**, a leading nobleman among the Swedish aristocracy in the kingdom united under Danish regency by the Union of Kalmar of 1397, was thrust into leadership after KING CHRISTIAN II attempted to suppress unrest in his Swedish provinces in the late 1510s. Resistance to royal attempts to impose the crown's power led to the Stockholm Bloodbath of 1520. In mid-1523, Vasa's fellow nobles elected him king of an independent Sweden, which embraced the Finnish territory within the Nordic realm as well, although the lands in the southwestern part of the Swedish peninsula remained under Copenhagen's control. Among Vasa's most trusted advisors were LAURENTIUS ANDREAE and OLAUS PETRI, two advocates of Wittenberg Reform. Vasa avoided imposing a confession of faith upon his church throughout his reign, and he moved slowly to promulgate a national liturgy. But his permissive attitude fostered the spread of Luther's way of thinking. A diet held at Västerås in 1527 affirmed the independence of the Swedish church from Roman obedience after bishops loyal to Rome had attempted to dethrone the king because of his support for reform. Andreae and Petri negotiated carefully to overcome their opponents' rhetoric in the diet, and disunity among the bishops turned the tide for the Reformers. A disputation was conducted between the two sides, and the estates decided that the evangelical side intended only to uphold God's word. Vasa repeatedly asserted his control of the church. When his two clerical advisors withheld from him information regarding a conspiracy that had been related to them in private confession in 1540, Gustav condemned them both to death, but later remitted. With varying degrees of success, royal policy attempted to place the king in absolute control of the church, but Olaus Petri's brother LAURENTIUS PETRI, as archbishop of Uppsala, resisted and managed to preserve an element of independence for the bishops and their dioceses. Gustav was succeeded in turn by three sons: Erik XIV favored Calvinist teaching but was opposed by the leadership of the church. Johan III guided the church in the direction of Rome, provoking a revolt, the leadership of which his younger brother, Karl IX, finally assumed. Also Calvinist in sentiment, Duke Karl submitted to the insistence on Lutheran theology voiced by his estates and their ecclesiastical leaders and became king. Karl's son, Gustav Adolf, entered the Thirty Years War to defend the Protestant churches.

And from England . . .

One example of a foreign ruler who did all he could to oppose Luther is ***Henry VIII, King of England*** **(1491–1547)**. Henry ascended the English throne hardly a generation after the end of the bitter and disastrous civil war, the War of the Roses, had ended with the victory of his father, Henry VII, of the Tudor family. As the second son, Henry did not receive the preparation for the throne that his older brother Arthur did, but Arthur died in 1502, seven years before the death of his father. Two concerns drove Henry as he became king: the preservation of peace in his kingdom—which was dependent to a significant extent on his having a male heir—and the improvement of England's position as a European power. The latter concern led him into a series of wars, particularly in France, but also with Scotland; concern for a male heir caused his divorce from his Aragonese wife, Catherine, daughter of Ferdinand of Aragon and Isabella of Castile, and thus aunt of the German emperor after 1519, CHARLES V. Henry worked closely with his chief minister, Thomas

Portrait of Henry VIII by Hans Holbein (ca. 1537)

Wolsey, archbishop of York and a cardinal in the Roman curia. Although Henry had asserted the long-claimed right of the English kings to govern the church in their lands in the 1510s, he won the title "Defender of the Faith" from Pope Clement VII in 1521 after he had written, with help from Wolsey and perhaps others, an *Assertion of the Seven Sacraments* against Luther's *Babylonian Captivity of the Church.* Under Wolsey and his successor, Thomas More, the royal government persecuted those who deviated from official church teaching and practice with energy and some regularity throughout Henry's reign. The king's frantic pursuit of a male heir to secure the succession and thus stability of his kingdom led to his divorce from Catherine of Aragon and, as a result, to his excommunication by Pope Clement VII. A turbulent period followed these events in 1532–34, resulting in the execution of Thomas More, the royal advisor who had nourished Henry's own humanistic interests in ancient texts, for his failure to support the policies stemming from the divorce and excommunication. More's successor at Henry's right hand, Thomas Cromwell, pursued a policy of negotiations with the Smalcald League, while he, in consort with the new archbishop of Canterbury, Thomas Cranmer, cautiously promoted the influx of evangelical ideas from the continent. By 1540, Cromwell had fallen from favor as the attempts at forming an alliance with the Smalcald League came to naught. Henry replaced the moderate "Ten Articles" of 1536 with a reaffirmation of medieval teaching and practice, his "Six Articles," in 1539. In his last years, Henry continued to prosecute and execute those accused of heresy, although his last queen, Catherine Parr, favored reform, and his only son, who succeeded him as Edward VI, turned the kingdom toward evangelical theology and practice.

Given the political constellation and religious climate of late medieval Europe, a broad popular movement would have had no chance of success without political support. Repeated reform movements of the Middle Ages demonstrate that, as does the limited success of the Bohemian reform led by Jan Hus and given support by Bohemian leadership. Rulers who did not commit themselves to Luther's way of thinking based their opposition on political considerations of various kinds, including their sincere fears of disorder. They also believed that a system of salvation that opposed hierarchical authority centered in Rome and that did not require the performance of good works for the winning of God's grace could only wreak havoc and destroy society. Others embraced Luther's Reforms, and some of those demonstrated a deeper understanding of his theology. Some exhibited a strong piety in the forms that Wittenberg Reformers tried to cultivate. Mixed motives are always present in human affairs, but not all sixteenth-century rulers who turned to reform movements did so out of greed for land or lust for power. Luther won the faith and hearts of many.

CHAPTER 8

LUTHER'S FOES: LUTHER'S CRITICS FROM ALL CORNERS

At the edges of the Wittenberg world stood the opponents of its Reformation. In addition to the princes discussed in chapter 7, church leaders and theologians reacted negatively and sharply against Luther's proposals for reform. Some criticized his program for the sake of personal gain and out of ambition, but most sincerely feared what his reforms would do to the understanding and practice of the Christian faith as they understood it. Others believed that Luther had not driven reform to its logical conclusion. Therefore, Luther's world took form under attack. It could not have been otherwise, because people resist change, and Luther broke the mold. His proposals for reform offended both those who took an establishment view of the church, society, and reality and those who held the old-fashioned dream for reform that had moved some in previous centuries.

The establishment maintained its conviction that the hierarchy of the church held the world together and that God was most effectively reached through sacred ritual and religious activity—albeit through works produced with the aid of God's grace at some point in their performance. In addition to earlier reformers who had worked within ecclesiastical structures particularly on the problem of the moral state of clergy and church or on ecclesiastical institutions and forms, some had held views that rejected the rules, regulations, and traditions of the official church and strove to have a simple, biblicistic view of the world. These reformers rejected the worth of most of the sacred rituals of the medieval establishment and promoted moral performance in imitation of Christ. Luther's emphasis on God's justifying action through Christ's work and the gift of faith through the Holy Spirit's activity with the external forms of God's Word contradicted both perceptions of God and the human creature. It is no wonder that Luther fell under repeated attack from the both Roman Catholic and Anabaptist heirs of these traditional ways of viewing the world.

In addition, some of those who shared Luther's conviction regarding God's justifying action in Christ were moved by their fear of what they regarded as medieval superstition concerning the divine power placed in material objects, such as the sacramental elements. They felt that Luther had betrayed the evangelical message and not properly understood how God works in the world by clinging to his insistence on the true presence of Christ's body and blood in the bread and wine of the Supper. Their perception of what God is saying in Scripture was influenced by the principle that the material creation can only represent and point to heavenly reality, whereas Luther was convinced that God comes into this down and dirty world and makes free use of selected elements of his created order to bestow the gifts of forgiveness, life, and salvation. Thus, conflict marked and shaped Luther's career. He found that natural, for he perceived human life after the fall into sin as a battleground between God and Satan, between God's truth and the devil's deception (John 8:44).

Luther's Jewish Conversation Partner

In a different category from the other opponents presented in this chapter, ***Josel von Rosheim*** **(ca. 1478–1554)** did not actively engage Luther in public polemic. Josel represented the Jewish community in the German-speaking lands. His family was prominent in that community: One relative, Jacob Jehiel Loans, served as personal physician for Emperor Frederick III. An uncle had been executed for allegedly taking part in a ritual murder of a Christian in 1470. Josel was a banker from the vicinity of Strassburg. The Jewish community in Lower Alsace elected him their leader after he had successfully defended Jews sent into exile from the town of Oberehnheim in 1507. Thereafter he served as representative of Jewish interests to the courts of MAXIMILIAN I, CHARLES V, and KING FERDINAND, as well as with other organs of the empire and the peasant forces in rebellion in 1525. From 1529, the Jewish community throughout the empire recognized him as its public representative. In that office, he defended Jews under pressure repeatedly and developed a good relationship with Emperor Charles V. He came to Wittenberg in 1537 to speak with Luther. Their conversation produced no positive results.

Roman Catholic Opponents

Luther's Ninety-Five Theses on Indulgences aroused immediate critique from the establishment, though not so much because of his views on indulgences. Neither the theology nor the practice of granting indulgences to diminish or eliminate the temporal punishment in purgatory due the sinner had been dogmatically fixed at Luther's time. It was the thinly veiled challenge to papal authority and power in the Theses that aroused opposition. Luther wanted to discuss proper pastoral care and the relationship of sinners to their gracious God. The Roman Catholic authorities were compelled to defend the order of things and to oppose with decrees and, if necessary, with fire and sword any threat such as Luther's to the orderly control of church and society by the established keepers of public harmony and stability.

That system depended, first of all, on the presupposition that God had placed at the head of Christendom the vicar of Christ, the bishop of Rome, the successor of Peter as chief of the apostles, the pope. The pope alone had the divine right to govern Christ's church. Challenges to that theory from those who wished to place power also in church councils had been beaten back over the course of the fifteenth century. Papal power may have still been a matter for private discussions, but publicly church officials simply accepted the pope's status as Christ's authoritative representative on earth as God's will. The popes who led the Western church during Luther's lifetime played little direct role in his life, but their decisions did dramatically affect the course of his career and his Reform.

When Luther journeyed to Rome in 1510, he visited the holy city under the rule of ***Pope Julius II, Giuliano della Rovere* (1443–1513)**, who rose in the church under the aegis of his uncle, Pope Sixtus IV. Julius's opposition to Pope Alexander VI sent him into exile in the 1490s, but he became Alexander's successor as pope in 1503. Gifted with political and military skills, he dedicated his decade in power to expanding the secular power of the papacy through expansion into lands in central Italy that his armies were able to conquer. To counter the call of the French king Louis XII for a general church council in Pisa in 1511, Julius organized the Fifth Lateran Council, which assembled in Rome in 1512 (and ended in early 1517). It affirmed the individuality and immortality of the soul against the theories of the Aristotelian philosopher Pietro Pomponazzi, who had argued that reason

Portrait of Pope Julian II by Raphael (1511)

cannot prove the soul's individuality and immortality. Instead, he proposed a theory of two versions of the truth, an idea also condemned by the council. Julius patronized the arts, promoting the careers of Michelangelo and Raphael among others, while neglecting pressing ecclesiastical matters. The nature of Julius's activities probably contributed to Luther's hardly mentioned disappointment with Rome as a holy city in reaction to his visit there.

***Pope Leo X, Giovanni de' Medici* (1475–1521)**, played a more significant role in Luther's life as the pope who condemned him to death as a heretic. Son of Lorenzo the Magnificent, ruler of Florence, Leo had pursued a career in the church as a papal diplomat and, after the restoration of his family's rule in 1512, governed the city of Florence with his younger brother after the death of the oldest brother. A protégé of POPE JULIUS II, he won election as pope with the support of those promoting reform in the church. In early 1517, he survived a plot to assassinate him by enemies of his family who were resisting his interference in the political affairs of the city of Sienna. Tensions with King Francis I of France at the beginning of Francis's reign gave way to a close association of the two, which led to Leo's support for the king as a candidate for the office of emperor in the German Empire in 1519. He also lent some support to the candidature of Elector Frederick the Wise. He later turned against France in league with Emperor Charles V. Leo's generally relaxed attitude toward theological and ecclesiastical matters stemmed at least in part from his love of the hunt and the arts. The dangerous challenge of Luther's call for reform aroused his ire, in part because his lavish expenditures had threatened to delay the completion of Saint Peter's church in Rome. Under his leadership the prosecution of the Wittenberg Reformer progressed, apparently without consideration of the theological core of his message. He issued the bulls *Exsurge Domine* (June 15, 1520) and *Decet Romanum Pontificum* (March 1, 1521) threatening and then ordering Luther's excommunication. Shortly before his death in 1521, he rewarded King Henry VIII with the title "Defender of the Faith" for his published attack on Luther's *Babylonian Captivity of the Church.*

Portrait of Pope Leo X; detail from a painting by Raphael (1518–19)

With deeper concern for the need and pressures for reform, the cardinals elected as his successor ***Pope Adrian VI, Adrian Florensz*** **(1459–1523)**, who came from reform-minded circles in the Netherlands. His theological works reflected the characteristics of the scholasticism of his time, but his life reflected his piety and desire for reform of the church's practice and organization. He served as tutor and then counselor for Charles V before Charles became emperor. As bishop of Tortosa in Spain and, after 1517, inquisitor and cardinal, Florensz exercised regency for Charles in Spain before becoming pope. He strove to introduce measures to counteract Luther's Reform movement, but opposition within the

Engraving of Pope Adrian VI by Théodore Galle (1598)

papal curia frustrated these attempts during the short time between his election in January 1522 and his death in September 1523.

The cardinals electing his successor returned to old form, choosing ***Pope Clement VII, Giulio de' Medici*** **(1478–1534)**, a cousin of POPE LEO X and member of the ruling family of Florence, uncle of Catherine de' Medici, the queen of France. The support of CHARLES V aided his rise to the papal office, but his diplomatic maneuvers to weaken imperial power in Italy through cooperation with Francis I of France resulted in the Sack of Rome in 1527 and the pope's imprisonment. His reconciliation with Charles V had taken place by the time of the Diet of Augsburg in 1530, but he continued to oppose the emperor on the issue of calling a council to address the church's problems, including Luther's Reformation. He also bungled negotiations over the appeal of KING HENRY VIII for an annulment of his marriage to Catherine of Aragon, the sister of Charles V's mother, Joanna. His ineffectual leadership provided little support to those opposed to the Reformation in the German lands.

Only with the election of ***Pope Paul III, Alessandro Farnese*** **(1468–1549)**, did the papacy find a leader capable of organizing forces to oppose reform with reform, and not only north of the Alps but also within Italy. The special relationship between Pope Alexander VI and Farnese's sister provided the latter with entrance into the papal service, and by 1494 he had been named to several bishoprics. CLEMENT VII raised him to the higher ranks of his bureaucracy in Rome. Highly educated and intelligent, his patronage of the arts, including sponsorship of projects under taken by Michelangelo, accompanied the unencumbered lifestyle of most at the papal court in this period. Nonetheless, as Paul III assumed office, he recognized the need for decisive change in the church. He named several reform-minded, theologically trained cardinals and used them as members of a special committee for reforming ecclesiastical practice and organization. He exercised papal power by excommunicating King Henry VIII for his annulment of his marriage to Catherine of Aragon and his seizure of church lands and ecclesiastical governance. However, Pope Paul did not thereby reach his goals. More successful were his restoration of the Inquisition in Italy and his pursuit of the meeting of a general council of the church. His plans to have the general council assemble in Mantua in 1537 collapsed, but he persevered until it finally convened eight years later, in Trent, in December 1545. His own pursuit of family interests and the promotion of family members, not all of good repute, for posts as rulers of parts of Italy distracted from his conciliar efforts and repeatedly alienated Charles V. Nonetheless, Pope Paul entered into an alliance with Charles in 1546 aimed at the military defeat and forceful eradication of the followers of Luther. The hostilities of the Smalcald War in late 1546 and 1547 caused the pope to move the council from Trent to Bologna, to the deep chagrin of Charles V. Pope Paul then suspended the council, which met again only in 1551, after his death.

Portrait of Pope Clement VII by Agnolo Bronzino

In the service of the popes, Italian officials of the papal court played key roles in the initial stages of the Reformation, largely because of their swift and harsh reactions to Luther's theses on indulgences. Among the most important were the following four papal bureaucrats.

***Silvester Mazzolini Prierias* (1456–1523)** joined the Dominican order in 1471. During his career as instructor of theology and vicar-general of the Dominican congregation in Lombardy, he published devotional literature that focused on God's love in sending his Son to the cross, a postil, and a *Summa of Cases of Conscience*. He assumed a professorship in Rome in 1514 and the next year became "Master of the Sacred Palace." That meant that he was serving Pope Leo X as chief theological advisor when Luther's case landed in Rome. The harshness of his early responses to Luther, filled with name-calling and arrogance, contributed to the sharpness of the tone of the early debates with German

Portrait of Pope Paul III by Titian (1545/6)

advocates of reform. Prierias was particularly concerned with issues of papal authority and, as a Thomist theologian, used Aquinas's texts against Luther's citations of the Bible and the ancient fathers, as well as canon law.

The first Italian representative of the papal court with whom Luther came face to face, ***Thomas de Vio, Cardinal Cajetan* (1480–1547)**, studied civil and canon law before entering into papal service. Ordained a priest in 1516, he became a member of the "Oratorium of Divine Love," an organization of those interested in reform and the renewal of the clergy. In 1518, the papal curia sent him to the imperial diet in Augsburg with the task of transporting Luther to Rome for trial as a heretic or obtaining his full submission to the papacy. FREDERICK THE WISE intervened, guaranteeing Luther protection. Luther and Cajetan met. The cardinal resisted the Reformer's attempts to discuss the theology and practice of indulgences and related questions. Luther fled Augsburg because he realized that Cajetan wished to have him arrested and brought to Rome. Following their meeting in Augsburg, Cajetan began to research the questions surrounding indulgence practice and wrote an authoritative treatise on the subject. Cajetan contributed significantly to Roman Catholic theology in the sixteenth century, both as a prominent leader of the revival of the theology of Thomas Aquinas and as a pioneering author of biblical commentaries. In 1518, he returned to his native Vicenza as a member of the Brotherhood of Saint Jerome and founded a hospice for the dying. With several others, including the future Pope Paul III, he organized the Order of the Theatines in 1524. His last years were spent in Venice and Naples in the work of his order and in arresting and prosecuting heretical followers of Jan de Valdés, Peter Martyr Vermigli, and Bernardino Ochino.

Luther and Cajetan, *painting by Franciso Salviati (1560)*

***Hieronymus Aleander* (1480–1542)** received a humanist preparation for his university education, which he gained in Motta, Pordenone, Venice, and Padua. He left a teaching post in Venice in 1508 to go Paris, where he introduced the study of Greek, exercised the office of rector of the university, and became secretary to the bishop of Paris, Etienne Poncher, who was at that time chancellor of King Louis XII. In 1515, Aleander became chief administrator at the court of Prince Bishop Erard von der Mark in Lüttich/Liege; the next year Cardinal Giulio de Medici called him to Rome as his personal secretary. POPE LEO X named him librarian of the Library Palatina in 1519 and sent him the following year to the court of EMPEROR CHARLES V to expedite the heresy proceedings against Luther. Frustrated in his attempts to prevent Luther's appearance at the Diet of Worms in 1521 and by the obvious popularity the Wittenberg professor enjoyed among the German populace, he did succeed in having the emperor issue the Edict of Worms, of which the nuncio had prepared the initial draft. POPE CLEMENT VII awarded him the archbishopric of Brindisi and sent him as nuncio to the French royal court. He continued to represent the papal court in the German Empire into the late 1530s.

***Lorenzo Campeggio* (1474–1539)** followed in his father's footsteps in the study of civil and canon law and joined him as professor in Bologna in 1499. He entered the service of the papal curia in 1510 as an auditor at the highest court of the papacy, the Rota Romana. The next year he entered the diplomatic service of the papacy and was dispatched to the court of EMPEROR MAXIMILIAN I. His success in diverting Maximilian's support from the rump council of Pisa, sponsored by the French king, Louis XII, to the papally called council, the Fifth Lateran, earned him appointment by POPE JULIUS II to the bishopric of Feltre in northern Italy. Julius sent Campeggio to the court of the Duke of Milan, Maximilian Sforza, but from 1513 to 1517 his post was again the court of Maximilian I. Named a cardinal in 1517, the next year Campeggio went to England as papal representative at KING HENRY VIII's court. His attempts at the imperial diet in Nuremberg in 1524 to win support for a strict enforcement of the Edict of Worms failed, but later that year he played a significant role in cooperation with CHARLES V's brother FERDINAND in organizing a league to oppose those governments that were introducing Wittenberg Reform measures. Papal assignments led him to Hungary in 1525 and England in 1528 and 1529, where success eluded him in finding a settlement to Henry VIII's maneuvering to obtain an annulment of his marriage to Catherine of Aragon. At the Diet of Augsburg in 1530 his negotiations with MELANCHTHON failed to reach a settlement, resulting in mutual recriminations between the two. Campeggio's opposition to Charles V's conclusion of a truce with the evangelical princes in 1532, "the Nuremberg Armistice," failed to attain its goal. At the time of his death, Campeggio was serving as a member of the papal reform committee and as the designated chairman of the papal council, which did not convene before his death.

Much more important for the Wittenberg efforts at reform were the German opponents, who struggled against the massive popularity of Luther and his colleagues and the efforts of princes and town councils to introduce meaningful reform in their lands or municipalities.

***Johann Tetzel* (ca. 1465–1519)** entered the Dominican order in the 1480s after studying in Leipzig. After serving as prior of the cloister in Glogau, he became the inquisitor for Saxony and taught in the cloister of his order in Leipzig. From 1504 to 1510, he worked

Portrait of Johann Tetzel taking an oath. At the top right of the image is Pope Leo X's papal bull Cum postquam, *which defined the doctrine of indulgences, and at the lower right is an indulgence. Illustration from book by Johann Jacob Vogel, published 1717.*

as a preacher of indulgences for the German knights in Livonia and was named inquisitor for Poland as well as Saxony in 1509. His connection to the court of FREDERICK THE WISE was sufficiently strong that the elector intervened on his behalf and won him pardon from capital charges of adultery. He became subcommissioner for indulgences in the bishopric of Meissen in 1516 and the following year was appointed general subcommissioner for the preaching of the indulgences for Saint Peter's cathedral in Rome by ARCHBISHOP ALBRECHT OF MAINZ. Tetzel's commission as Albrecht's representative for the sale of the indulgence was to raise funds for the building of Saint Peter's Cathedral in Rome. When his sale of the indulgence provoked Luther's Ninety-Five Theses, members of his order at the University of Frankfurt an der Oder, particularly KONRAD WIMPINA, arranged for him to receive his doctorate in theology. Abandoned by church officials, he retired to the cloister in Leipzig, where he died of the plague. Luther sent him a letter of consolation in his last days.

Konrad Wimpina (Koch) **(ca. 1460–1531)** left his home in the Odenwald for the University of Leipzig in 1485 and received his doctorate in Bible there in 1503 after serving as rector and later vice-chancellor of the university. He was ordained around 1500. He fell into dispute with his former instructor and friend MARTIN POLLICH VON MELLERSTADT, defending the scholastic method against Pollich's advocacy of the methods of biblical humanism. In 1505 Wimpina moved to Frankfurt an der Oder and shaped the theological faculty there. He supported his friend and former student JOHANN TETZEL in the dispute provoked by Luther's challenges in the Ninety-Five Theses to Tetzel's indulgence sales methods. Wimpina synthesized his earlier critiques of Luther's theology in a work entitled *Anacep halaeosis*, published in 1528. He was actively involved in negotiations with MELANCHTHON and his colleagues at the Diet of Augsburg in 1530 and participated in the preparation of the "Papal Confutation" of the Augsburg Confession.

Skilled in political maneuvering, in church and at princely courts, and well-trained in scholastic theology, ***Johann Eck*** **(1486–1543)** was among the brightest and best of the theologians who defended the "old faith" in the last quarter century of his life. A normal course of studies had brought him to the universities of Heidelberg, Tübingen, Cologne, and Freiburg, where he became committed to the "*via moderna*." By 1510 he had become a doctor of Bible at the University of Ingolstadt, which the dukes of Bavaria had founded in 1472. He proved to be a faithful representative of his university and his dukes in their opposition to the upstart university in Wittenberg. Eck had a budding reputation as a public interpreter of the church's thought as he ventured to argue against the prohibition of charging interest; it was said that he was in the pay of the Fugger banking family in Augsburg. Indeed, he served its interests with his public disputations and publications. In 1514, he published a treatise on grace and predestination, defending the Franciscan view of the importance of works in gaining access to grace and subsequently to salvation. However, he also championed reforms in church life and dedicated himself to the study of Scripture and Augustine as well as Dionysius the Areopagite and ancient Neoplatonic thinkers. His initial reaction to Luther's writings had been receptive. The threat to the old order, which Eck saw both in Luther's developing views of papal authority and in what he regarded as the Wittenberg Reformer's threat to public morality in his view of salvation by faith alone, however, soon aroused Eck's opposition. His *Obelisci*, a critique of Luther's argumentation in the Ninety-Five Theses, elicited Luther's *Asterici* (1518). While others dawdled, Eck seized the initiative in opposing Luther, challenging his Wittenberg colleague Andreas Karlstadt to debate critical issues raised by Luther. His intent, to draw Luther into the public disputation, came to fruition after Duke Georg of Saxony arranged for the debate at his university in Leipzig in June and July 1519. Eck drew from Luther the admission that councils as well as popes could err, and that elicited from Eck the accusation that Luther accepted the theology of the Bohemian heretic, Jan Hus, who had been condemned by the Council of Constance and burned in 1415. Eck personally traveled to Rome to expedite the excommunication of Luther by the papal authorities and to gain the commission to bring the bull *Exsurge Domine*, threatening Luther with excommunication, to Germany. At the same time, he campaigned for reform of indulgence practices and of the bestowal of church offices for money. He also called for deeper theological study and better pastoral care. Often in fear of his life because of opposition from the populace, he gingerly distributed the bulls threatening and executing Luther's excommunication.

Johann Eck

In the years following Luther's excommunication, Eck's battle against evangelical theology and practice continued. His publications included a dogmatic textbook, entitled *Handbook of Topics against the Lutherans* (1525), aimed to counter MELANCHTHON'S *Loci communes*; it enjoyed great success, with sixteen editions by 1529, thus one of the most widespread early summaries of Roman Catholic teaching. Other writings addressed the breakdown in public order and the misrepresentation of the Christian tradition that he found in Wittenberg publications. He played vital roles in negotiating with the evangelical theologians and governments at the Diet of Augsburg in 1530, contributing significantly to the composition of the "Papal Confutation" of the Augsburg Confession. He led papal theologians in negotiations at the imperial diets in Hagenau, Worms, and Regensburg (1540–41). His participation in the negotiations at Regensburg and the production of a statement of agreement on key issues insured a fair representation of the Roman party's concerns, but from his sickbed he subsequently criticized and rejected the settlement. In so doing, he remained faithful to his own principles and to the politics of his dukes in Bavaria.

***Jacob Hoogstraten* (1460–1527)** studied at Leuven/Louvain, near his home in Brabant, and became a Dominican as he moved to Cologne for further study. He was called to be professor of theology there in 1504 and also held offices in his order as supervisor of studies and prior of the cloister in Cologne. He was appointed inquisitor for the ecclesiastical province that embraced the archdioceses of Cologne, Mainz, and Trier. He exercised this office with diligence and severity. His avid support for the campaign of the converted Jew Johannes Pfefferkorn against the study and use of Jewish literature and particularly against JOHANNES REUCHLIN aroused protests from the biblical humanists that culminated in the *Letters of Obscure Men* edited by ULRICH VON HUTTEN, appearing in two editions, 1515/1517. Hoogstraten responded in two published defenses of his position. He was instrumental in the condemnation of Luther by the theological faculty in Cologne in 1519. His command of Augustine's writings enabled him to mount a critique of Luther's understanding of the justification of sinners through Christ's death and resurrection; he perceptively viewed Luther's view of original sin and concupiscence as the key to the Reformer's theology. He also countered Luther's teaching on the veneration of the saints, good works, and the freedom of the will.

***Johannes Cochlaeus (Dobeneck)* (1479–1552)** received a humanist education in Nuremberg before beginning studies at the University of Cologne in 1504. He returned to Nuremberg as rector of the school of Saint Lorenz parish six years later and, in 1515, became tutor for the nephews of WILLIBALD PIRCKHEIMER. With them he traveled to Italy

Johannes Cochlaeus

and received a doctorate in theology at the University of Ferrara in 1517. Ordained that year in Rome, he settled the next year in Frankfurt am Main as dean of the Foundation of Our Lady. A friend of the papal nuncio Hieronymus Aleander, he assisted in negotiations with Luther in Worms in 1521, seeking to persuade the Wittenberg professor to recant. The next year the first of his long series of attacks on Luther appeared in print. After a brief period in the service of Archbishop Elector Albrecht of Mainz, Cochlaeus assumed a position as chaplain and counselor of Duke Georg of Saxony in 1528. He actively participated in the politics of opposition to reform at a number of meetings of the imperial diet in the 1520s, and at Augsburg in 1530 he contributed to the composition of the "papal Confutation." In 1539, as a consequence of the death of Duke Georg and the subsequent reformation of his lands by his brother and successor Heinrich, Cochlaeus took up residency in Breslau as a canon at its cathedral. From 1543 to 1548 he served as a canon in Eichstätt, returning to Breslau in 1549. Among his works criticizing Luther was his assessment of what he found to be contradictions in Wittenberg theology, his *Seven-Headed Luther*. With no little theological imagination, he reclaimed Jan Hus as a moderate advocate of proper reform for the papal party. Cochlaeus's *Commentaries on the Deeds and Writings of Martin Luther, the Saxon* (1549) offered the first longer biography of Luther and pioneered the genre of polemical biography with its mixture of fact, misrepresentation, and fabrication.

***Hieronymus Emser* (1478–1527)** received his theological training in Tübingen and Basel. Ordained a priest during his studies, he served the papal legate Raimund Peraudi, who was preaching an indulgence to support a crusade against the Turks, in the years following 1502. Emser's humanistic studies informed his lectures at the University of Erfurt, where Luther heard him. He turned to the study of canon law, became a secretary and chaplain for DUKE GEORG OF SAXONY, edited a new printing of ERASMUS's *Handbook of the Christian Soldier*, and favored Luther's initial call for reform. With his prince, he began to attack Luther publicly in 1519, and Luther returned fire on both of them. Emser issued a translation of the New Testament into German in 1527; its text was largely borrowed from Luther's translation.

***Thomas Murner* (1475–1537)** placed his humanist training in the service of the opposition to Luther through direct polemic and satire. A Franciscan, he was ordained in 1494. Study at the universities of Freiburg, Cologne, Paris, Rostock, Cracow, Prague, Vienna, Trier, and Basel culminated in his earning his doctorate in theology in 1506 in Freiburg and his doctorate in civil and canon law in 1519 in Basel. EMPEROR MAXIMILIAN I recognized his literary skills by awarding him the title of poet laureate in 1505. Murner served in leadership positions in at least six Franciscan cloisters over the years, became a pastor in Lucerne in 1527, and later served the parish in Oberehnheim near Strassburg. Controversy came easy for this Franciscan. In 1502, he attacked fellow humanist Jacob Wimpfeling over the question of whether Alsace belonged to the German Empire. He promoted moral and institutional reform of the church in his *Conspiracy of Fools*, modeled after Sebastian Brant's *Ship of Fools*. He pursued this theme with his *On the Great Lutheran Fool* (1522). His critique of Luther's theology found expression in a number of other published works including *On Dr. Martin Luther's Teachings and Sermons* (1520) and *Whether the King of England or Luther is a Liar* (1522). He also defended the papal church against JOHANN OECOLAMPADIUS in treatments of the disputation in Baden in 1526 (in which he did not directly participate).

***Hieronymus Dungersheim (Ochsenfort)* (1465–1540)** studied and taught in Leipzig and Cologne beginning in 1484 and completed his education with doctorates in theology and canon law in Bologna and Sienna (1504). He returned in 1506 to Leipzig and served as professor there until his death. Thomas Aquinas shaped his theology. In 1514 and 1515 he published attacks on the Bohemian Brethren, one branch of the followers of Jan Hus. He consistently opposed Luther and his colleagues, including in his *Repudiation of the False Pamphlet of Martin Luther on Both Kinds in the Venerable Sacrament* (1530), *Against Martin Luther and the Anabaptists* (ca. 1530), and *Critique of the Confession or Flawed Lutheran Testament* (1530).

The Dominican ***Johann Dietenberger* (ca. 1475–1537)** became prior of his house in Frankfurt am Main in 1510. After studying in Cologne and Heidelberg, he received his doctorate in theology in Mainz in 1515. He returned to his cloister in Frankfurt in 1516 and then became the head of cloisters in Trier and later Koblenz before returning to Frankfurt as prior (1510–26). He closed out his career with a decade of service in Koblenz as prior of the Dominicans there. Among his contributions to Roman Catholic reform were his work on the "Confutation" of the Augsburg Confession in 1530, his German catechism, and his Bible translation. It adhered closely to that of Hieronymus Emser, which largely reproduced Luther's translation, with the translation of the Apocrypha copied from the Zwinglian Leo Jud.

***Augustin Alveldt* (ca. 1480–ca. 1535)** served in leadership positions in Franciscan monasteries in Leipzig and Halle in the first decades of his membership in the Observantine wing of the order. He showed concern for the upright life of the brothers. In 1529–32 he led his province of the Observant Franciscans. Bishop Adolf of Merseburg and the papal legate Karl von Miltitz commissioned Alveldt to refute Luther's critique of papal power; his *On the Apostolic See* of 1520 provoked Luther's reply *On the Papacy in Rome, Against the Famous Romanist in Leipzig*. Alveldt followed this work with a number of other treatises against Luther. He edited a second edition of Hieronymus Emser's translation of the New Testament, which added to Luther's translation notes conforming to papal teaching.

***Johann Fabri* (ca. 1470/75–1530),** a smith's son from Leutkirch in Allgäu, made his way through secondary education and initial university studies before entering the University of Tübingen in 1505. Ordained there as a secular priest, he completed doctorates in civil and canon law at the University of Freiburg in 1509. He became vicar-general of the diocese of Constance in 1517 and in 1521 suffragan bishop. His friendship with Erasmus led him to greet Luther's initial calls for reform positively, and he admired the preaching of Wolfgang Capito and Johannes Oecolampadius. In 1521 at the Diet of Worms he advocated the calling of a council to address Luther's concerns. By 1522, he had turned against Luther and in 1523 began his criticism of Zwingli. In 1523 the Habsburg Archduke Ferdinand engaged him as an advisor, and Fabri was active in opposing Anabaptists, including Balthasar Hubmaier. Electeded bishop of Vienna in 1530, he participated in the negotiations with MELANCHTHON and other evangelical representatives at Augsburg and contributed to the composition of the "Papal Confutation" of the Augsburg Confession.

***Kaspar Schatzgeyer* (1463–1527)** studied at the university of his Bavarian dukes in Ingolstadt in the 1480s and joined the Observant Franciscan order in 1482. As provincial head of the order from 1514, he strove for reform of life in the houses under his supervision. More open than most prominent advocates of the old faith, Schatzgeyer attempted to initiate a dialogue over Luther's criticisms of medieval practices and teaching in 1522, but his treatises *Examination of Holy Scripture for the Reconciliation of Dissenting Dogmas* (1522) and *On True Christian and Evangelical Freedom* (1524) also rejected Luther's teaching on grace and the freedom of the will, justification of sinners, good works and Christian freedom, the mass, and monastic vows. At the same time, he strove to make clear that good works cannot save and that the doctrine of transubstantiation was not a biblical concept. He simply did not recognize the doctrinal basis of Luther's call for reform and profound change in his perception of the underlying structure of what it means to be Christian. Schatzgeyer went on to attack more fiercely those who left the Franciscan order, such as JOHANN EBERLIN VON GÜNZBURG, and ANDREAS OSIANDER in nearby Nuremberg.

***Georg Witzel* (1501–1573)** studied in Erfurt beginning in 1516 and soon joined the group of biblical humanists there. His attraction to Luther's teaching drew him to the University of Wittenberg in 1521, and he was ordained the following year and then married. After being dismissed from his parish in Vacha, he served two other congregations before returning to the Roman obedience in 1531. He became priest in Eisleben in 1533 and entered into controversy with JOHANN AGRICOLA there. In 1538 DUKE GEORG OF SAXONY appointed him his counselor. After the introduction of the Reformation in ducal Saxony in 1539, he met with MARTIN BUCER to formulate a path to reconciliation of the papal party with the evangelical Reformers. He left Dresden in 1541 for Fulda to serve as counselor to the abbot there. From 1554 to his death, he resided in Mainz, where EMPEROR FERDINAND consulted him for advice from time to time. He strove to create a bridge between the Wittenberg Reformers and the Roman Catholic Church with Erasmian positions on many issues. He took part in negotiations with the followers of Luther, for instance, in

Georg Witzel (engraving, sixteenth century)

Regensburg in 1541 and Worms in 1557. He participated in the creation of the Augsburg Interim of 1548. He abandoned attempts to reconcile the two sides with the rise of Jesuit influence in Germany and the issuance of the canons and decrees of the Council of Trent.

The father of ***Julius Pflug* (1499–1564)** had served as chancellor at the ducal Saxon court in Dresden. He sent Julius to study in Bologna and Rome, where he absorbed some influences of the biblical humanist movement and immersed himself in the writings of ERASMUS. He also admired and used the publications of MELANCHTHON. DUKE GEORG OF SAXONY took interest in Pflug and furthered his career. His lack of theological training did show itself in what he himself produced. He participated in the Roman Catholic committee that negotiated with the evangelical delegation headed by Melanchthon at the colloquies in Hagenau, Worms, and Regensburg in 1540 and 1541. He was named to membership in the foundations of Meissen, Zeitz, Merseburg, and Magdeburg in the course of the 1530s, and in 1541 the chapter of the diocese of Naumburg and Zeitz elected him bishop. ELECTOR JOHANN FRIEDRICH OF SAXONY thwarted Pflug's assuming that office by imposing NIKOLAUS VON AMSDORF on the chapter to lead the diocese, the population of which had largely become Lutheran by that time. Pflug continued to serve the sons of DUKE HEINRICH even though they introduced and promoted the Reformation in their lands. In 1547–48, Pflug was a leading voice in the committee that composed the Augsburg Interim. ELECTOR MORITZ also named him to the committee that fashioned the Saxon Leipzig Proposal or "Interim." At the same time, the victory of CHARLES V over the Smalcald League placed Pflug on the episcopal throne in Zeitz. As bishop, he played a leading role in the German delegation to the Council of Trent in 1551–52. EMPEROR FERDINAND named him chair of the colloquy of Worms in 1557. After its failure, Pflug campaigned for his own program of reform, which emphasized humanistic learning for priests and abolition of many superstitious practices. His criticism of the moral life of the clergy was clear and severe.

The Reformed Foes

Among those who turned from support for Luther to sharp critique of his position on the Lord's Supper were the following five German-speaking theologians from southern German lands and Switzerland. JOHN CALVIN muted his critique of Luther, though he finally publicly supported the position of HEINRICH BULLINGER, whose respectful but decisive rejection of the true presence of Christ's body and blood in the sacramental elements remained constant in his polemical exchanges with defenders of Luther's position to the end of his life.

***Ulrich Zwingli* (1484–1531)** grew up as the son of a well-to-do peasant family in the Toggenburg valley in lands subject to the Swiss abbey of Saint Gall. He began schooling at home and under tutelage of an uncle who was priest in Wesen and then Basel. After completing his preparatory education, he attended lectures at the University of Vienna from 1498 to 1502 and then transferred to the University of Basel. His education steeped him in the *via antiqua* with its realist philosophy, which shaped his thought just as Luther's Ockhamist orientation in the *via moderna* determined his framework for interpreting Scripture. Basel also provided Zwingli with exposure to the biblical humanists. He was ordained in 1506 in Glarus and accompanied local troops to war, participating in the battle of Marignano in 1515. He had contact in these years with ERASMUS and purchased his edition of the Greek New Testament when it appeared in 1516. In that year he became priest at the

Benedictine abbey in Einsiedeln, a pilgrimage site, and ministered to pilgrims who sought the indulgences offered there. He immersed himself in ancient fathers, including Jerome, Ambrose, and Cyprian. In 1518 Zwingli sought the position of priest of the Grossmünster in Zurich, and upon promising to break off his relationship with a peasant woman, he was called to the position. His first sermon included the announcement that he would reject the pericopal system and would be preaching through the Gospel of Matthew. His powerful preaching won him a following. His reading of Luther's early writings caused him to acclaim the Wittenberg professor as the third Elijah. He found that Luther spoke to his own humanistic concerns for the reform of the life and administration of the church. His preaching called increasingly for changes, and in January 1523 the Zurich city council organized a disputation for which Zwingli prepared *Sixty-Seven Articles*, theses on the reform of the church for public debate. In October 1523, a second disputation took place,

Portrait of Ulrich Zwingli by Hans Asper (1549)

with results reflecting the fact that under Zwingli's leadership the will to reform had taken hold in the city. In 1525 he, with LEO JUD and KONRAD PELLIKAN, organized the "*Prophezei*," a continuing education program for priests in the jurisdiction of Zurich. In 1525 he had the town council abolish the medieval liturgy of the mass. By this time his revulsion against its superstitious elements led him to reject and openly attack Luther's teaching on the true presence of Christ's body and blood in the Lord's Supper. The two fell into often acrimonious controversy, which was calmed but not resolved in the Marburg Colloquy of 1529. While the Swiss and south German theologians accompanying Zwingli there could agree on most issues with Luther and his followers, the Lord's Supper remained a serious obstacle to full agreement. After the appearance of Zwingli's personal confessions of faith, the "*Ratio fidei*" prepared for presentation to EMPEROR CHARLES V at the Diet of Augsburg in 1530 and the "*Expositio fidei*" he wrote to win the French king Francis I in 1531, Luther also criticized Zwingli's belief that the noblest of ancient Greek and Roman thinkers could be saved apart from faith in Christ. Zwingli died accompanying Zurich's military forces in a battle with Roman Catholic cantons at Kappel in October 1531.

***Leo Jud* (1482–1542)** had gone to secondary school with MARTIN BUCER in their native Alsace, at Schlettstadt. In 1498, he began university studies at Basel and formed a friendship with ULRICH ZWINGLI. He abandoned the study of medicine for theology and was ordained in Rome in 1507, then serving in Basel and Sankt Hippolyt in Alsace. In 1519, he followed Zwingli in the pastorate in Einsiedeln and began to work for reform of church practice. In 1522, he was called to Zurich as pastor of the Church of Saint Peter. From that time on, he stood at Zwingli's side, preaching, teaching, and also translating key works of patristic, medieval, and contemporary figures, including Luther. He aided his Zurich colleagues KONRAD PELLIKAN and Theodor Bibliander in translating the Bible, which appeared beginning in 1525. After several months of criticism of Zurich's Erastian organization of the church, which placed it under the control of the city council, Jud capitulated to HEINRICH BULLINGER's continued support of the arrangement created under Zwingli's leadership. Jud assisted in the composition of the *First Helvetic Confession* of 1536; his German translation of the Latin became its official text. At the time of his death he was in the midst of a translation of the Old Testament.

***Konrad Pellikan* (1478–1556)** returned to his birthplace, Ruffach in Alsace, after studying at the University of Heidelberg in 1491–92, to assist the schoolmaster. He entered the Franciscan order and rose quickly to administrative posts, with time dedicated to further education at the University of Tübingen. The cloister in Basel also needed his services,

Leo Jud (engraving, sixteenth century)

and there he became involved with printers because he had learned sufficient Hebrew in Tübingen to compose the first German introduction to the Hebrew language, with grammatical instruction and a rudimentary dictionary. It appeared in 1501, and the next year the printer Johann Amerbach put Pellikan to work. Pellikan's close association with ERASMUS while in Basel made a significant impact on his thinking. Officials of the order returned him to Ruffach to serve as instructor in their cloister there, and then he was transferred to Pforzheim before becoming secretary to the order's provincial head, whom he accompanied on journeys that afforded him the opportunity to meet, among others, JACQUES LEFÈVRE D'ÉTAPLES. Further time in Basel immersed Pellikan deeper in the publication of works in Hebrew as he worked for ADAM PETRI, who also had him work on the preparation of a new edition of Luther's writings. This fired his long-felt desire for reform in the church, and by 1523 his commitment to reform in something of Luther's manner was well known.

Konrad Pellikan (engraving, sixteenth century)

Deprived of his leadership posts in the order, he entered into a public disputation in February 1524 over clerical celibacy. At the end of 1525 ZWINGLI called him to be a professor of Hebrew in Zurich. He served in that role faithfully for thirty years. He rejected Luther's understanding of the true presence of Christ's body and blood in the Lord's Supper. He was one of the contributors to the First Helvetic Confession of 1536.

***Heinrich Bullinger* (1504–1575)** exercised an even stronger influence on the development of the Reformed tradition than did his predecessor and mentor, ZWINGLI. His father had served in Bremgarten in the Aargau as a priest, and he there began his education. After further preparation in Emmerich, he entered the University of Cologne and absorbed the realist philosophy dominant there. His reading of Luther's early writings and MELANCHTHON's *Loci communes* of 1521 won him to their teaching. In early 1523, he became the chief teacher at the Cistercian monastery at Kappel, where he began to produce commentaries on the New Testament books. He instituted the abolition of the mass there in 1525 and 1526 and took part in the disputations that brought the Reformation to Zurich and Bern. He became pastor at Bremgarten in 1529 and married Anna Adlischwyler the same year. After the defeat of Zurich and its allies at the battle at Kappel in 1531, he fled with his family to Zurich, and he there was appointed to Zwingli's post as antistes, the head of Zurich's church. His literary activity as well as his preaching made him a widely influential figure. His commentaries, some derived from his preaching, and his catechetical sermons, the *Decades*, provided pastors with basic materials for their preaching and teaching. His development of the concept of covenant shaped the teaching of many in the Reformed tradition. His view of the covenant held that one covenant existed between God and his faithful throughout human history, and it was bilateral. Trust in God and love of neighbor were required on the human side. Thus, his theology, while indeed shaped by Zwingli's, went beyond it in significant ways. Bullinger and Calvin worked out an agreement that moved Calvin away from his belief that Christ is indeed spiritually present in the Lord's Supper to a more symbolic view of the sacrament. Bullinger's commitment to a doctrine of single predestination did not move Calvin in the same way. Calvin also did not accept Bullinger's commitment to Zwingli's understanding of the governing role of the civil government in the life of the church, insisting instead on the church's relative independence from civil authorities.

Portrait of Heinrich Bullinger by Hans Asper (1550)

***Johann Oecolampadius* (1482–1531)** came from a family of means and was sent to Bologna to study law before he began his study of theology in Heidelberg, Tübingen, and Basel. In Heidelberg, the influence of biblical humanists decisively shaped his mindset.

Befriended by Jakob Wimpfeling, he became tutor for the sons of Elector Philip of the Palatinate, who were studying in Mainz. His parents endowed a position for their son at Weinsberg, his hometown, and there he was ordained in 1510. His first published work appeared in 1512, a devotional mediation on the last words of Jesus. In 1513, he returned to university studies at Tübingen and then Heidelberg, making the acquaintance of MELANCHTHON, JOHANNES REUCHLIN, and WOLFGANG CAPITO, among others. In 1515, JOHANN FROBEN hired him to work at his press in Basel as proofreader and editor. There, Oecolampadius assisted ERASMUS in preparing his *Annotations*. In 1516, he returned to Weinsberg. In 1518, he went back to Basel, then assumed the position of cathedral preacher and confessor in Augsburg after completing his doctorate. Two years later, he found quiet in a monastery near Augsburg to sort out the various streams of thoughts he had encountered. In 1522, he found his way back to Basel to work for ANDREAS CRATANDER in his

Portrait of Johann Oecolampadius by Hans Asper (1550)

printing operation. Oecolampadius cultivated a friendship with ZWINGLI at that time that did not immediately damage his continuing relationship with Melanchthon and Luther but did lead to a break with Erasmus by 1525. However, by 1525 Oecolampadius felt compelled to criticize the Wittenberg position on the Lord's Supper in print. In May 1526, Oecolampadius took part in the disputation at Baden and defended a symbolic view of the presence of Christ in the Lord's Supper. He bore the brunt of the debate with Luther and his supporters over the Lord's Supper in the second half of the 1520s and was supported by Zwingli at the Marburg Colloquy with the Wittenberg theologians, at which Oecolampadius served as the official head of the Swiss and Strassburg delegation.

***Wolfgang Musculus* (1497–1563)** left his home in Dieuze in Lorraine to gain a secondary education in the Alsace. He became a Benedictine monk and rose to the office of preacher of the monastery in Lixheim. As Luther's writings began to appear in 1518, Musculus eagerly read them and advocated his theology. In 1527 he married, left the monastery, and became first MARTIN BUCER's secretary, then MATTHÄUS ZELL's assistant in Strassburg. There he learned Greek and Hebrew. In 1531 he became a pastor in Augsburg, and in 1536 he joined Bucer in accepting the Wittenberg Concord. He participated in the discussions between Roman Catholic and evangelical theologians in Hagenau, Worms, and Regensburg in 1540–41. Driven from Augsburg by the imposition of the Augsburg Interim in 1548, he briefly found residence in several Swiss towns before accepting a professorship of theology in Bern in 1549. There he returned to his earlier convictions, rejecting the true presence of

Wolfgang Musculus

Christ's body and blood in the Lord's Supper. His biblical commentaries were widely read, including in Lutheran circles, and his *Loci communes* of 1560 became a classical expression of the Reformed faith.

Following the direction of his father, a trustee of the cathedral chapter in Noyon (in Picardy in northern France), ***John Calvin* (1509–1564)** began the study of theology in 1523 in Paris. When his father lost his position with the chapter, he directed Calvin to study law in Orléans. Calvin's early education had acquainted him with the piety of the Brethren of the Common Life, and in Orléans he met an instructor in Latin and Greek, Melchior Wolmar, a German who also had immersed himself in the Greek New Testament and had read Luther's works extensively. Calvin followed his example. After his study in Orléans, Calvin pursued learning the biblical languages and reading ancient Christian and pagan sources at the College Royal in Paris, where he absorbed the biblical humanism of Erasmus and Lefèvre and published his first book, a commentary on the Stoic thinker Seneca's *On Mercy*. He moved into the reform-minded group gathered by Bishop Guillaume Briçonnet of Meaux. There he further deepened his acquaintance with Luther's writings. When his friend Nicolas Cop became rector of the University of Paris in late 1533 and advocated a doctrine of justification by faith in his inaugural oration, the French courts charged with the prosecution of heresy intervened, and Calvin fled Paris, first going to Basel. There, he wrote the first edition of his *Institute of the Christian Religion*, published in 1536, which drew heavily from Luther's two catechisms, his *Freedom of the Christian*, and his *On the Babylonian Captivity of the Church* and particularly on Melanchthon's *Loci communes*. As he was passing through Geneva in 1536, the local leader of ecclesiastical reform, Guillaume Farel, insisted Calvin remain to aid in the completion of reform measures for the city. His time as "lecturer in Holy Scripture" in Geneva ended in the spring of 1538 when the city council exiled Farel and Calvin. Calvin spent three years in Strassburg as pastor of the French-speaking congregation before being invited to return to Geneva, where he spent the rest of his life, becoming the leading voice of French-speaking Reformed theology. He continued to admire and borrow from Luther, although the two never met, and Luther expressed approval of the little he heard about Calvin. Calvin and Melanchthon maintained a correspondence until the latter's death, although they disappointed each other, Calvin with his—what seemed to Melanchthon—deterministic doctrine of predestination, Melanchthon with his expressions regarding the freedom of the will and with his compromise in the Leipzig Proposal, or Interim, of 1548. Calvin did join in the sharp rejection of the doctrine of justification advanced by Andreas Osiander. Originally, Calvin formulated a doctrine of the presence of Christ in the Lord's Supper that could be labeled "spiritual": Christ is truly present but in his whole person, not specifically in his body and blood in the reception of the sacrament. Calvin's training had convinced him of a divide between spiritual and material that avoided the materialistic veneration of the elements and their magical use. He did not understand Luther's interpretation, based on principles regarding God's omnipotence that were taken from William of Ockham, whose influence on Calvin was negligible. Joachim Westphal and Calvin fell into controversy over Calvin's acceptance of a compromise with Heinrich Bullinger in Zurich, the *Zurich Consensus* (1549), in which Calvin abandoned his emphasis on Christ's presence in the Lord's Supper for a more symbolic interpretation of the sacrament. Although Melanchthon was accused of adopting Calvin's view, he steadfastly refused to do so in his last years, seeking his own formulation of the doctrine of Christ's true presence that did not use Luther's terminology but insisted on that presence. Luther's followers and Calvin's fell into acrimonious disputes by the end of the century, in which the confrontation between Calvin's successor in Geneva, Theodore Beza, and Jakob Andreae at Mömpelgaard (Montbéliard) in 1586 played a significant role.

Portrait of John Calvin at age fifty-three by René Boyvin (1562)

The Anabaptists, Spiritualists, and Antitrinitarians

For at least a half millennium, Western Christendom had experienced chiefly localized and usually short-lived (the Albigensians in southwestern France an exception) movements for reform. Although connections between most of them cannot be documented, most shared some common characteristics. They were biblicistic, insisting that the rules of church officials and their appeals to the tradition of the church had no place in the truly Christian life. They were, at the same time, heavily moralistic, rejecting the medieval church's dependence on sacred or religious acts of piety as the pinnacle of the good life and imitating instead the ethical commands of Scripture. Often arising from upwardly mobile social groups, such as the peasants who had come to the towns to find work, they opposed the power of the clergy and the hierarchy in general. This anticlericalism issued into anti-sacramentalism since the sacraments served as instruments to reinforce the power of the clergy. Many of these groups were millenarian, often believing that they themselves were called to be God's instruments in establishing God's kingdom on earth or at least bringing the world of sin and injustice to an end. This medieval pattern of reform hung in the air at the beginning of the sixteenth century, and elements of it surfaced in the thinking of a rather wide spectrum of individuals and groups calling for reform.

ANDREAS KARLSTADT exhibited some of these characteristics as he developed his own alternative to Luther's kind of reform. In Zurich at much the same time, individuals disgusted with the slow pace and incomplete nature, from their perspective, of ZWINGLI's reform organized small groups of the pious and began practicing rebaptism. Within months, in several locations within the German-speaking lands, similar small groups arose and began to propagate their own plans for reform. They were often led by young men, the majority of them with no university training though often with an extensive command of the Bible. Because they refused to submit to governmental authority when its rules conflicted with Scripture, such as the requirement for oaths, they were regarded as treasonous, holding beliefs that undermined society and tore the social fabric. Thus, they were persecuted by Roman Catholic and Protestant authorities, although Lutheran governments preferred exile to execution, putting very few to death. The Reformers often grouped with them a variety of spiritualists, although the spiritualists, unlike the Anabaptists, paid little attention to any outward forms of God's word. The Anabaptists emphasized dependence on Scripture and the use of baptism as a human confession of faith and commitment to God. Several prominent leaders among the Anabaptists met in Schleitheim in the canton of Schaffhausen in February 1527, where they produced "Articles," in the twentieth century relabeled a "confession," summarizing their protest against the established church; several of these leaders participated in what came to be called "The Martyrs' Synod" in Augsburg in August 1527.

Luther saw these *Schwärmer* (ravers), to use the word he invented to describe them, as a threat to proper biblical understanding of how God brings salvation to his people. Their reliance on the inner movement of the Spirit deprived those in true struggles over their guilt before God of the consolation of God's word coming with certainty from outside themselves. Although Luther was aware of significant differences among those he so labeled, he did not distinguish between those who relied on inner revelation alone (spiritualists) and those who accepted biblical authority (Anabaptists). Dependence on the inner voice of the Spirit and a failure to acknowledge that the Holy Spirit uses the oral, written, and sacramental forms of God's word as the instruments for accomplishing God's will, as well as their frequent argument that good works do contribute to salvation, earned the Anabaptists and spiritualists sharp critique from Wittenberg. The Wittenberg Reformers engaged these Schwärmer at several levels, but chiefly in writings designed to warn readers against being enticed into false belief by them.

***Thomas Müntzer* (ca. 1490–1525)** studied in Leipzig and Frankfurt an der Oder before being ordained by the bishop of Halberstadt in early 1514. He became a priest in Braunschweig, where he developed friendships with leading merchants. He studied in Wittenberg during the years 1517–19, becoming acquainted with Karlstadt and Luther. During a period of travel that brought him to preach in a number of places, he began to read sermons by Johannes Tauler, the fourteenth-century mystical theologian whose works Luther also appreciated. Müntzer's reading, however, took him in a spiritualistic direction, in which he heard special direct revelations and dismissed the worth of outward forms of God's word. From May 1520, he found employment as a preacher in the Saxon town of Zwickau for a year. Dismissed in April 1521 he traveled to Bohemia, preaching until forbidden to do so by governmental authorities, who found his message unsettling. In Prague he wrote a *Protest*, which related his private, personal revelations from God concerning the total corruption of the church. He returned to Wittenberg in 1522 but found no welcome there, nor in his home town of Stolberg, or in Nordhausen. In early 1523, the town of Allstedt in Thuringia called him as pastor without obtaining permission of the church's patron, Elector Frederick the Wise. There, Müntzer married, introduced a reformed, vernacular liturgy, and sought reconciliation with Luther. Luther's continued suspicion of Müntzer provoked the latter's attack on Wittenberg theology, culminating in his *Well-Grounded Defense and Answer against the Soft-Living Flesh at Wittenberg* and *Express Exposure of the False Faith of the Unfaithful World* in 1524. Müntzer also antagonized neighboring rulers, including Count Ernst of Mansfeld and Duke Georg of Saxony. His attempt to win the favor of Elector Frederick and his brother Elector Johann failed and elicited Luther's *Letter to the Princes of Saxony Concerning the Rebellious Spirit.* In August 1524,

Portrait of Thomas Müntzer from Pansebia *by Alexander Ross, printed 1683*

Müntzer began to preach in an imperial town in Thuringia, Mühlhausen, with the support of a preacher there, Heinrich Pfeiffer. They were sent into exile, and Müntzer began another preaching pilgrimage, returning in early 1525 to a pastorate in Mühlhausen. There, he organized forces to support rebellious peasants and assumed what he deemed a Gideon-like role as their leader. His rebel band was defeated at the battle of Frankenhausen in May 1525. Müntzer was captured and executed. Müntzer commanded public attention into the seventeenth century as an example of the dangers of spiritualistic reliance on direct revelation; indifference to, if not outright rejection of the oral, written, and sacramental forms of God's word; and the use of force to pursue religions goals. Only much later did he become a cult figure of Marxist thinkers.

A different personality type, with a different kind of spiritualism, ***Kaspar Schwenckfeld von Ossig* (1489–1561)** supported Luther enthusiastically for a time before departing from his teaching on the necessity of the oral, written, and sacramental forms of God's word in delivering the gospel and from his convictions regarding justification by grace through faith in Christ. Schwenckfeld renounced his claim on part of the family's holdings in Silesia. After studying at the University of Cologne from 1505 to 1507 and at the University of Frankfurt an der Oder thereafter, he entered service in the courts of two small Silesian principalities and in 1521 joined the court of Duke Friedrich II of Liegnitz-Brieg-Wohlau. After two years on Duke Friedrich's staff, he resigned because of worsening problems with his hearing. His reading of Luther's writings attracted him, and he actively argued for the introduction of the Wittenberg Reformation in Silesia. In 1525 he visited Wittenberg, but by that time his views of the Lord's Supper had turned in a decidedly Zwinglian direction. Luther criticized him sharply in treatises focused on the aberrant position of his colleague Andreas Karlstadt and Zwingli. Schwenckfeld was also discontented with the moral laxity he found among Luther's followers and insisted that the leading of a godly life contributes to salvation. Schwenckfeld's return to Silesia did not last long, for in 1528 King Ferdinand, who exercised sovereignty over the Silesian principalities, ordered a severe crackdown on every type of reform. In 1529 Schwenkfeld found his way to Strassburg, where his contacts with the church's leadership were initially friendly. In 1534, however, he and Martin Bucer openly opposed each other. Schwenkfeld began a pilgrimage that brought him to Speyer and then to Ulm, where he had influential supporters, then to Augsburg and Esslingen. His attempt to find common ground with South German theologians through a dialogue in Tübingen in 1535 failed because of disagreement on several issues. These included Schwenkfeld's

Kaspar Schwenkfeld (engraving, sixteenth century)

vehement rejection of the efficacy of all external forms of God's word and his contention that Christ's humanness was in fact "celestial," that is, not creaturely but a special form of existence sent to earth from heaven. By 1539, he openly defended the view that Christ was not a creature according to his humanity but that his flesh was "celestial" and he is "totally our God and Lord." This earned him banishment from Ulm. The Smalcald League formally condemned him repeatedly; Luther took issue with his Christology in a disputation in Wittenberg in 1540. A nobleman provided him refuge near Ulm (1541–47), and there he authored some fifty published treatises. However, the victory of CHARLES V in the Smalcald War ended the nobleman's ability to shelter him. In the 1550s, MATTHIAS FLACIUS challenged Schwenckfeld's theology with a series of thorough critiques. Schwenckfeld hid where he could and traveled widely, seeking converts and encouraging followers, until his death in Ulm.

Distinct in their teaching from such spiritualists, though not always differentiated from them by their opponents, were those who emphasized the outer means of the sacraments as symbols and the Bible as the source of the necessary information for living the godly life, the Anabaptists. Their initial leadership had many former university students in its ranks, although most came to despise formal theological education. The Anabaptist movement had many distinct streams of thought, and Luther had personal contact with some representatives of some of them; in other cases, he read their publications or based reactions on the reports of others.

When peasant forces occupied the Benedictine monastery of Saint Peter of the Black Forest in 1525, its prior, ***Michael Sattler* (ca. 1490–1527)**, apparently joined them, if not physically, at least in spirit. He had worked for reform in the monastery, although he seems not to have been influenced significantly by Luther's writings. He began preaching rebaptism and strict Christian discipline in the area surrounding Zurich and then near Strassburg. Conversations with BUCER and CAPITO at that time made a positive impression upon them. He composed the "Schleitheim Articles" at the meeting in the Swiss village of Schleitheim of several Anabaptist leaders in February 1527. Shortly thereafter, he moved to Horb in Württemberg to become pastor of an Anabaptist congregation, was arrested, and was tortured and executed by burning in May 1527.

***Hans Hut* (d. 1527)** was born not far from the birthplace of HANS LUDER in western Thuringia. He learned the trade of bookbinding and became a traveling bookseller as well, visiting Wittenberg on occasion in the 1520s. He aired his doubts about infant baptism there, without receiving what were satisfactory answers to his growing skepticism. In the midst of the Peasants Revolt of 1525, the preaching of Thomas Müntzer drew him into the peasant army assembled at Frankenhausen. When the peasant force was defeated, he fled the battlefield but was arrested. He quickly won release, but soon thereafter governmental authorities came to regard him as the leader of the Anabaptists. Rebaptized by Hans Denck in 1526, Hut became a traveling preacher, seeking converts to his movement across southern German-speaking areas. At the center of his preaching stood Jesus Christ, who had paid the price for the world's sins. His own views accepted governmental authority, but he urged believers not to submit to requirements that went against God's commands and not to take part in government service of any kind. He rejected the necessity of communal sharing of goods, but he also rejected infant baptism and the presence of Christ in the Lord's Supper, teaching that baptism is a commitment to God that must produce true obedience to divine commands. His message asserted the impending return of Christ

Hans Hut, gravure by Christoffel van Sichem (1567)

and promised that the kingdom of Christ would soon be established on earth. In late 1526, his encounter with BALTHASAR HUBMAIER in Nikolsburg and their disagreements led to two disputations between the two on proper biblical teaching. Hut departed on a wide-ranging missionary journey that brought him to Steyr in Austria, where he barely eluded arrest and execution (some of his converts there did not), to several other Austrian towns, and to Augsburg. His participation in the Martyrs' Synod there landed him in jail, where he died in a fire while awaiting execution.

***Hans Denck* (ca. 1500–1527)** was born and raised in southern Bavaria and attended the universities in Ingolstadt and Basel, benefitting from humanist instruction in Greek and Hebrew. His theological roots sprang, however, from the monastic-mystical tradition represented by the writing edited by Luther, the *Deutsche Theologie* (*German Theology*). JOHANN OECOLAMPADIUS, his instructor in Basel, recommended him to become rector of Saint Sebald school in Nuremberg. Along with the painter Sebald Behaim and several colleagues, Denck suffered banishment from the city because of their opinions on baptism and the Lord's Supper. He rejected the Lutheran doctrine of justification by faith, emphasizing the necessity of a pious life for salvation. His confession composed for the courts in Nuremberg became an important formulation of Anabaptist thought, although his belief that all would be saved offended other Anabaptists. He settled in Augsburg as a tutor after traveling around Switzerland and contacting some Anabaptists there. In Augsburg he may have been rebaptized by BALTHASAR HUBMAIER. Denck assumed leadership of the Anabaptist congregation upon Hubmaier's departure. His own departure followed a disputation with URBANUS RHEGIUS and other Lutheran pastors. His subsequent stay in Strassburg ended with a similar disputation. His next residence was Worms, where he aided Ludwig Haetzer in the translation of the Old Testament prophetic books. In early 1527 he participated in the "Martyrs' Synod" in Augsburg, although he died of the plague in Basel a month after the synod. In two works published in 1527, he set forth an Anabaptist dogmatics of sorts, a work which influenced others. Toward the end of his life, he abandoned an emphasis on baptism and drifted into a more mystical theology that needed no outward signs. Whether he also tended toward antitrinitarian thinking is debated by scholars.

***Melchior Rinck* (1490–after 1551)** studied in Leipzig and Erfurt, where he received a good foundation in Greek. As schoolmaster in Hersfeld, he openly advocated Luther's theology and earned dismissal from his position at the foundation of canons there. He became a pastor in villages near Eisenach, married, but then fell under the influence of THOMAS MÜNTZER. He publicly criticized the doctrine of justification by faith in Christ and promoted a doctrine of salvation through faith and works. He denied that original sin merits condemnation until its fruits appear in the years in which children can think for themselves. He rejected baptismal regeneration and called for a second baptism as the commitment of the individual believer to serve God. He also denied the true presence of Christ's body and blood in the Lord's Supper. These views became clear in a disputation held in Marburg, sponsored by the government of Philip of Hesse in 1528. Until 1531 Rinck wandered, preaching where he could, without much success in gathering people for his cause. In November 1531, he was arrested by the electoral Saxon government and never emerged from prison, though his confinement was eased.

***Balthasar Hubmaier* (ca. 1480–1528)** came from the vicinity of Augsburg to the University of Freiburg in 1503 and studied under Johann Eck. After his ordination, he followed Eck to Ingolstadt for further study and became a preacher at the cathedral in Regensburg and the first chaplain of the chapel built on the site of the razed Jewish synagogue. In the chapel's earliest years, it had experienced miracles, which Hubmaier recorded. A call to Waldshut in Breisgau brought him to the shores of the Rhine River in 1521, where he began to read Luther's writings. After a brief return to Regensburg, his arrival back in Waldshut in 1523 began an intensive engagement with the ideas of Luther and Zwingli that led to his alienation from medieval practice and teaching and to conflict in Waldshut that the Habsburg government ended with force. A life of wandering began. He sided with the Anabaptists in Zurich against Zwingli and encouraged the peasants who were seizing arms in the assertion of their traditional rights in 1524–26. After trying to marshal peasant resistance in several areas, he returned to Zurich a fugitive, and therewas tortured and forced to recant. He secretly left the city, spending time in Augsburg as leader of its Anabaptist community and settling in the summer of 1526 in Nikolsburg in Moravia. There he gathered a large Anabaptist community. The Augsburg printer Simprecht Sorg (also known as Froschauer) moved his press to Nikolsburg and, with Hubmaier as author, launched a print campaign for Anabaptist theology. In August 1527, Hubmaier was arrested and imprisoned by Habsburg authorities. He appealed to his friend from university days, Johann Fabri, the bishop of Vienna, who visited him, as did a number of other theologians, in attempts to induce him to recant. He wrote a confession of faith for the emperor's brother, Ferdinand, administrator of Austria, which failed to convince the Habsburg prince of his orthodoxy. He was burned at the stake March 10, 1527.

***Pilgram Marpeck* (ca. 1495–1556)**, one of the most prolific and sophisticated of the sixteenth-century Anabaptist writers, came from a prominent family in Rattenberg in

Tirol. As a mechanic or engineer in the mines of that region, Marpeck became a member of the governing councils of Rattenberg in the mid-1520s. His refusal to take part in the arrest of Anabaptists who were coming into the area led to his dismissal from his positions in 1527. After a brief period of interest in Luther's thought, he turned to Anabaptist teaching and became a leader of the Anabaptist congregation in Strassburg in 1530. He quickly fell into controversy with MARTIN BUCER and his colleagues in the municipal ministerium. When Marpeck persisted in his rejection of infant baptism, he was sent into exile in 1532. For twelve years he traveled, making contacts with and ministering to Anabaptist congregations in southern German lands, Moravia, and Swiss cantons. From 1544 to his death, he resided in Augsburg, working for the city government as the manager of its water system and other public works. Repeated warnings regarding his religious views from city officials did not bring about a change of his teaching but also did not result in another exile. He wrote extensively against KASPAR SCHWENCKFELD's attack on the "externalism" of the Anabaptists, in which he allegedly charged that this led them to neglect the inner spirit. Although the two had become friends during Marpeck's residence in Strassburg, Schwenckfeld's attitude toward the Bible and the rites of the Christian community aroused Marpeck's sharp critique.

***Melchior Hofmann/Hoffmann* (ca. 1495–1543),** a furrier from Schwäbisch-Hall, found early spiritual nourishment from the mystical work the *Deutsche Theologie* (*German Theology*), which Luther edited in 1516. He became a follower of Luther and began to preach, though not ordained, in 1523 while in Livonia, in Wolmar and Dorpat (Tartu). He won approval for his preaching in the latter town from the Lutheran pastors in Riga. His visit to Wittenberg in 1525 brought him into personal contact with Luther and BUGENHAGEN, who wrote a letter of support to the Livonian officials in his behalf. An accompanying letter from Hofmann confessed justification by faith alone but also accentuated the fruits of faith, good works, and hinted at his millenarian views. A brief return to Dorpat and brief activity in Reval (Tallinn) led only to tensions with and rejection by local officials. Forced to leave Livonia and Estonia, he became pastor of the German congregation in Stockholm, where he began to publish short treatises that exposed his millenarian teaching (he predicted the end of the world in 1533) and his denial of the presence of Christ's body and blood in the Lord's Supper. His return to Wittenberg in May 1527 and his attempt to visit NIKOLAUS VON AMSDORF in Magdeburg at the same time ended in his frustration, for he encountered a cool attitude in Wittenberg and outright hostility in Magdeburg. Hofmann made his way to Kiel and impressed local officials and the Danish government. He received

Melchior Hofmann, gravure by Christoffel van Sichem

a pastorate but almost immediately fell into conflict with another pastor. A disputation between Hofmann and his opponents held in Flensburg was chaired by Bugenhagen in the presence of Duke Christian of Holstein. It ended in the banishment of Hofmann, who joined with Andreas Karlstadt in East Friesland briefly before going to Strassburg. In this period, he was producing short treatises on a variety of subjects; his millenarian teaching, gained from the visionary Anabaptists Lienhart and Urusula Jost, formed the underlying structure for his thought from this time forward. In 1530, he returned to East Friesland, where his rebaptism of some three hundred individuals led to his ouster. He hid out in Strassburg, with a brief trip to Amsterdam to rebaptize followers, and concentrated on writing. Jailed by Strassburg authorities in 1533, he spent the last decade of his life in ever stricter confinement. His rejection of the natural humanity of Jesus and certain of his expressions on the Trinity combined with his rejection of baptismal regeneration and the true presence of Christ's body and blood in the Lord's Supper made him a persona non grata in Wittenberg eyes.

***Bernhard Rothmann* (ca. 1495–ca. 1535)** was born and raised near Münster and became pastor in that episcopal city around 1529. He visited MELANCHTHON in Wittenberg in 1531 but did not meet Luther while there. He went to Strassburg to seek counsel from MARTIN BUCER and his colleagues and maintained contact with them over the next months. In the course of their correspondence, the Strassburg preachers criticized Rothmann's turn from infant baptism to believers' baptism. The ideas of ERASMUS and other biblical humanists in the Netherlands and Rhine Valley shaped his thought; Luther's theology interested him little. As pastor of the Church of Saint Lambert in Münster, he introduced the Reformation in 1532, searching for the formula for the life of the church and its teaching that best fitted his Erasmian convictions. Luther and Melanchthon both wrote to him regarding his anti-sacramental tendencies, but Rothmann rejected their admonitions, introducing a Zwinglian form of the Lord's Supper in early 1533. His rejection of Anabaptism in late 1532 quickly turned to acceptance through his association with the "preachers of Wassenberg" in the nearby duchy of Jülich—a group, united by a rejection of papal governance, who had a variety of theological directions, including Anabaptist tendencies. Rothmann accepted the Anabaptist leaders JAN MATTHIJSZ and JON BOCKELSON VAN LEYDEN when they came to the city in 1534. They persuaded Rothmann to be rebaptized and to marry eight additional wives when they instituted polygamy for their kingdom. It is most likely that he died in the final battle against the Münsterite "kingdom" in 1535.

This "kingdom" was established by ***Jan Matthijsz* (d. 1534)**, who left his native Haarlem after being baptized by MELCHIOR HOFMANN and organizing a small group of Anabaptists; among its members was ***Jan Bockelson van Leyden* (d. 1536)**. Matthijs abandoned his wife for another, who upon his death became the spouse of Bockelson and reigned with him as Queen Divara in Münster for the last year of the Anabaptist establishment there. Matthijsz followed Bockelson to Münster in early 1534, and they took command of the city in defiance of Bishop Franz von Waldeck. Bockelson was crowned King David; his government introduced communal property, appropriating the possessions of Münster's middle class for the increasing number of Dutch Anabaptists, mostly poorer people, who were coming to join the new kingdom. When the bishop and forces of PHILIP OF HESSE and other neighboring princes besieged the city, Matthijsz led a foray against the army surrounding Münster and died in fighting. Bockelson, a native of Leiden, had earned a living as a tailor, then a merchant, then an innkeeper. After his baptism in November 1533 by

Portrait of Jan Bockelson van Leyden as King of Münster by Heinrich Aldegrever shortly before Bockelson's execution in 1536

Matthijsz, he was sent as a preacher into several Dutch cities. He came to Münster in January of 1534. His rhetorical gifts propelled him to the leadership of the government the Anabaptists established as they overthrew the municipal government in Münster in 1534. By early summer, Bockelson had assumed rule of the city, displacing ROTHMANN and replacing Matthijsz after the latter's death. In September, he had himself crowned King of Zion or New Jerusalem. At the fall of the Anabaptist kingdom on June 25, 1535, he was arrested, put on display at several princely courts, and then executed in Münster in January 1536.

***Menno Simons* (ca. 1496–1561)** was born in West Frisia and ordained in 1524 in Utrecht. In his first parish, the influence of late medieval Dutch anti-sacramental thinking propagated by Cornelis Hoen and others influenced him and drove him into intensive study of the Bible, which he read in the context of his reading of Luther's works. Encounters with followers of MELCHIOR HOFMANN around 1530 led him to reject infant baptism, and he formally left the Roman obedience in 1536. The practices of the Anabaptist kingdom in Münster and its defeat on the battlefield in 1535 led Menno into a spiritual crisis, out of which he developed his convictions that Christians dare never use force. From 1536 to 1544, he was continually on the move, ministering to Anabaptist groups in the region of Groningen and Frisia, while governmental authorities sought his arrest and execution. When the Countess Anna of East Frisia bowed to imperial pressure to crack down on heretical groups in her domains, she entrusted the negotiations with them to the Reformed pastor in Emden, Jan à Lasco. His conversation with Menno ended in disagreement regarding the incarnation of Christ because Menno held to the view that Christ's flesh differed from normal human flesh as the celestial flesh he had brought with him from heaven. Menno then worked briefly in the archbishopric of Cologne, where he ran afoul of the reforming

Portrait of Menno Simons by Jacob Burghart (1682)

archbishop Hermann von Wied. He continued his life as a wandering preacher until his death.

Modern scholars have associated Anabaptists and spiritualists with antitrinitarians, of which there were very few in the first half of the sixteenth century who attracted public attention. Two examples demonstrate the role they played in Wittenberg.

***Michael Servetus* (ca. 1510–1553)**, left his home in Villanueva de Sijena in the kingdom of Aragon for study in Toulouse, the beginning of a scholarly career that led him to spend time in Strassburg, Basel, and Paris, concentrating on medical studies but also absorbing the Erasmian spirit and dedicating himself to broad studies of ancient texts in geography, theology, and other fields. He contributed to the debate between Arabic and Greek approaches to medicine, advancing the first description of pulmonary circulation of the blood. His reading of the patristic debates over the Trinity with various heretical groups led him initially to a modalistic doctrine of God, teaching that the one God revealed himself in various times and places through a variety of names, including Jesus. His early works advancing these views, particularly his *On the Errors of the Trinity* of 1531, attracted attention in Wittenberg, eliciting Melanchthon's attacks. This volume provided occasion for the conduct of academic disputations at the University of Wittenberg on the doctrine of the Trinity in Luther's later years. Servetus moved further in the direction of Arian views, regarding Jesus as a subordinate divine figure. His thought reflected his studies in rabbinic exegesis and Neoplatonic treatises, including that of Hermes Trismegistus. After some fifteen years of practicing medicine and editing various ancient treatises, including Ptolemy's *Geography*, in Vienne, southern France, Servetus's identity as the author of heretical texts was discovered, and he was jailed by Roman Catholic authorities in Vienne. To escape execution, he fled imprisonment. While he made a stop in Geneva, he revealed his identity and was arrested and executed according to Roman law, which condemned Trinitarian heretics to death. His position continued to influence Wittenberg treatments of the doctrine of the Trinity, which countered his arguments.

Closer to home, the only other prominent opponent of the orthodox doctrine of the Trinity was a native of the province of Limburg in the Low Countries, ***Johannes Campanus* (ca. 1500–1574)**, who was attracted to Luther's way of thinking. He attended the Marburg Colloquy in 1529 but was not permitted to participate in the mediating role he offered to play. In correspondence with Melanchthon, he aroused Melanchthon's anger with his ditheistic position: God the Father and Christ are one being but two distinct persons, though Christ is inferior to the Father, he argued, also concluding that the Holy Spirit is not a person at all, but rather the power of the other two. With protection from nobles in the duchy of Jülich-Cleve-Berg, Campanus managed to avoid prosecution for his views. He attempted to advise HERMANN VON WIED, the archbishop of Cologne, on the introduction of the Reformation in the 1540s. In the mid-1550s, Duke Wilhelm of Cleve did arrest him, and several Roman Catholic theologians tried to convince him to recant, a course he apparently rejected. Little is known about his last years.

GLOSSARY

apocalyptic—From the Greek word for "revelation," with reference to the final book of the Bible, the Apocalypse of Saint John, used today for a particularly cataclysmic end of the world and, derivatively, for any situation of severe crisis.

Augsburg Interim—The religious policy formulated for the German Empire and for Emperor CHARLES V in 1548, which mandated observance of medieval doctrine and covenant, with some reform of practices viewed as superstitious and two concessions to evangelical Christians: the suspension of clerical celibacy requirements and the offering of the chalice of Christ's blood in the Lord's Supper to the laity. It was designed as an interim policy until the Council of Trent (1545–63) would make its final decisions and was imposed only on the Protestant territories and towns of the empire.

biblical humanism—A movement promoting education reform, arising in the fourteenth and fifteenth centuries in Italy, arriving north of the Alps in the late fifteenth century. It favored a return to original sources for theology and to the original Greek and Hebrew of the biblical texts, and an emphasis on rhetoric or effective communication of ideas.

Brethren of the Common Life—A group of lay people and priests dedicated to a simple style of life that imitated Christ's practices of love and mercy and emphasized education and the reading of Scripture. Founded in the fourteenth century by Gerhardt Groote in the Netherlands, the movement maintained houses dedicated to supporting or conducting education and social welfare. Members did not take lifelong binding vows, but they did live together and shared meals and a common devotional life.

cabala—A method of mystical interpretation of the Old Testament using allegorical principles, grounded in a Neoplatonic worldview, that arose among Jewish scholars in the twelfth and thirteenth centuries, above all in Spain. It spread to Christian Europe as the study of Hebrew arrived around 1500.

disputation—A form of instruction and examination in the medieval university that posed short thetic statements for debate. Instructors or students formulated the theses, and the student had to demonstrate his ability to defend the theses with good, logical argument. Professors could also offer theses for debate when testing new ideas or new approaches to topics.

Gnesio-Lutherans—A group of Luther's and MELANCHTHON's students and followers who, in the aftermath of Luther's death, the Smalcald War, and the Augsburg Interim, held a more radical interpretation of Luther's thought, in opposition to their Philippist fellow students, who hewed closer to medieval concerns in certain issues of doctrine and practice.

Leipzig Proposal or Interim—A proposal for religious policy in the domains of ELECTOR MORITZ OF SAXONY, offered to and rejected by the Saxon diet in December 1548. Its aim was to make it appear to EMPEROR CHARLES V that Saxony was complying with the Augsburg Interim by making concessions in "adiaphora," neutral matters neither forbidden nor commanded by Scripture, while preserving Lutheran teaching. MELANCHTHON and his Wittenberg colleagues aided in the formulation in order to prevent imperial-Spanish invasion of Saxony, in the hope that this would preserve Saxon Lutheran pulpits for Lutheran preachers.

Neoplatonism—An adaptation of the thought of Plato that arose in the third century, maintained its prominence into the sixth century, and revived in Renaissance circles in the late fifteenth century. It defined the ultimate reality as pure Spirit, an impersonal essence, and described a network of hierarchies descending from that pure Spirit into the spark of spirit entrapped in human bodies. Its deprecation of the material or physical sometimes contributed to Christian mystical thinking and to a dismissal of God's use of material elements, particularly the elements of the sacraments, to convey his power.

nuncio—An envoy representing the papal court at other European rulers' courts.

Ockhamism—A philosophical and theological school following the thinking of William of Ockham (1285–1347), which predominated in the late medieval university and its theological faculty. It held a "nominalistic" view of reality, regarding terms as deductions from human encounters with specific things of a common category, as opposed to the "realist" view that reality resides in divine ideas or the term itself, and specific things are only shadows of those ideas. Luther's training came from those largely influenced by Ockham. This way of thought contributed positively to Luther's own thinking through its emphasis on God as totally sovereign and almighty and on the goodness of the material order as God's creation. Negatively, he revolted against its proposal that believers must "do what is in them" or do their best to win an initial grace with congruent merit, which is not truly worthy of God's favor, and with the aid of the grace won by congruent merit, to perform works of condignent merit, which save.

Philippists—A group of Luther's and Melanchthon's students and followers who, in the aftermath of Luther's death, the Smalcald War, and the Augsburg Interim, defended Philip Melanchthon's efforts to reach a compromise with Emperor Charles V for Elector Moritz of Saxony. Initially, Philippists held a more conservative interpretation of Luther's thought, in opposition to their Gnesio-Lutheran fellow students, who embraced more of the more radical positions in Luther's teaching and practice.

Pomesania—A diocese in Prussia, along the Baltic coast, established in 1243 and, from 1523 to 1587 (when it was secularized), administered by Lutheran bishops.

realism—The view of reality that regarded specific things encountered on earth as mere reflections or shadows of divine ideas or heavenly forms. This view was held by Thomas Aquinas and his followers, as opposed to the nominalist or terminist view of William of Ockham.

quadrivium—The second stage of medieval education, following the trivium, consisting of the mathematical subjects, arithmetic, geometry, music, and astronomy.

Schwärmer—A word invented by Luther for those who rejected external forms of God's word as the means of bestowing grace. Derived from the word for "swarm" in German, it designated those who refused to rely on God's address to them in oral, written, or sacramental forms of his word but instead relied in part or whole on their own inner feelings or on reason.

Smalcald Articles—A document composed by Martin Luther in December 1536 and January 1537, designed to provide Protestant rulers with a basis for instructing their theologians for dialogue at the council called by the pope. It was also regarded as a kind of doctrinal last will and testament of the Reformer. A committee of Wittenberg colleagues and others met to aid him in its composition. It became a confessional document of Lutheran churches beginning in the 1540s and 1550s.

Smalcald League—A league of principalities and towns formed in 1531 to defend the Wittenberg Reformation. It fell apart with the approach of the Smalcald War of 1546–47.

Smalcald War—The military conflict that began with Emperor Charles V's act of naming Elector Johann Friedrich of Saxony and Landgrave Philip of Hesse outlaws in June 1546. Deserted by key Protestant princes, including Duke Moritz of Saxony, Johann Friedrich and Philip were defeated at the battle Mühlberg in April 1547 and condemned to death. Charles remitted their sentences but subjected them to several years of harsh imprisonment.

sodality—A group formed to pursue specific purposes of an intellectual or pious nature.

spiritualistic view of the Lord's Supper—The definition of the presence of Christ in the Lord's Supper as a spiritual view, that is, denying the presence of his body and blood in or with the elements of bread and wine, but affirming a presence that is more than merely symbolic.

Swabian League—A league of territorial rulers, nobles, and towns in southwestern Germany, formed in 1488 to keep the peace and ward off enemies. It dissolved in 1534.

trivium—The basic stage of medieval education, which set forth the fundamental language skills necessary for good communication: grammar, logic or dialectic, and rhetoric.

Truce of Passau—The agreement reached in 1552 that ended hostilities between the Habsburg forces under King Ferdinand and an alliance of princes of the empire, among whom were Elector Moritz of Saxony. The truce reversed the policies of the Habsburgs in force since the Habsburg victory in the Smalcald War in 1547 aimed at the suppression of Protestant governments and their religious reforms. The Augsburg Interim was laid aside as official imperial policy, some Protestant rulers were restored to their lands and rights, and Wittenberg Reforms were permitted to continue in force. The Truce of Passau led to the Religious Peace of Augsburg of 1555.

Variata of the Augsburg Confession—The revision of the Augsburg Confession prepared by the Wittenberg theologians in response to the request of Elector Johann Friedrich for a more explicit statement on justification by faith in the negotiating document that he and his colleagues wanted to guide the evangelical theologians at the religious colloquy called by Emperor Charles V, which took place in Regensburg in 1541.

via antiqua—Another term for the realist school of philosophy and theology.

via moderna—Another term for the nominalist school of philosophy and theology.

BIBLIOGRAPHY

The biographies in this volume have been constructed out of a variety of sources that the author has encountered over the years and consulted specifically for this project. Many anecdotes appeared first in his other works. Here are the secondary sources to which readers can turn for the source of the descriptions of these individuals and for further reading.

Benzing, Josef, and Helmut Claus. *Lutherbibliographie: Verzeichnis der gedruckten Schriften Martin Luthers bis zu dessen Tod.* Baden-Baden: Heitz, 1966.

Brecht, Martin. *Martin Luther.* 3 vols. Minneapolis: Fortress Press, 1985–94.

Buchberger, Michael. *Lexikon für Theologie und Kirche.* Edited by Josef Hofer and Karl Rahner. 14 vols. 2nd ed. Freiburg: Herder, 1957–68.

———. *Lexikon für Theologie und Kirche.* Edited by Walter Kasper. 11 vols. 3rd ed. Freiburg: Herder, 1993–2001.

Controverisa et Confessio. Die Akademie der Wissenschaften und der Literatur Mainz. http://www.controversia-et-confessio.de.

Domröse, Sonja. *Frauen der Reformationszeit: Gelehrt, Mutig, und Glaubensfest.* Göttingen: Vandenhoeck & Ruprecht, 2010.

Frauen der Reformationszeit. Wittenberg: Drei Kastanien, 2004.

Hendrix, Scott H. *Martin Luther: Visionary Reformer.* New Haven: Yale University Press, 2015.

Herbermann, Charles G., ed. *The Catholic Encyclopedia.* 16 vols. New York: Appleton, 1907–14.

Hillerbrand, Hans J., ed. *The Oxford Encyclopedia of the Reformation.* 4 vols. Oxford: Oxford University Press, 1996.

Historische Kommission bei der Königl. Akademie der Wissenschaften. *Allgemeine Deutsche Biographie.* 56 vols. Leipzig: Duncker & Humblot, 1875–1912.

Köstlin, Julius. *Martin Luther: Sein Leben und seine Schriften.* 2nd ed. Elberfeld: Friderichs, 1883.

Krahn, Cornelius, ed. *The Mennonite Encyclopedia.* 5 vols. Hillsboro, KS: Mennonite Brethren Publishing House, 1982–93.

Krause, Gerhard, and Gerhard Müller, eds. *Theologische Realenzyklopädie.* 36 vols. Berlin: de Gruyter, 1977–2004.

Neue Deutsche Biographie. Berlin: Duncker & Humblot, 1953–.

New Catholic Encyclopedia. New York: McGraw-Hill, 1967–96.

Reske, Christoph. *Die Buchdrucker des 16. und 17. Jahrhunderts im deutschen Sprachgebiet.* Wiesbaden: Harrassowitz, 2015.

Sadie, Stanley, ed. *The New Grove Dictionary of Music and Musicians.* 29 vols. 2nd ed. New York: Grove, 2002.

Scheible, Heinz, ed. *Melanchthons Briefwechsel, Band 11–12.* Personen. Stuttgart-Bad Cannstatt: Fromann-holzboog, 2003–.

Index of Featured Individuals